Communication in Accounting Education

Accounting, often described as 'the language of business', requires a diverse set of written, listening and oral communication skills if those who practise it are to be effective. Given the pace of change relating to, for example, the evolution of international accounting standards and the demands for greater transparency, accountants must be clear, responsive, and audience-focussed communicators.

Employers of accountants consistently comment on the need for their new graduate recruits and trainees to have strong written, oral, and interpersonal communication skills. In this light, accounting educators face the challenge of designing and delivering programmes that reflect professional expectations on the part of employers and clients, and educating students on how to make informed communication choices in order to achieve desired results and to build good working relationships.

The chapters in this book deal with such topics as accounting students' perceptions of oral communication skills; competence-based writing skills; and the development of listening skills.

This book is a compilation of papers originally published in *Accounting Education: an international journal*.

Richard M.S. Wilson is Emeritus Professor of Business Administration & Financial Management at Loughborough University, UK. He has worked as an accounting educator in more than a dozen countries; has published widely; is the founding Editor of *Accounting Education: an international journal*; and holds two Lifetime Achievement Awards (one specifically for his work in the field of accounting education).

F. Elizabeth Gray is Associate Head of the School of Communication, Journalism, and Marketing at Massey University, New Zealand, where she teaches courses in professional writing, editing and publishing. She has ongoing research interests in written and oral communication demand in scientific and business workplaces, as well as in the field of nineteenth-century journalism.

Lynn Hamilton is Associate Professor and Director of Management Communication Programs at the McIntire School of Commerce, University of Virginia, USA. She teaches managerial writing, communication strategy, oral presentation skills, media relations, and crisis communication. She has a particular interest in organizational and professional storytelling.

Communication in Accounting Education

Edited by
Richard M.S. Wilson, F. Elizabeth Gray and Lynn Hamilton

Routledge
Taylor & Francis Group

LONDON AND NEW YORK

First published 2015 by Routledge

2 Park Square, Milton Park, Abingdon, Oxfordshire OX14 4RN

711 Third Avenue, New York, NY 10017

Routledge is an imprint of the Taylor & Francis Group, an informa business

First issued in paperback 2017

British Library Cataloguing in Publication Data
A catalogue record for this book is available from the British Library

ISBN 13: 978-1-138-82919-0 (hbk)
ISBN 13: 978-1-138-47838-1 (pbk)

Typeset in Times New Roman
by RefineCatch Limited, Bungay, Suffolk

Publisher's Note
The publisher accepts responsibility for any inconsistencies that may have
arisen during the conversion of this book from journal articles to book chapters,
namely the possible inclusion of journal terminology.

Disclaimer
Every effort has been made to contact copyright holders for their permission to
reprint material in this book. The publishers would be grateful to hear from any
copyright holder who is not here acknowledged and will undertake to rectify
any errors or omissions in future editions of this book.

Contents

Citation Information

The chapters in this book were originally published in various issues of *Accounting Education: an international journal*. When citing this material, please use the original page numbering for each article, as follows:

Chapter 1

Guest Editorial: Communication in Accounting Education
F. Elizabeth Gray, Lynn Hamilton and Richard M.S. Wilson
Accounting Education: an international journal, volume 23, issue 2 (April 2014)
pp. 115–118

Chapter 2

The Communication Skills of Accountants: What we Know and the Gaps in our Knowledge
Harshini P. Siriwardane and Chris H. Durden
Accounting Education: an international journal, volume 23, issue 2 (April 2014)
pp. 119–134

Chapter 3

'Lights, Camera, Action!' Video Technology and Students' Perceptions of Oral Communication in Accounting Education
Craig Cameron and Jennifer Dickfos
Accounting Education: an international journal, volume 23, issue 2 (April 2014)
pp. 135–154

Chapter 4

A Business Communication Module for an MBA Managerial Accounting *Course: A Teaching Note*
David E. Stout
Accounting Education: an international journal, volume 23, issue 2 (April 2014)
pp. 155–173

Chapter 5

Effects of Interspersed versus Summary Feedback on the Quality of Students' Case Report Revisions
Fred Phillips and Susan Wolcott
Accounting Education: an international journal, volume 23, issue 2 (April 2014)
pp. 174–190

Chapter 6

A Successful Competency-Based Writing Skills Development Programme: Results of an Experiment
Russell Craig and C. Nicholas McKinney
Accounting Education: an international journal, volume 19, issue 3 (June 2010)
pp. 257–278

Chapter 7

'A distinguishing factor': Oral Communication Skills in New Accountancy Graduates
F. Elizabeth Gray and Niki Murray
Accounting Education: an international journal, volume 20, issue 3 (June 2011)
pp. 275–294

Chapter 8

A Qualitative Exploration of Oral Communication Apprehension
Marann Byrne, Barbara Flood and Dan Shanahan
Accounting Education: an international journal, volume 21, issue 6 (December 2012)
pp. 565–581

Chapter 9

Developing Accounting Students' Listening Skills: Barriers, Opportunities and an Integrated Stakeholder Approach
Gerard Stone, Margaret Lightbody and Rob Whait
Accounting Education: an international journal, volume 22, issue 2 (April 2013)
pp. 168–192

Chapter 10

Accounting Students in an Australian University Improve their Writing: But How Did it Happen?
Gillian Dale-Jones, Phil Hancock and Keith Willey
Accounting Education: an international journal, volume 22, issue 6 (December 2013)
pp. 544–562

Please direct any queries you may have about the citations to
clsuk.permissions@cengage.com

Notes on Contributors

Marann Byrne, Dublin City University, Ireland

Craig Cameron, Griffith University, Australia

Russell Craig, Victoria University, Australia

Gillian Dale-Jones, University of Western Australia, Australia

Jennifer Dickfos, Griffith University, Australia

Chris H. Durden, James Cook University, Australia

Barbara Flood, Dublin City University, Ireland

F. Elizabeth Gray, Massey University, New Zealand

Lynn Hamilton, University of Virginia, USA

Phil Hancock, University of Western Australia, Australia

Margaret Lightbody, University of South Australia, Australia

C. Nicholas McKinney, Rhodes College, USA

Niki Murray, Massey University, New Zealand

Fred Phillips, University of Saskatchewan, Canada

Dan Shanahan, Dublin Institute of Technology, Ireland

Harshini P. Siriwardane, James Cook University, Singapore

Gerard Stone, University of South Australia, Australia

David E. Stout, Youngstown State University, USA

Rob Whait, University of South Australia, Australia

Keith Willey, University of Technology, Sydney, Australia

Richard M.S. Wilson, Loughborough University, UK

Susan Wolcott, CA School of Business, Canada

Communication in Accounting Education

Fifty years ago, Roy and MacNeill inquired into the common body of knowledge that US Certified Public Accountants (CPAs) should possess at the outset of their careers. 'What is the outstanding deficiency of college graduates?' the authors asked of respondents. CPAs replied 'in unison – the inability to communicate orally or in writing' (Roy and Mac-Neill, 1963, p. 58). In the years since 1963, the need to impart communication skills as part of accounting education has been universally recognised. The International Accounting Education Standards Board (IAESB) has summed up the need for strong written and oral communication skills in accounting, stating in *International Education Standard 3* that accounting professionals should be able to 'present, discuss, report, and defend views effectively through formal, informal, written and spoken communication' (IAESB, 2010, p. 50).

Adding to a large and growing body of research, recent international studies demonstrate how consistently communication skills are regarded as being essential to professional success in accounting. A New Zealand-based study by Bui and Porter (2010, p. 45) noted that employers from the Big Four accounting firms place greater importance on 'well-developed analytical, critical and creative thinking skills, and oral presentational and writing skills' than on 'technical accounting skills'. In another New Zealand study, this time of 130 practising auditors, Chaffey, Van Peursem and Low (2011, p. 153) analysed survey responses regarding 'practices, subjects and techniques that might be of value to future audit professionals'. In their comments, respondents highlighted 'the importance of a professional's communication skills and public persona' (p. 162), and the qualitative data reinforced that 'the most-preferred, and agreed, skill is [...] communication' (p. 165).

Crawford, Helliar and Monk (2011, p. 116) surveyed 124 academics and 321 practising chartered accountants in the United Kingdom to gather perceptions regarding '16 generic skills that may be important to the accounting and auditing profession'. Academic respondents viewed analytical skills and written communication skills as being the most important of the generic skills included in the survey. And while practitioners considered all 16 skills important, 'ranking of their importance showed that analytical skills, presentation skills, and written communication skills were the most important' (p. 129).

Finally, a 2010 study by Frecka and Reckers surveyed more than 500 practising auditors, recent graduates of Master of Accountancy programmes in the USA, to assess the workplace relevance of current coursework and to identify and prioritise future curriculum initiatives. The auditors ranked 'report writing/written communication skills' as being the most important area to develop in the curriculum, sounding a clear challenge to accounting educators.

Today, accounting educators do not need to be persuaded regarding their students' need for such skills as much as they need meaningful, research-driven direction as to *how they can impart* those skills. As the editors of this themed issue we strongly concur with the summation in a recent review of accounting education literature (Apostolou *et al.*, 2013, p. 146), which notes:

> The literature consistently shows that core professional competencies (e.g., communication, analytical skill, critical thinking) are important for success in accounting. Research must shift away from documenting the importance, which is now generally accepted, toward identifying the best ways to teach or learn these competencies, or the appropriate place in an individual's career where these competencies should be learned/acquired.

This themed issue of *Accounting Education: an international journal* responds by placing a strong emphasis on the teaching and learning of communication skills and competencies, as well as sounding the call for ongoing, international research that will bring together educators, practitioners, and communication specialists, to more thoroughly equip accounting students for the varying and dynamic communication challenges they will face in the twenty-first-century global workplace.

Outline of the Issue's Genesis

Our Call for Papers reflected that:

> *evolving international accounting standards and demands for increased transparency require accountants to be clear, responsive, audience-focused communicators. In addition, employers consistently report their need for accounting graduates with strong written, oral, and interpersonal communication skills. Accounting educators face the challenge of designing and delivering programmes that reflect current and evolving standards, meet employers' and clients' expectations, and educate students to make informed communication choices in order to achieve desired results and build relationships.*

We invited papers on a range of communication and pedagogy topics, and received 13 submissions, seven of which were sent out for double-blind peer review. Four were subsequently accepted for revision and ultimate publication.

A truly international interest in the role of communication in accounting was reflected in the responses to our call for papers, which represented research institutions from France to South Africa; and we believe an international perspective is represented in these final articles. Phillips and Wolcott report on a Canadian study; Cameron and Dickfos report on a pedagogical approach developed on the Gold Coast of Australia; Stout offers a Teaching Note developed over a number of years in an MBA programme in the United States; and Siriwardane and Durden have collaborated between Singaporean and Australian universities. The editors for this themed issue hail from Wellington, New Zealand, and Charlottesville, Virginia, USA.

As quoted by Professor David Stout in his Teaching Note in this issue, 'despite academia's best efforts there still remains a gap in communication skills desired by business practitioners and those delivered by new graduates' (Conrad and Newberry, 2012, p. 112). Addressing, narrowing, and ultimately eliminating that gap is the goal of many passionate and committed accounting educators.

Conclusion

We thank all the authors for their diligence, their patience, and most of all for their generosity in seeking to share with their community of scholars the fruits of many years of research and hard-won teaching expertise. We owe our sincere thanks as well to the reviewers who so thoughtfully provided their feedback and guidance. As Siriwardane and Durden have identified in their survey study, tantalising gaps in the literature still exist. It is the hope of the editors that this themed issue highlights that communication skills are *special* in the sense of being significant, rather than in the sense of being odd or supernumerary, and that research into communication pedagogy will continue to be regularly published in this and other leading journals.

F. Elizabeth Gray
Massey University, New Zealand

Lynn Hamilton
University of Virginia, USA

Richard M.S. Wilson
Loughborough University, UK

References

Apostolou, B., Dorminey, J. W., Hassell, J. M. and Watson, S. F. (2013) Accounting education literature review (2010–2012), *Journal of Accounting Education*, 31, pp. 107–161.

Bui, B. and Porter, B. (2010) The expectation-performance gap in accounting education: an exploratory study, *Accounting Education: An International Journal*, 19(1–2), pp. 23–50.

Chaffey, J., Van Peursem, K. A. and Low, M. (2011) Audit education for future professionals: perceptions of New Zealand auditors, *Accounting Education: An International Journal*, 20(2), pp. 153–185.

Conrad, D. and Newberry, R. (2012) Identification and instruction of important business communication skills for graduate business education, *Journal of Education for Business*, 87(2), pp. 112–120.

Crawford, L., Helliar, C. and Monk, E. A. (2011) Generic skills in audit education, *Accounting Education: An International Journal*, 20(2), pp. 115–131.

Frecka, T. J. and Reckers, P. M. J. (2010) Rekindling the debate: what's right and what's wrong with Masters of Accountancy programs: the staff auditor's perspective, *Issues in Accounting Education*, 25(2), pp. 215–226.

Gray, F. E. and Murray, N. (2011) 'A distinguishing factor': oral communication skills in new accountancy graduates, *Accounting Education: An International Journal*, 20(3), pp. 275–294.

International Accounting Education Standards Board (IAESB). (2010) *Handbook of International Education Pronouncements*, 2010 edn (New York, NY: International Federation of Accountants). Available at http://www.ifac.org/sites/default/files/publications/files/handbook-of-international-e-2.pdf

Roy, R. H. and MacNeill, J. H. (1963) A report of plans and progress: study of the common body of knowledge for CPAs, *Journal of Accountancy*, 116(6), pp. 55–58.

The Communication Skills of Accountants: What we Know and the Gaps in our Knowledge

HARSHINI P. SIRIWARDANE* and CHRIS H. DURDEN**

*James Cook University, Singapore; **James Cook University, Australia

ABSTRACT   *This paper critically reviews 19 studies published between 1972 and 2012 that investigated the written and/or oral communication skills of practicing accountants. The core aim of the review was to identify skills considered important and highlight gaps regarding what is known about existing and desired communication skills in the accounting profession. Key findings include that most studies did not detail the basis used to select the skills examined, used very broad skill-set categories and/or did not sufficiently incorporate information already established in the literature. Differing views on the importance of communication skills were found between educators and accountants. Knowledge gaps identified relate to the communication skills considered most important at varying career stages and different career paths, the specific types of oral and written communication skills needed and the role and importance of oral versus written and informal versus formal communication skills. A fundamental concern is that much of the existing communication skills research is crucially out of date. Of the 19 studies reviewed, only three have been published in the past decade. This suggests that further research is needed in the area.*

1.   Introduction

The importance of communication skills for accountants has been emphasized in the literature for more than 50 years. In 1963, following a two-year study, Roy and MacNeill (1963) reported on the common body of knowledge that a Certified Public Accountant (CPA) in the USA should possess at the outset of his/her career. In this context, the authors commented: 'What is the outstanding deficiency of college graduates? The answer has come back in unison — the inability to communicate orally or in writing'

This paper was edited and accepted by Richard M. S. Wilson.

(Roy and MacNeill, 1963, p. 58). Since this early study, many researchers have undertaken studies focusing on the communication skills of accountants, and universities across the globe have attempted to better integrate communication skills into accounting programs.

Despite the efforts of accounting educators and numerous studies of communication skills in accounting, there is a continuing perception that accountants are poor communicators (Lin *et al.*, 2010; Maubane and van Rheede van Oudtshoorn, 2011; Witherspoon, 2010). Possible reasons for this perception include:

- accounting educators have not grasped the communication requirements of practicing accountants and therefore communication skills taught in universities do not sufficiently meet professional needs (Gros, 1976; May and May, 1989; Maupin and May, 1993);
- communication requirements of practicing accountants have been identified, but higher education providers have not been successful in developing the necessary transferable communication skills (de Lange, Jackling and Gut, 2006; May, 1992);
- communication skills necessary for career success evolve over time and professional accounting bodies have failed to provide adequate continuing education in this area (Addams, 1981);
- students who select accounting as a major have a communication apprehension and therefore do not develop the necessary skills (Ameen, Jackson and Malgwi, 2010); and
- the perception that accountants have poor communication skills may in fact be wrong.

Regardless of the reasons for, or the validity of, this perception, an underlying question remains unresolved: are accountants sufficiently skilled in the areas of written and oral communication? Moreover, most of the research on the communication skills of accountants is crucially out of date. Of the 19 studies appearing in major accounting and communication journals reviewed in this paper, only three are from the past decade. This suggests a need for further research in the area. The number of studies reviewed has been deliberately delimited: while numerous studies of generic skills in accounting have been undertaken, these treat communication as only one general item among a range of competencies (e.g. Ashiabor, Blazey and Janu, 2006; Beck and Halim, 2008; Bui and Porter, 2010; Hancock *et al.*, 2009). This paper's point of focus is on studies that investigate specific oral and/or written communication skills.

Accounting educators can play a key role in integrating oral and written communication skills into accounting programs, thereby helping to improve the communication abilities of accounting graduates. If conducting research in the field of communication skills in accounting aims to improve the communication skills of accounting graduates, it is essential that educators are aware of what has been established in the literature and where knowledge gaps exist. It is also essential to understand how various dimensions of communication skills are prioritized within the accounting profession, including across varying career stages and different areas of specialization.

This paper reviews 19 studies on the written and/or oral communication skills of accountants published between 1972 and 2012. The purposes of the paper are fourfold.

- First, it provides a summary and critical overview of empirical research on communication skills of accountants published over the past 40 years.
- Second, it highlights key gaps in our knowledge about the communication skills of accountants.
- Third, it attempts to identify communication skills that are considered important to practicing accountants.

● Finally, contrasting views held by educators and accountants regarding communication skill needs are identified.

By addressing these four areas, we hope to provide better insights into critical issues about communication skills and to provide a basis for further research and for the development of accounting programs that better incorporate communication skills.

The remainder of the paper is organized as follows. Section 2 describes the method used to conduct the literature review and introduces the 19 articles reviewed; the following section provides a critical overview of the studies and addresses the fourfold purpose described above; and the final section evaluates the findings of the literature review, highlights key weaknesses of prior studies, identifies communication skill areas that should be addressed by educators and the accounting profession and makes suggestions for future research.

2.   Method

For the purpose of this paper, 34 databases were searched using keyword combinations of 'communication' and 'accountant' or 'accounting'. In addition, relevant articles listed in the reference lists of the articles identified through the keyword search were examined. As articles were appraised, they were placed into emerging classifications. After all the articles had been appraised, a final taxonomy of communication skill themes was identified as follows:

● communication difficulties (or effectiveness),
● communication tasks undertaken,
● importance of communication skills,
● performance on communication tasks,
● communication training needs,
● pedagogy/curriculum,
● communication apprehension of accounting students and
● other.

This resulted in a list of 53 articles. However, pedagogy/curriculum- and communication apprehension-related articles were removed from the list because they did not directly address the use of communication skills by accountants in practice. The core focus of this study is to identify communication skills that are important to the accounting profession. To meet this focus, only empirical studies that examined communication skills from a practitioner perspective were identified for critical review.[1] Nineteen articles published between 1972 and 2012 met this criterion.

The 19 articles reviewed were: Andrews and Koester (1979), Ingram and Frazier (1980), Addams (1981), Andrews and Sigband (1984), Juchau and Galvin (1984), Gingras (1987), Hanson (1987), Hiemstra, Schmidt and Madison (1990), McLaren (1990), Maupin and May (1993), Zaid and Abraham (1994), Moncada, Nelson and Smith (1997), Morgan (1997), Goby and Lewis (1999), Nellermoe, Weirich and Reinstein (1999), Stowers and White (1999), Christensen and Rees (2002), Gray (2010) and Jones (2011). The studies of the communication skills of auditors by Goby and Lewis (1999) and of management accountants by Hiemstra, Schmidt and Madison (1990) were included even though these two studies concentrate on specific accounting career sub-paths.

3.   Findings

Table 1 provides a summary overview of empirical research on communication skills of accountants published over the past 40 years.

The majority of studies in Table 1 examined the skills needed by professional accountants in general and did not address communication skill needs that might relate to different career stages or career specializations. Studies were focused either on recently graduated accountants (RGAs) or experienced accountants. However, given that the responsibilities undertaken by accountants vary widely according to career stage and specialization, it seems reasonable to expect that the communication skills needed to be successful will change in kind or degree as a career develops. For example, in a study of the skills necessary to achieve promotion, Blanthorne, Bhamarnsiri and Guinn (2005) found that the importance of communication skills increases as accountants ascend the career ladder.

In terms of the types of communication skills examined, three broad categories are evident in Table 1:

- oral communication skills;
- written communication skills and
- communication skills more generally (oral and written or oral, written and interpersonal).

However, this broad categorization itself represents a potential deficiency in that specific skills are not identified. In this context, Gray (2010, p. 41) noted that, in spite of numerous studies on communication skills, '... formal studies of communication competencies to this point have tended to the quite general, utilizing the umbrella term *oral communication skills* or even vaguer term *generic skills*'. Jones (2011, p. 249) also expressed a similar view regarding the overly general use of the term *effective writing*: 'what is not clear from literature is what the profession means by "effective writing" or what should be included in the accountant's written communication skill set'. The majority of studies reviewed display this lack of precision. For example, Andrews and Koester (1979) asked respondents to rate *oral communication skills* and *written communication skills* of recent graduates. Addams (1981) used the term *writing ability* and Gingras (1987) used the term *writing skills*. By way of contrast, Ingram and Frazier (1980) contributed an early study that identified specific communication skills: 20 in total.

Most of the studies examined did not distinguish between communication tasks (activities), skills (abilities) and elements (attributes or qualities). All were referred to generically as 'communication skills' and not individually considered. As a result, it is difficult to conclude which communication tasks are most frequently undertaken in accounting, which skills are most needed to successfully complete a certain accounting task and/or which elements of communication are needed to effectively complete the accounting task. According to the Education Committee of the International Federation of Accountants (IFAC, 1998), competency is 'the ability to perform the tasks and roles expected of a professional accountant'. This was subsequently revised (IFAC, 2003, p. 12) as follows:

> Competence is being able to perform a work role to a defined standard with reference to real working environments.

Based on this definition, accountants should have the appropriate communication skills to perform communication tasks. Examples of oral communication tasks include giving presentations, conducting small group meetings and answering clients' questions. Examples of oral communication skills include informal speaking skills, formal presentation skills and listening skills. Effectiveness of oral communication also depends on various elements of speech such as clarity, brevity and tone. In a similar manner, written communication tasks require different skills and elements.

Table 1. Summary overview of empirical studies on the written and oral communication skills of practicing accountants published between 1972 and 2012.

Author(s)	Location	Focus	Respondent	Communication skill examined	Theme addressed	Key findings
Andrews and Koester (1979)	USA	Recently graduated accountants (RGAs)	• RGAs and practicing accountants (who worked with RGAs) • Accounting educators • Senior accounting students	Oral and written	• Importance of communication skills • Communication difficulties • Communication tasks undertaken • Communication training needs	• Educators and practitioners: oral communication skills of RGAs are better than written communication skills • Practitioners held higher education providers responsible for poor communication skills of graduates
Ingram and Frazier (1980)	USA	RGAs	• Accountants • Accounting educators	Oral and written	• Importance of communication skills • Performance on communication tasks	• Educators and practitioners: accountants are inadequately trained in communication skills
Addams (1981)	USA	RGAs from Big 8 (mostly from audit)	• RGAs from Big 8 (self-assessment)	Written	• Communication difficulties • Communication training needs • Other	• Basic writing skills the most important • Professional firms should provide communication training

(Continued)

Table 1. Continued

Author(s)	Location	Focus	Respondent	Communication skill examined	Theme addressed	Key findings
Andrews and Sigband (1984)	USA	RGAs	• Managing partners of public accounting firms • Department chairs of business schools	Oral, written and interpersonal	• Communication difficulties • Importance of communication skills • Performance on communication tasks • Communication training needs	• Practitioners: oral communication skills of RGAs are better than written communication skills
Juchau and Galvin (1984)	Australia	Staff accountants (junior accountants with less than three years' experience)	• Chief accountants and corporate accountants (supervisors of staff accountants) • Accounting department chairs	Oral and written	• Importance of communication skills • Performance on communication tasks • Other	• Overall: reading comprehension most important followed by listening attentiveness and memoranda and informal report writing • Educators and practitioners: informal report writing skills more important than formal report writing skills • Educators and practitioners: informal oral presentation skills more important than formal oral presentation skills • Practitioners: stylistic and mechanical skills are the most problematic • Educators: mechanical skills are the most problematic

(Continued)

Table 1. Continued

Author(s)	Location	Focus	Respondent	Communication skill examined	Theme addressed	Key findings
Gingras (1987)	USA	CPAs	• CPAs (self-assessment)	Written	• Communication difficulties • Importance of communication skills • Communication tasks undertaken • Communication training needs	• Importance of communication skills varies with career stage • Professional bodies should provide writing skills training • Main writing tasks undertaken are informal
Hanson (1987)	USA	Accountants in public accounting firms	• Accountants in public accounting firms	Oral	• Importance of communication skills • Communication tasks undertaken	• Informal oral communication skills more important than formal communication skills
Hiemstra, Schmidt and Madison (1990)	USA	Certified Management Accountants (CMAs)	• CMAs	Oral and written	• Importance of communication skills • Communication tasks undertaken • Communication training needs	• Importance of communication skills varies with career stage • Listening is the most important communication skill • Informal oral communication skills are more important than formal communication skills • Informal writing skills are more important than formal writing skills

(Continued)

Table 1. Continued

Author(s)	Location	Focus	Respondent	Communication skill examined	Theme addressed	Key findings
McLaren (1990)	New Zealand	Accountants	• Chartered Accountants • Accounting educators	Written and oral	• Importance of communication skills • Performance on communication skills	• Practitioners: the most important skills are correspondence writing and listening • Educators: rated formal writing skills as more important than practitioners • Practitioners: informal oral communication skills are more important than formal skills • Educators: formal and informal oral communication skills are equally important • Educators and practitioners: formal report writing skills are more important than informal report writing skills
Maupin and May (1993)	USA	Accountants	• Business communication professors • Accounting practitioners	Written	• Other	• Educators: formal reports more important than informal reports • Practitioners: informal reports more important than formal reports

(Continued)

Table 1. Continued

Author(s)	Location	Focus	Respondent	Communication skill examined	Theme addressed	Key findings
Zaid and Abraham (1994)	Australia	Graduate Accountants (RGAs)	• Employers hiring accountants • Heads of accounting departments • Accounting graduates	Written and oral	• Importance of communication skills • Communication training needs	• Educators and practitioners: casual verbal presentation and intelligent analysis are the most important communication skills • Formal writing skills more important than informal writing
Moncada, Nelson and Smith (1997)	USA	Accountants	• CPAs	Written	• Communication tasks undertaken	• Compiling working papers is the most commonly undertaken task • Main writing tasks undertaken are informal
Morgan (1997)	UK	Accounting trainees	• Accounting practitioners (CPAs and CMAs) • Accounting educators	Written and oral	• Importance of communication skills • Performance on communication tasks • Communication skills training needs	• Educators and practitioners: listening is the most important oral communication skill for RGAs • Informal writing skills more important than formal writing skills • Educators: formal oral communication skills are more important than informal oral communication skills • Practitioners: informal oral communication skills are more important than formal skills

(*Continued*)

Table 1. Continued

Author(s)	Location	Focus	Respondent	Communication skill examined	Theme addressed	Key findings
Goby and Lewis (1999)	Singapore	Auditors	• Auditors in different career stages	Written and oral	• Communication training needs	• Informal writing skills more important than formal writing skills • Documentation of work is the most commonly undertaken communication task
Nellermoe, Weirich and Reinstein (1999)	USA	CPAs	• CPAs	Written and oral	• Importance of communication skills • Communication tasks undertaken	• Informal writing skills are more important than formal writing skills • Main writing tasks undertaken are informal • More time is spent on writing than speaking or listening • CPAs held higher education providers responsible for poor communication skills of graduates
Stowers and White (1999)	USA	CPAs	• CPAs at different career stages in public accounting firms	Written, oral, and interpersonal	• Importance of communication skills • Performance on communication tasks • Communication training needs	• Importance of communication skills varies with career stage • Listening the most important communication skill

(Continued)

Table 1. Continued

Author(s)	Location	Focus	Respondent	Communication skill examined	Theme addressed	Key findings
Christensen and Rees (2002)	USA	RGAs	• CMAs and CPAs	Written and oral	• Importance of communication skills • Performance on communication tasks	• Listening skills are the most important for RGAs • Writing skills are less important than oral communication skills • Of the writing skills, basic writing mechanics are the most important
Gray (2010)	New Zealand	RGAs	• Practicing accountants	Oral	• Importance of communication skills • Performance on communication tasks	• Listening is the most important oral communication skill • Conveying attitude of respect and interest to clients is extremely important
Jones (2011)	USA	RGAs	• Employers	Written and computer-mediated	• Importance of communication skills • Performance on communication tasks	• Of the writing skills, basic writing mechanics are the most important • The only computer-mediated skill that employers regard as essential is effective use of email

In the studies examined, oral communication skills were commonly ranked by practicing accountants as being more important than written communication skills, especially for RGAs. However, beyond the RGA level it is less clear which communication skills, oral or written, are more important. Three studies of experienced accountants included listening skills as a specific category and identified listening as a key communication skill considered important by practicing accountants (Hiemstra, Schmidt and Madison, 1990; McLaren, 1990; Stowers and White, 1999). Several studies considering RGAs also identified listening as a key communication skill (Christensen and Rees, 2002; Gray, 2010; Juchau and Galvin, 1984; Morgan, 1997). Other skills rated highly for RGAs include reading comprehension and casual verbal presentation (Juchau and Galvin, 1984; Zaid and Abraham, 1994).

Studies often distinguished between formal and informal communication skills. There is evidence that informal oral communication skills are perceived by practicing accountants as being more important than formal oral communication skills (Hanson, 1987; Hiemstra, Schmidt and Madison, 1990; McLaren, 1990). Similarly, informal writing skills appeared higher on the important skills lists of practicing accountants than formal writing skills (Hiemstra, Schmidt and Madison, 1990; Maupin and May, 1993). The two most recent studies that examined the written communication skills of RGAs suggest that basic writing skills are more important than more formal writing skills (Christensen and Rees, 2002; Jones, 2011). However, the distinction between formal and informal writing is not precise. For example, it is not clear whether email and memorandum writing is a formal or informal writing skill. Similarly, with oral communication, the formal-informal distinction needs clarification. This issue is important because the International Accounting Education Standards Board (IAESB) in *International Education Standard 3* also used the terms formal and informal: 'Accounting professionals should be able to present, discuss, report, and defend views effectively through formal, informal, written, and spoken communication' (IAESB, 2010, IES3:17(f)).

While the studies directly addressed the communication skill needs of practicing accountants, the overall findings are only tentative. There is some consensus that informal oral and written communication skills are considered to be most significant by practicing accountants. However, ambiguity surrounding the meaning of informal versus formal communication, variations across studies in terms of the skills lists examined and the fact that most of the studies are quite dated all create uncertainty about the communication skill priorities of practicing accountants. Further research is needed to better understand whether informal communication skills are of more value than formal communication skills, and how to balance emphasis on each.

Finally, the research revealed some contrasting views between educators and accounting practitioners about how communication skills should be prioritized. For example, Maupin and May (1993) reported the results of a study that surveyed the opinions of business communication educators and accounting practitioners with respect to the topics emphasized in business communication textbooks. The topics emphasized in textbooks and the views of business communication educators were closely aligned. However, the views of practitioners diverged from what was emphasized in textbooks. This divergence highlights the need for greater collaboration between accounting educators, communication specialists (to help design courses) and the accounting profession (to identify critical skills) in order to improve the communication skill levels of accounting graduates.

Other key differences in the views of educators and practitioners that are evident from the 19 studies include the following:

- Educators placed greater emphasis on formal communication (both oral and written), while practitioners placed greater emphasis on informal communication (Maupin and

May, 1993; McLaren, 1990; Morgan, 1997; Zaid and Abraham, 1994). This divergence appeared stronger for written communication skills than oral communication skills.

- Practitioners viewed universities as being primarily responsible for the poor communication skills of accountants. Fewer educators than practitioners held the view that universities should be held responsible for the development of communication skill capability in accountants (Andrews and Sigband, 1984; Zaid and Abraham, 1994).
- Practitioners considered that basic informal communication skills were more important than the formal mechanical and stylistic aspects of written communication (Juchau and Galvin, 1984; Morgan, 1997).

4.   Discussion and Conclusions

The importance of communication skills for accountants has been researched and discussed for over half a century. However, many basic questions remain unanswered or unresolved. One reason for this lack of clarity may be weaknesses in the taxonomies of communication skills considered in prior studies. Most studies did not detail the bases used to select the skills examined, adopted outdated skill lists, used very broad skill-set categories and/or did not sufficiently incorporate information already known. For example, the US-based Accounting Education Change Commission (AECC), in its *Position Statement Number 1* (AECC, 1990, p. 5), identified a composite profile of capabilities needed by accounting graduates. Within the category of communication skills, the statement lists: ability to present, discuss, and defend views effectively through formal and informal, written and spoken language; ability to listen effectively; and ability to locate, obtain, organize, report, and use information from human, print, and electronic sources. However, of the six communication skills studies undertaken in the USA after 1990, three did not include listening skills; none included the ability to locate and obtain information; and none mentioned retrieving information from electronic sources.

Another limiting factor in prior studies may be incomplete literature reviews. Even though each study included a literature review, these reviews either excluded much of the prior communication skills research or included studies that were not directly related to communication skills (i.e. generic accounting skills competency studies). As a result, communication studies over time have not successfully built a body of knowledge using prior research and have not overcome weaknesses of prior studies. The studies do not adequately identify or address information gaps from earlier work.

In addition, much of the existing communication skills research about accountants is outdated, narrow in scope and of limited geographic reach. Only three communication skills studies have been undertaken in the past decade. Jones (2011) completed a study in the USA that examined only written communication skills, and the respondents were limited to employers of the accounting graduates of one university. Gray (2010) completed a recent study in New Zealand on the oral communication skills of RGAs. The work of Christensen and Rees (2002) was US-centred and covered both written and oral communication skills. However, the survey questions were based on a business skills inventory developed by Warner in 1995, which was long before the current accounting, regulatory, and socio-economic environment unfolded. Out of the 19 studies reviewed, two were based in Australia, two in New Zealand and one each in the UK and Singapore, with the remainder all US-focused. Relatively little is known about the nuances of communication skills required outside of a US-centric context. There is a notable dearth of data regarding the types of communication skills considered necessary for accounting graduates and accountants in Asian countries. Lin, Xiong and Liu (2005) replicated Albrecht and Sack's (2000) US study with the aim of identifying core accounting skill sets relevant in a Chinese context. The results indicated that both educators and accounting professionals in China rated the importance of communication skills lower than did their counterparts in the USA. However, the study did not examine specific oral or written communication skills or tasks.

A key challenge for accounting educators is to help students develop transferable skills that align with the most frequently performed communication tasks in accounting. To achieve this, collaboration is necessary between accounting educators, practitioners and, in particular, communication specialists to identify relevant communication skills needs and implement these in accounting programs. According to Smythe and Nikolai (1996, p. 436), educators who are engaged in incorporating communication skills into accounting programs must '... assess the effectiveness of instruction in providing useful, transferable skills for the practicing professional'. Being able to complete a task does not constitute a transferable skill. For example, Hanson (1987) identified *using the telephone* as being an important oral communication task. However, it would be problematic and arguably a waste of academic resources for an accounting department to train its students to manage telephone conversations effectively. Instead, it would be more practical and realistic to improve skills and elements of communication that are necessary for successful telephone conversations. For example, if educators can improve accounting students' effective listening skills and elements of speech such as clarity and brevity, then the ability of graduates to use the telephone as well as to answer questions, give oral presentations and conduct meetings should all improve.

There are potentially two ways to address this challenge:

1. accounting educators could engage communication specialists to identify the skills and elements of communication that are most crucial to effectively complete various accounting-related activities; and
2. accounting educators could collaborate with communication specialists in designing research studies so that specific transferable skills are identified and included.

Greater levels of collaboration between the accounting profession, accounting educators and communication specialists is especially critical, given the differences in perception that have been observed among the three groups (Maupin and May, 1993).

There is presently only limited information about the types of communication skills considered most essential at varying career stages and across different career specializations within accounting. Accordingly, in terms of the relationship between communication skills and accounting career development, this knowledge gap should be addressed. Furthermore, most of the existing communication skills research is dated and may not reflect the communication competencies now required in an accounting role. As a starting point, a range of communication skills considered important for RGAs should be determined. Additionally, communication skills deemed important at other career stages and across different specializations should also be identified. Future research studies exploring communication skills should specifically cover career stage and career specialization to expand the body of knowledge in these areas. Educators could then better account for the needs of RGAs when designing accounting programs, and professional accounting bodies and employers could better account for career stage and specialization when designing continuing education programs, professional examinations and on-the-job training.

As noted, practicing accountants appear to rate the importance of informal communication skills higher than formal communication skills. Merz (1989), for example, stressed the importance of accountants having the ability to communicate abstract concepts to a non-accountant audience in an informal setting. Educators, on the other hand, tend to rank formal communication skills above informal communication skills. This suggests a disconnect and implies that accounting programs might not be emphasizing or prioritizing the communication skills considered most critical to the profession. In this respect, the distinction between formal and informal communication skills needs to be more clearly established and understood. Information on the relative significance of formal versus informal communication skills, across both oral and written dimensions and the underlying attributes and elements that support these, should be delineated through carefully designed research studies.

In conclusion, this paper has reviewed the existing literature and identifies various communication skills knowledge gaps. It provides a foundation for future researchers who are interested in exploring the communication skills of accountants. By more precisely identifying the needs and expectations of practicing accountants, accounting educators will be better able to target specific communication skills and elements through accounting program design and innovative pedagogies. It is our hope that a more systematic approach might evolve in helping to address the communication needs of accountants.

Note

[1]In addition to a practitioner's perspective, some of these studies also included educators' and students' perspectives

References

Accounting Education Change Commission (AECC). (1990) *First Position Statement – Objectives of Education for Accountants.* Available at http://aaahq.org/AECC/pdf/position/pos1.pdf (accessed 7 September 2012).

Addams, L. H. (1981) Should the Big 8 teach communication skills?, *Management Accounting*, 62(11), p. 37.

Albrecht, W. S. and Sack, R. J. (2000) *Accounting Education: Charting the Course Through a Perilous Future* (Sarasota, FL: American Accounting Association).

Ameen, E., Jackson, C. and Malgwi, C. (2010) Student perceptions of oral communication requirements in the accounting profession, *Global Perspectives on Accounting Education*, 7, pp. 31–49.

Andrews, J. D. and Koester, R. J. (1979) Communication difficulties as perceived by the accounting profession and professors of accounting, *The Journal of Business Communication*, 16(2), pp. 33–33.

Andrews, J. D. and Sigband, N. B. (1984) How effectively does the new accountant communicate? Perceptions by practitioners and academics, *The Journal of Business Communication*, 21(2), pp. 15–15.

Ashiabor, H., Blazey, P. and Janu, P. (2006) *Investigation, Integration and Implementation of Generic Skills within a Business Law Curriculum* (Sydney: Macquarie University).

Beck, J. E. and Halim, H. (2008) Undergraduate internships in accounting: what and how do Singapore interns learn from experience?, *Accounting Education: An International Journal*, 17(1), pp. 1–22.

Blanthorne, C., Bhamornsiri, S. and Guinn, R. E. (2005) Are technical skills still important?, *The CPA Journal*, 75(3), pp. 64–65.

Bui, B. and Porter, B. (2010) The expectation-performance gap in accounting education: an exploratory study, *Accounting Education: An International Journal*, 19(1–2), pp. 23–50.

Christensen, D. S. and Rees, D. (2002) An analysis of the business communication skills needed by entry-level accountants, *Mountain Plains Journal of Business and Economics*, Fall, pp. 1–13.

de Lange, P., Jackling, B. and Gut, A. (2006) Accounting graduates' perceptions of skills emphasis in undergraduate courses: an investigation from two Victorian universities, *Accounting and Finance*, 46, pp. 365–386.

Gingras, R. (1987) Writing and the certified public accountant, *Journal of Accounting Education*, 5, pp. 127–137.

Goby, V. and Lewis, J. H. (1999) Auditors' communication requirements: a study of five MNCs in Singapore, *Business Communication Quarterly*, 62(4), pp. 41–52.

Gray, F. E. (2010) Specific oral communication skills desired in new accountancy graduates, *Business Communication Quarterly*, 73(1), pp. 40–67.

Gros, R. J. (1976) The communication package in the business curriculum. Why? *ABCA Bulletin*, 39(4), pp. 5–8.

Hancock, P., Howieson, B., Kavanagh, M., Kent, J., Tempone, I. and Segal, N. (2009). *Accounting for the Future: More than Numbers*, Vol. 1 Final Report. Sydney: Australian Teaching and Learning Council.

Hanson, G. A. (1987) The importance of oral communication in accounting practice, *The CPA Journal*, 57(12), pp. 118–122.

Hiemstra, K. M., Schmidt, J. J. and Madison, R. L. (1990) Certified management accountants: perceptions of the need for communication skills in accounting, *Business Communication Quarterly*, 53(4), pp. 5–9.

Ingram, R. W. and Frazier, C. R. (1980) *Developing Communication Skills for the Accounting Profession* (Sarasota, FL: American Accounting Association).

International Accounting Education Standards Board (IAESB). (2010) *Handbook of International Education Pronouncements*, 2010 edn (Ney York, NY: International Federation of Accountants).

International Federation of Accountants (IFAC). (1998) *Competence-Based Approaches to the Professional Preparation of Accountants*. Available at http://www.javeriana.edu.co/personales/hbermude/areacontable/particulars/EDC-competence.pdf (accessed 5 July 2012).

International Federation of Accountants. (2003) *Towards Competent Professional Accountants*, International Education Paper 2, New York: IFAC.

Jones, C. G. (2011) Written and computer-mediated accounting communication skills: an employer perspective, *Business Communication Quarterly*, 74(3), pp. 247–271.

Juchau, R. and Galvin, M. (1984) Communication skills of accountants in Australia, *Accounting and Finance*, 24, pp. 17–32.

Lin, J. Z., Xiong, X. and Liu, M. (2005) Knowledge base and skill development in accounting education: evidence from China, *Journal of Accounting Education*, 23(3), pp. 149–169.

Lin, P., Grace, D., Krishnan, S. and Gilsdorf, J. (2010) Failure to communicate, *The CPA Journal*, 80(1), pp. 63–65.

May, G. S. and May, C. B. (1989) Communication instruction: what is being done to develop the communication skills of accounting students, *Journal of Accounting Education*, 7(2), pp. 233–244.

Maubane, P. and van Rheede van Oudtshoorn, G. (2011) An exploratory survey of professional accountants' perception of interpersonal communication in organisations, *Journal of Public Affairs*, 11(4), pp. 297–302.

Maupin, R. J. and May, C. A. (1993) Communication for accounting students, *The International Journal of Educational Management*, 7(3), pp. 30–30.

McLaren, M. C. (1990) The place of communication skills in the training of accountants in New Zealand, *Accounting and Finance*, 30(1), pp. 83–83.

Merz, C. M. (1989) Accountants: mind your bedside manner, *Management Accounting (CMA)*, 71, pp. 35–8.

Moncada, S. M., Nelson, S. J. and Smith, D. C. (1997) Written communication frequently composed by entry-level accountants, *New Accountant*, 12(4), pp. 26–28.

Morgan, G. J. (1997) Communication skills required by accounting graduates: practitioner and academic perceptions, *Accounting Education: An International Journal*, 6(2), pp. 93–107.

Nellermoe, D. A., Weirich, T. R. and Reinstein, A. (1999) Using practitioners' viewpoints to improve accounting students' communications skills, *Business Communication Quarterly*, 62(2), pp. 41–60.

Roy, R. H. and MacNeill, J. H. (1963) A report of plans and progress: study of the common body of knowledge for CPAs, *Journal of Accountancy*, 116(6), pp. 55–58.

Smythe, M. and Nikolai, L. A. (1996) Communication concerns across different accounting constituencies, *Journal of Accounting Education*, 14(4), pp. 435–451.

Stowers, R. H. and White, G. T. (1999) Connecting accounting and communication: a survey of public accounting firms, *Business Communication Quarterly*, 62(2), pp. 23–40.

Warner, K. (1995) Business communication competencies needed by employees as perceived by business faculty and business professionals, *Business Communication Quarterly*, 58(4), pp. 51–56.

Witherspoon, C. (2010) Creating compelling client communications, *The CPA Journal*, 80(4), p. 10.

Zaid, O. A. and Abraham, A. (1994) Communication skills in accounting education: perceptions of academics, employers and graduate accountants, *Accounting Education: An International Journal*, 3(3), pp. 205–221.

'Lights, Camera, Action!' Video Technology and Students' Perceptions of Oral Communication in Accounting Education

CRAIG CAMERON and JENNIFER DICKFOS

Griffith University, Australia

ABSTRACT   *This paper examines the influence of an authentic assessment item on three dimensions of oral communication in accounting education: skills, self-efficacy, and relevance. An explanatory mixed methods design is used to explore students' perceptions of their development. The results indicate that an elevator pitch assessment has a positive impact on all three dimensions. In particular, the employed video technology fosters greater self-awareness and a more accurate perception of skill levels, and enhances students' self-efficacy. The contextualised learning experience also enables students to better appreciate the relevance of oral communication to their future careers. The paper extends the literature on video technology, self-efficacy, and generic skills development in accounting education, and provides relevant stakeholders with evidence of an authentic activity that can assist with bridging the skills-expectation gap.*

Introduction

Accreditation bodies and employers have identified oral communication as an integral part of an accounting student's desired generic skill set (ICAA and CPA, 2009; Jackling and de Lange, 2009; Kavanagh and Drennan, 2008; Tempone *et al.*, 2012). Despite the imperative to develop accounting students' generic skills, there remains a gap between employers' expectations and oral communication skill levels of accounting graduates (skills-expectation gap) (Kavanagh and Drennan, 2008; Tempone *et al.*, 2012). The literature reveals

---

This paper was edited and accepted by Richard M. S. Wilson.

two potential reasons for the gap. First, generic skills are context-dependent (Jones, 2010). As such, academics and employers perceive and define generic skills differently (Gray, 2010; Levenson, 2000; Tempone *et al.*, 2012), which may in turn lead to differences in the expectations of both parties regarding the skills that accounting graduates should possess (Bui and Porter, 2010). The second reason is that students may not fully appreciate the importance of skills such as oral communication to their future careers (Gray and Murray, 2011). The skills-expectation gap suggests that tertiary institutions may not be equipping graduates with context-specific oral communication skills or conveying their importance to students in terms of graduate employability and career success.

The challenge for tertiary institutions is to develop learning activities and assessments that not only assure the learning of oral communication skills for accreditation purposes, but are also relevant to the workplace environment, and which instil its relevance in accounting students. To address this challenge, the authors developed an elevator pitch assessment using video technology as part of a comprehensive blended learning strategy in *Company Law*, a second-year undergraduate accounting course at an Australian university. The assessment is an example of what Smythe and Nikolai (2002) identify as the most productive form of oral communication assessment, as it combines an individual performance with a roleplaying activity. This paper provides preliminary evidence, based on students' self-reporting and interviews, that the mastery experience of this authentic learning activity, combined with video technology, has a positive influence on three dimensions of oral communication: skills, self-efficacy, and relevance.

The remainder of this paper is structured as follows. The next section provides a theoretical background to oral communication skills, contextualisation (relevance) and self-efficacy. This discussion is followed by an overview of the assessment. (A more detailed description of the learning activity, including its evolution and impact on students' self-reflection and assessment practice, has been addressed elsewhere; Dickfos, Cameron and Hodgson, forthcoming.) A subsequent section addresses the research methods. The preliminary results, which include students' self-reported data from a survey instrument and interviews with students, indicate the positive impact of the elevator pitch assessment on students' oral communication skills, self-efficacy, and relevance. This paper concludes with limitations and potential for future research.

Theoretical Background

Oral Communication

Oral communication is a generic skill demanded by employers and professional accounting bodies but not necessarily acquired by accounting students during their programme of study (Jackling and de Lange, 2009; Jackson *et al.*, 2006; Kavanagh and Drennan, 2008). Two recent studies have expanded the literature on the skills-expectation gap in accounting education by exploring and measuring the meanings that employers ascribe to oral communication. In Tempone *et al.* (2012), the authors interviewed a wide cross-section of Australian employers of accounting graduates concerning their perceptions of skill importance and meaning. The subsequent analysis revealed that oral communication, categorised as 'verbal skills, speaking, listening, negotiation and feedback', was the most frequently cited generic skill. Oral communication included the ability to:

- talk to clients;
- make a presentation (involving more than using *PowerPoint*);
- hold a conversation at a cocktail party;

- discuss difficult topics;
- conduct boardroom negotiations;
- engage in active listening;
- get maximum information from a client;
- provide feedback;
- communicate clearly and succinctly; and
- engage in professional conduct (Tempone *et al.*, 2012, p. 49).

Gray (2010) conducted a quantitative study of New Zealand accounting employers involving 27 predetermined dimensions of oral communication skills. The two most important skills were 'listening attentiveness' and 'listening responsiveness' (Gray, 2010, p. 48). Rounding out the top seven most highly valued oral communication skills, in rank order, were:

- conveying professional attitude of respect and interest in clients;
- asking for clarification or feedback from management;
- speaking on the telephone/making conferences calls with clients;
- describing situations accurately and precisely to superior/s; and
- conveying a knowledgeable and confident demeanour to clients (Gray, 2010, p. 49).

By contextualising oral communication, Tempone *et al.* and Gray make an important contribution to the current academic debate concerning generic skills and curriculum reform in accounting education.

Contextualisation

Oral communication should be taught and assessed in a contextualised manner; that is, it must be relevant to the workplace environment if it is to meet the professional demand for work-ready accounting graduates. The studies of Tempone *et al.* and of Gray reveal that oral communication in a business context goes beyond that of the traditional tertiary context of students making a presentation to their peer group on an accounting issue or topic (Grace and Gilsdorf, 2004) or participating in class discussion (Dallimore, Hertenstein and Platt, 2004). A key element in contextualising the accounting curriculum is authenticity. This entails the provision of authentic learning activities, that is activities that are also carried out in professional practice (Gulikers, Bastiaens and Kirscher, 2004), and authentic assessment of learning within the activities (Herrington and Oliver, 2000). Unfortunately, the accounting education literature contains scant discussion of authentic learning and assessment of oral communication. The Professional Development Programme (PDP), a three-year generic skills programme offered by one Australian university, directly addresses authentic learning: in this programme, accounting students participate in business networking, drama classes and speed interviewing activities, and complete a professional presentation at a student-industry conference. The PDP demonstrates that authentic learning activities influence students' perceptions of their oral communication skills, as well as of the relevance of oral communication to their future careers (Freudenberg, Brimble and Cameron, 2010, 2011).

Self-efficacy

Self-efficacy refers to 'the judgements of one's capabilities to organise and execute the courses of action required to produce given attainments' (Bandura, 1997, p. 3). Self-efficacy is positively related to academic performance (Pintrich and Degroot, 1990), career choice, and career competency because it influences the choices, effort, and persistence of human behaviour (Bandura, 1982; Gist and Mitchell, 1992). For example, students with low self-efficacy or an inaccurate perception of their oral communication skills may drop out of the accounting degree, avoid elective courses involving oral communication assessment, or not exert the effort required to improve or apply their oral communication skills. While students may possess oral communication skills, a lack of self-efficacy can inhibit task performance. Fortunately, a person's self-efficacy is not static, but can be increased through mastery experiences, social persuasion, physiological states, and modelling (Wood and Bandura, 1989).

- Mastery experiences are the most influential factor in developing self-efficacy, by giving students an opportunity to learn a particular concept or skill (Bandura, 1982; Wood and Bandura, 1989). Success in accomplishing specific tasks in oral communication strengthens students' beliefs in their abilities, which can be manifested in different activities (Bandura, 1977).
- Social persuasion entails receiving realistic encouragement or feedback from credible persuaders (Zimmerman, 2000) who may include educators, peers, and accounting professionals.
- Actions which can modify students' physiological states (e.g. fatigue, anxiety, and stress) can enhance their self-efficacy levels (Wood and Bandura, 1989).
- Modelling builds self-efficacy by enabling students to observe the performance of others in a situation similar to that which the student will encounter and by making social comparisons. Students see others succeed as a result of sustained effort and so adopt the attitude: 'If they can do it, I can do it'. Modelling can be further classified into three categories: exemplary, peer, and self-modelling. Being exposed to exemplary models with proficient skills can help raise the learners' beliefs in their own capabilities for success (Bandura, 2001). However, the research suggests that the best models are those that share the same attributes (Bandura, 1997; Schunk and Hanson, 1985). Nevertheless, Bandura acknowledges 'the wide applications' of self-modelling and its potential to enhance self-efficacy, particularly with 'inveterate self-doubters' (Bandura, 1997, p. 94). All three forms of modelling occur in the elevator pitch assessment, which is discussed in the section that follows.

Assessment Design

The elevator pitch was implemented in *Company Law*, a second-year undergraduate accounting course in 2011. As at the end of 2012, four cohorts on two different campuses had completed this assessment. Cohort 1 presented the elevator pitch in person to their colleagues, whereas Cohort 2 students (and subsequent cohorts) pre-recorded their presentation. A detailed description of context, including the logistical, technological, assessment, and behavioural issues related to the elevator pitch, has been addressed elsewhere (Dickfos, Cameron and Hodgson, forthcoming). Students were required to complete a three-minute elevator pitch in which the student was placed in the role of a promoter. In company law, a promoter is a person who either stands to gain from or takes active steps in incorporating an entity. One such step is raising capital. The elevator pitch is a mastery experience that replicates the situation of a person having the duration of an elevator ride to pitch an idea, product, service or business (the item) to a potential investor. In this scenario, the promoter's hypothetical client (an entity yet to be incorporated) owns the item and, in return for investment, the investor may become a substantial shareholder in the entity yet to be incorporated. The potential 'investor' has agreed to listen to the presentation. In summary, the elevator pitch is an authentic learning activity that combines students' technical legal knowledge on promoters and share capital, their accounting knowledge, in that they have to communicate cash flow, balance sheet, and/or profit and loss projections, and a generic skill (oral communication).

Students received substantial online resources to assist them in identifying an item to promote, the financial and legal content to cover, and an appropriate structure to adopt when making the presentation. Cohort 2 students had access to a series of video presentations performed and narrated by academic staff of 'good' elevator pitches (exemplary modelling) and 'bad' elevator pitches, which could be considered a form of peer modelling. Students recorded their individual presentation in groups of three using a university-supplied Sony Bloggie video camera outside class time. It has been reported that the use of small groups is capable of changing physiological states: 'students were less anxious with completing a video presentation within their self-selected groups than in front of a large class' (Dickfos, Cameron and Hodgson, forthcoming). Whilst this was not a group work assessment, as students were assessed individually, grouping the students facilitated peer modelling and social persuasion. Groups could borrow a camera to practice with before the assessment, and had limited time whilst completing the assessment to review and provide feedback on each student's pitch. Students acted in the role of camera operator, promoter, and potential investor and rotated roles after each presentation. The group members had one hour to record and select their 'best' individual presentation, upload them to the university's learning management system, review their presentation to ensure it addressed the assessment instructions and criteria (self-modelling), and make a personal copy.

The presentation was then assessed using an electronic rubric within a custom-built web application. Electronic rubrics are not a foreign concept to assessment of oral communication in accounting education (Anderson and Mohrweis, 2008). The rubric for Cohorts 1 and 2 comprised eight criteria (Introduction; Content; Organisation of Presentation; Voice; Pace; Visual Aids; Audience Engagement; and Conclusion), and seven criteria (after deletion of Visual Aids) for Cohorts 3 and 4. Visual aids were removed as an assessment criterion for two reasons. First, they are not a common feature of elevator pitches. Second, it was difficult for the teacher to view (and therefore properly assess) visual aid use in the video presentations of Cohort 2. Students were not discouraged from using visual aids as a form of audience engagement and to demonstrate originality, but they were not compulsory (Dickfos, Cameron and Hodgson, forthcoming).

A weighting was assigned to each criterion with five standards of performance attached to each criterion (Excellent: 100%; Very good: 84%; Good: 67%; Satisfactory: 50%; Unsatisfactory: 33% or 0). Teachers could provide customised student feedback for each criterion. Modifications to the web application also enabled teachers to vary the performance percentages in respect of Cohort 4. The rubric for Cohorts 3 and 4 is included in Table 1.

Following the assessment of Cohort 4, the authors posted four downloadable video presentations of excellent elevator pitches by students (peer modelling) to assist their peers in preparing for future oral assessment items. One significant additional assessment element in Cohort 4, relevant to the elevator pitch, involved self-modelling (Bandura, 1977). In this cohort, students in *Company Law* were subject to two random tutorial spot checks during the teaching period, worth 2.5% each. One tutorial question in the second to last week of the teaching period required students to review their video presentations, refer to the completed rubric emailed to them and complete three short answer questions: *What were the best aspects of your presentation and why?*; *What aspects are in need of improvement and why?*; and *How will you address these aspects in future presentations?* This reflective exercise was one of the two spot checks.

Table 1. Electronic rubric.

Criteria	Excellent	Very good	Good	Satisfactory	Unsatisfactory
Introduction (weighting 10%)	Topic, key points and purpose of the presentation are introduced in a clear and interesting way which captures the audience's attention	Topic, key points and purpose of the presentation are introduced in a clear and interesting way	Topic, key points and purpose of the presentation are introduced with clarity	Topic introduced, but the introduction is underdeveloped in terms of key points and/or purpose of presentation	No topic, key points and/or purpose is introduced or the introduction is irrelevant to assessment item
Content (weighting 25%)	The student has a thorough knowledge of the content and consistently demonstrated originality in its presentation	The student has a very good knowledge of the content and demonstrated originality (at times) in its presentation	The student has an adequate knowledge of the content and demonstrated originality (at times) in its presentation	The student has some knowledge of the content, but demonstrated little or no originality in its presentation	The student has little or no understanding of the content and demonstrated little or no originality in its presentation
Organisation of presentation (weighting 10%)	Presents information and ideas in a logical and interesting sequence which the audience can easily follow	Presents information and ideas in a logical sequence which the audience can follow	Presents information and ideas at a reasonable level of logical sequence which the audience finds difficult to follow at times	Presents information and ideas at a basic level of logical sequence which the audience generally finds difficult to follow	Presents information in a poorly-developed and illogical sequence which the audience cannot follow
Voice (weighting 10%)	The student has a clear voice, is expressive throughout the presentation, uses precise pronunciation of terms, enabling the audience to understand the presentation	The student has a clear voice, is expressive at times, in most instances uses precise pronunciation of terms, enabling the audience to understand the presentation	The student has a clear voice, but is not expressive and/or pronounces some words incorrectly	The student's voice is not clear at times, not expressive and/or the student pronounces a number of terms incorrectly	The student mumbles, incorrectly pronounces terms, is not expressive

Criteria					
Pace (weighting 10%)	Presentation at a good pace, without any inappropriate pauses	Presentation at a good pace, occasional inappropriate pauses but they do not detract from the audiences' understanding of the presentation	Delivery is slightly fast or slow or there are occasional inappropriate pauses that detract from the audience's understanding of the presentation	Delivery is too fast or too slow in parts, or there are several inappropriate pauses that detract from the audience's understanding of the presentation	Delivery is too fast or too slow throughout, or there are several lengthy and inappropriate pauses that detract from the audience's understanding of the presentation
Audience engagement (weighting 25%)	The student demonstrates all the following attributes: enthusiasm for the topic, successful techniques to engage the audience, appropriate eye contact, poise and body language	The student has demonstrated all of the following attributes: successful techniques to engage the audience, and appropriate eye contact, poise and body language	The student demonstrated three of the following attributes: successful techniques to engage the audience, and appropriate eye contact, poise and body language	The student has demonstrated two of the following attributes: successful techniques to engage the audience, and appropriate eye contact, poise and body language	The student has demonstrated only one or none of the following attributes: successful techniques to engage the audience, appropriate eye contact, poise and body language
Conclusion (weighting 10%)	Clear and concise summary with effective links to the introduction and body of the presentation	Clear and concise summary of the presentation with links to the introduction and body of the presentation	The conclusion provided links to the introduction and body of the presentation, but was not concise or clear at times	The conclusion provided some links to the introduction and body of the presentation, but was not concise or clear	No conclusion or no links established to the introduction and body of the presentation

Research Method and Ethics

An explanatory mixed methods design (Creswell, 2008) was used to address the research question: *Did the elevator pitch assessment influence students' communication skills, self-efficacy, and relevance and, if so, why?* Greater weight is afforded to the qualitative data and analysis in this paper because the authors were particularly interested in whether the contextualisation and video technology employed in the elevator pitch explained the survey results. The use of qualitative research to help explain the quantitative results in more depth is consistent with this type of mixed methods design (Creswell, 2008, p. 566).

The mixed methods study in this paper involves Cohort 2 (C2), Cohort 3 (C3) and Cohort 4 (C4) after they completed the assessment. First, a survey instrument was administered in class at the beginning of the teaching period (week 1: C3 and C4; week 2: C2) to measure students' initial perceptions of communication skills, self-efficacy, and relevance. The instrument was then re-administered in class at the end of the teaching period. The survey instrument included three sections: demographic information; perceptions of self-efficacy; and communication skills/relevance. The behaviourally-specific statements in the communication skills/relevance section (refer to Appendix) were based on those used to evaluate the impact of the PDP on accounting students at an Australian university (Freudenberg *et al.*, 2010), which were adapted from Lizzio and Wilson (2004). Students self-evaluated for each statement on a seven-point scale, from 1 (not at all a characteristic of me) to 7 (very characteristic of me). The five statements in the self-efficacy section (refer to Appendix) were aligned to four assessment criteria: voice, audience engagement, organisation of presentation, and visual aids. This alignment ensured that task-specific self-efficacy was measured, namely the survey instrument was directly related to the elevator pitch assessment. Students rated the strength of their self-efficacy on a five-point scale from 1 (not confident at all) to 5 (very confident). A copy of the survey instrument is contained in the Appendix.

Students in each cohort were invited via email to participate in individual or (if they requested) group interviews of 5–30 minutes duration at the end of the teaching period. The interview included questions on the assessment item (best aspects and aspects in need of improvement), self-reflection, self-efficacy, communication skills, and relevance. The qualitative analysis in this paper addresses the three dimensions of communication from the C4 sample only, for two reasons.

- First, the authors had very small sample sizes in the other two cohorts (C2: 8 students; C3: 2 students), whereas the sample size in C4 was 18 students (17.5% of the cohort). The sample is also fairly representative of the cohort in terms of gender (10 male; 8 female) and average mark for the assessment item (7.25 sample; 7.26 cohort).
- Second, the qualitative data associated with self-reflection and the assessment item itself from C2 and C3 has been reported separately in the literature (Dickfos, Cameron and Hodgson, forthcoming).

The authors acknowledge that restricting the qualitative data to a single snapshot of one cohort is a significant limitation of this study. For example, comparisons cannot be drawn between the students' experiences of the elevator pitch assessment in other cohorts, nor can the interview data be used as a reliable basis for explaining the survey results for C2 and C3. Nevertheless, the authors contend that the qualitative data for C4 is of greater value for accounting educators wishing to employ some or all of the elevator pitch assessment than the qualitative data derived from the two previous cohorts. C4's greater value is that it provides the most recent snapshot of students' experiences involving an elevator pitch assessment that has reached the final stage of its evolution. Since C2, the authors have made a number of changes to the assessment, including the requirement for students to treat the camera lens as the 'eye' of the investor when making the presentation; a quicker process for uploading presentations; the use of a single office for all presentations to ensure consistent recording quality; the ability of students to borrow a Sony Bloggie camera to practise before their presentation (Dickfos, Cameron and Hodgson, forthcoming); the formal assessment of students' reflection of their video presentation; and the removal of visual aids as an assessment criterion. Accounting educators will be more interested in the final version of the elevator pitch assessment, a product of the lessons learned from the previous three cohorts, when considering its implementation. Consequently, the authors suggest the students' experiences attached to that final version (C4) are of greater significance to accounting educators than the small sample of interview responses from C2 and C3.

The survey instrument and interview process received university ethics approval. Before participating in the survey, students were presented with an information sheet which included, amongst other things, details about the research project, in particular its purpose; how the data would be used, including the use of demographic data (i.e. that it is used for analytical purposes and not to identify the student); that participation in the research was voluntary; how the data would be stored; the steps taken to protect the student's anonymity; a contact person if the student had any concerns with the research; and implicit consent to use the data by completing the survey. Student interviewees were also required to sign a consent form confirming their understanding of the information sheet prior to the interview. All student interviews were audio-taped and fully transcribed.

Descriptive Statistics

Selected summary descriptive statistics for each cohort are provided in Table 2. The low number of survey responses in C3 is due to class size (41 students compared with 135 students in C2 and 103 students in C4). Given the class size, the authors suggest that the respective response rates in each cohort were acceptable. The response rate is the number of participants from the sample who returned the survey expressed, in percentage terms. The sample for C2, C3, and C4 represents all students who attended the lecture when the survey instrument was administered. The class size referred to above represents the population, not the sample, and not all students attend lectures. Unfortunately, those who administered the survey instrument did not conduct a head count of students to calculate the sample. Nevertheless, the response rate using the population as the denominator was: C2 (35% and 46%); C3 (78% and 51%); and C4 (80% and 53%) (refer to Table 2). Whilst there is no universally accepted benchmark for a 'good' response rate, a higher response rate minimises sample bias and improves the prospects of generalising the results from the sample to the defined population (Creswell, 2008). In the context of educational research, Creswell (2008, p. 402) notes that a response rate of 50% or better is characteristic of 'many survey studies in leading educational journals'. The authors posit that the response rate, given the use of population not sample as the denominator, appears to be consistent with survey studies reported in educational research.

Unlike the case with C3 and C4, there were fewer students in C2 who completed the survey instrument before than after engaging with the assessment. This may be explained by the administration of the survey to C2 in the second week and not the first week of the teaching period, where, in the authors' experience, student attendance is at its peak. C3 also had no international respondents. This is due to the unique nature of the undergraduate degrees attached to this cohort. Students can either undertake their degree in an accelerated

Table 2. Descriptive statistics.

	Cohort 2		Cohort 3		Cohort 4	
Item	Before	After	Before	After	Before	After
N^a	47	62	32	21	82	55
Gender n (%)						
Male	15 (33)	18 (30)	16 (50)	11 (52)	39 (48)	27 (49)
Female	31 (67)	43 (70)	16 (50)	10 (48)	43 (52)	28 (51)
Type n (%)						
Domestic	36 (78)	47 (76)	32 (100)	21 (100)	52 (65)	41 (75)
International	10 (22)	15 (24)	0 (0)	0 (0)	28 (35)	14 (25)
Age n (%)						
Less than 20	18 (39)	17 (27)	7 (22)	5 (24)	15 (18)	12 (22)
20–30	25 (53)	39 (63)	16 (50)	10 (48)	58 (71)	35 (64)
31–40	2 (4)	4 (7)	7 (22)	5 (24)	6 (7)	6 (11)
> 40	2 (4)	2 (3)	2 (6)	1 (4)	3 (4)	2 (3)
Oral (degree)						
None	8 (17)	1 (2)	3 (9)	0 (0)	9 (11)	0 (0)
1 to 2	31 (66)	32 (51)	22 (69)	2 (10)	48 (59)	15 (27)
3 to 4	5 (11)	23 (37)	6 (19)	15 (71)	18 (22)	34 (62)
> 4	3 (6)	6 (10)	1 (3)	4 (19)	7 (8)	6 (11)
Oral (semester)						
None	32 (68)	37 (60)	17 (55)	9 (43)	43 (54)	38 (69)
1	12 (26)	21 (34)	11 (35)	10 (47)	24 (30)	12 (22)
2	2 (4)	2 (3)	3 (10)	1 (5)	8 (10)	4 (7)
> 2	1 (2)	2 (3)	0 (0)	1 (5)	5 (6)	1 (2)

Note: ^aSome n results differ because students did not answer the question.

mode or complete a two-year paid internship with an accounting firm as well as the PDP (Freudenberg et al., 2010), but visa work restrictions mean that international students cannot enrol in the internship. C3 has a higher number of mature age respondents (over 20%), but generally the vast majority of students in all cohorts are in the 30-and-under category. One other significant demographic statistic was the high percentage of female respondents in C2 (67–70%) compared to the approximate 50/50 male/female split in C3 and C4.

Company Law is offered after accounting students have completed half of their three-year degree (or 12 courses). At that time the majority of students (60–70%) have completed only one or two oral communication assessments. The 'oral (semester)' demographic represents the number of oral assessments the students completed during the semester (excluding the elevator pitch). The majority of students completed no oral assessments other than the elevator pitch. Approximately 90% of students reported completing no oral assessment or only one oral assessment. The purpose of including this statistic is to suggest that any positive results for the three dimensions of communication studied are more likely to be attributable to the elevator pitch rather than to other oral assessments completed during the degree or semester.

Results and Discussion

Summary survey results for skill, self-efficacy, and relevance measures across the three cohorts and at two points in time (beginning and end of the teaching period) are contained in Table 3. A detailed analysis of the survey results and the qualitative data for each measure follows.

Table 3. Oral communication: skills, self-efficacy and relevance.

Skill	Cohort 2 (C2)			Cohort 3 (C3)			Cohort 4 (C4)		
	Before	After	% Change	Before	After	% Change	Before	After	% Change
When I give verbal instructions or directions to people they usually clearly understand 'first time' what I mean (clarity)	4.51	4.87	8	4.86	4.86	0	4.59	4.89	6.5
When I make a presentation it seems to stimulate a fair level of interest amongst the listeners (audience engagement)	3.94	4.43	12.4	4.08	4.76	16.7	4.33	4.63	6.9
I know how to design a presentation to facilitate people's learning (organisation)	3.87	4.67	20.7	3.89	4.33	11.3	4.04	4.48	10.9
I know that I can make a persuasive argument in a group for something that is important to me (persuasiveness)	4.36	5.03	15.4	5.08	5.19	2.2	4.70	5.00	6
Average	4.17	4.75	13.9	4.48	4.79	6.9	4.42	4.75	7.5
Self-efficacy: how confident are you in your ability to …									
… be clear when presenting your ideas (voice; pace)	3.11	3.33	7.1	2.88	3.24	12.5	3.13	3.41	8.9
… present your ideas in a logical way which the audience can easily follow (organisation)	3.11	3.38	8.7	3.00	3.48	16	3.22	3.48	8.1
… present your ideas in a way which captures the audience's attention (audience engagement)	2.53	3.13	23.7	2.63	3.33	26.6	3.04	3.19	4.9
… use visual aids in a way which supports the presentation of your ideas (visual aids)	3.23	3.20	(0.9)	3.00	3.57	19	3.30	3.42	3.6
… use appropriate eye contact and body language when presenting your ideas (audience engagement)	2.83	3.34	18	2.97	3.57	20.2	3.22	3.39	5.3
Average	2.96	3.28	10.8	2.90	3.44	18.6	3.18	3.38	6.3
Relevance									
How relevant do you consider 'Oral Communication Skills' will be to your future work or career?	4.91	5.45	11	6.05	5.95	(1.7)	5.57	5.98	7.4

Oral Communication Skills

Students from each cohort reported an improvement in all four elements of oral communication skills measured over the evaluation period. The average increase was 13.9% (C2), 6.9% (C3), and 7.5% (C4), with a similar average 'after' score of between 4.75 and 4.80 across the three cohorts. The most significant gains for C3 and C4 were the elements *I know how to design a presentation to facilitate people's learning* (organisation) (11.3% and 10.9%, respectively), and *When I make a presentation it seems to stimulate a fair level of interest amongst the listeners* (audience engagement) (16.7% and 6.9%), with C2 experiencing the largest increase in the organisation element (20.7%). The smaller increases concerning the other two elements (clarity and persuasiveness) can be explained by their significantly higher reported 'before' scores compared to the organisation and audience engagement elements. Nevertheless, it is pleasing that the second highest score for all cohorts was clarity, as that is an aspect of communication raised by employers as a matter of skill-importance in the studies of Tempone *et al.* (2012) and Gray (2010).

The value of video-recording talks was the dominant theme (12 of 18 responses) in students' responses to the general interview question: *How has the promoter presentation affected your oral communication skills?* This dominance suggests that a key factor in the positive survey result for oral communication skills was the use of the Sony Bloggie cameras and the associated online resources. The opportunity for students to review the presentation during and after the assessment facilitated greater self-awareness of particular elements of their oral communication skills that required improvement, most notably pace, voice, audience engagement, and the conclusion. During the follow-up interviews, students frequently mentioned body language and the use of 'umms' and 'aahs'. They identified particular habits which detracted from the quality of their presentations, such as:

> crossing my arms or holding my wrist which is defensive [and that] I rocked back almost out of shot then rocked back in.

One student:

> could see the areas where you could tell that I was rehearsed with hand gestures it was obvious [...] if I didn't watch that, I wouldn't have picked up on that.

Students were also more aware of the pace of their delivery (four responses), in particular that they spoke too fast, affecting the investor's understanding of the pitch. As one student put it:

> I think I'm going to be more self-conscious about how quickly I speak [...] because that was a problem in the video. Like, I'd rush through something, and people would just be taken back, like "what did you just say?" it came out a little mumbly.

Another common error made by students was that they often did not have a proper conclusion with a clear take-away message and appropriate links to the introduction and body of the pitch. This problem was acknowledged by students on video review:

> The conclusion really surprised me actually [...] I slacked off at the end of it; and I'm more aware, watching that I sort of did tail off, so I realise that you have to conclude properly.

The combination of the video resource on 'good' and 'bad' elevator pitches and the assessment guidelines that were addressed in the video resource also had a positive impact on the organisation or structuring of presentations (five responses):

> You gave a really precise structure that we needed to follow, and this really helped me a lot during the construction and everything.

The interview responses support the significant improvement in organisation as reported by students in the survey results. Of most concern to the authors were students' comments that exemplars and guidelines (exemplar modelling) had not been provided to students in previous oral assessment items:

> everywhere else I haven't been taught how to structure a speech […] I've just kind of been winging it in other speeches.

This reveals one potential reason for the skills-expectation gap identified in the literature: accounting educators may assess generic skills but not necessarily deliver teaching and learning activities associated with those skills.

Self-efficacy

The self-efficacy measure contained five elements, with students in each cohort reporting an improvement in all but one element (C2: visual aids) over the evaluation period. C4 reported the lowest average improvement in self-efficacy (6.3%) but had the highest 'before' reported score (3.18). It may be that students in C4 were a little over-confident compared to students in C2 and C3. Self-reported improvement in visual aids had the smallest change in C2 (-0.9%) and C4 (3.6%). This is not surprising given that the visual aids component was worth only 10% of the overall mark for the assessment item in C2, that this component was not a separate criterion with respect to C3 and C4, and that the length of the elevator pitch (three minutes) minimised the use of visual aids. The largest reported increases in self-reported scores were for the elements *Present your ideas in a way which captures the audience's attention* (audience engagement) (C2: 23.7%; C3: 26.6%) and *Be clear when presenting your ideas* (voice; pace) (C4: 8.9%). The highest reported 'after' score for all three cohorts was *Present your ideas in a logical way which the audience can easily follow* (organisation) (C2: 3.38; C3: 3.48; C4: 3.48). This result is consistent with the significant self-reported increase in the organisation element within the oral communication skills measure, and thereby provides further support for the positive impact of the assessment on students' ability to design and deliver a well-organised presentation.

The usefulness of the video technology (seven responses) was the major theme identified in students' responses to the interview question: *How has the promoter presentation affected your confidence in oral communication?* In particular, students identified the self-modelling that occurred in reviewing their presentation. Prior to the assessment, students were not confident in their oral communication skills. The physiological state described by many students was nervousness. One student commented that:

> when I heard about this oral presentation last year, I felt really sick about it.

However, on viewing the presentation (self-modelling), students had a more accurate (and positive) perception of their communication skills, which in turn influenced their self-efficacy. As one student put it:

> I actually did kind of look at it and I thought, geez I really did look confident in what I was actually doing but I didn't feel it at the time […] I realise I come across much more confident in the actual video itself.

Conveying a confident demeanour is particularly important in oral communication, given that confidence is an aspect demanded by employers (Gray, 2010), and confidence can have a positive effect on students' self-efficacy when preparing for future oral communication activities, whether at university or in the workplace.

The presentation technology also corrected the students' misguided assumption that their physiological state was 'exposed' to audience members and the teacher in such a way that it would have a negative effect on their grade:

> now I'm actually aware that even though I feel horrible doing it, it might not actually be perceived as horrible when I actually deliver it.

Trepidation and negativity following submission of the assessment was replaced by relief and confidence upon its subsequent review:

> when I handed it in I thought this is going to be a rubbish mark you know. This is not going to be good. So then when I looked at it again, I was like, well it wasn't that bad.

Thus the video technology not only facilitated self-modelling, but moderated students' fears about the impact of their physiological state.

Relevance

The relevance measure on the survey contained a single element: *How relevant do you consider 'Oral Communication Skills' will be to your future work or career?* The students' self-reported 'before' and 'after' relevance scores for C2 (4.91 and 5.45) were disappointing, and of particular concern because the authors had selected the elevator pitch to assess oral communication skills based on relevance. Pitching is a generic skill that can be applied in a variety of business contexts before and after graduation, from job interviews to networking events and annual pay reviews. The elevator pitch assessment also relates to the regulation of promoters, a major topic covered in the company law curriculum (Dickfos, Cameron and Hodgson, forthcoming). In response to the disappointing scores in C2, the authors spent more time at the beginning of the C4 teaching period explaining to students the difference between generic skills and technical knowledge; justifying the assessment; and emphasising the importance of generic skills such as oral communication in the 'real world' of accounting. This effort appears to have influenced students' perceptions of relevance in C4, with a reported 'after' score of 5.98, an increase of 7.4%. The relatively high 'before' score for C3 (6.05) can be explained by previous research concerning members of this cohort, many of whom had completed one year of the PDP and commenced their paid internship (Freudenberg, Brimble and Cameron, 2011).

The self-reported survey results were supported by students' explanations as to how the assessment was relevant to the workplace and their future career. Students appreciated the contextualised learning experience and distinguished the pitch from a traditional presentation of technical knowledge (three responses). The pitch was better than:

> doing a presentation about Section 494 [Corporations Act 2001 (Cth) ...] because for me that would have been just burping up whatever information.

Students also recognised that the oral communication skills associated with the pitch could be used in a variety of workplace contexts, such as the following.

- Human resources: conveying the workplace ethos and culture to a new employee.
- Accounting: presenting an analysis of a client's financial statements or tax advice or presenting to colleagues on an accounting topic at a meeting.
- Sales: selling the business that you work for or a product or service.

- Investment: seeking money from a potential investor.
- Graduate employment: promoting yourself at job interviews, for example the ability to answer a common interview question: *Why should we recruit you?*
- Employer-employee relations: asking for a day off or communicating a resignation.
- Client communication: sitting in a business context and talking to a client.
- Self-promotion: selling your skill to a client.

Limitations and Further Research

The findings of this study should be viewed in the light of several limitations, including: the preliminary nature of the evidence; the use of students' perceptions as data; the variations in the pre- and post- assessment survey sample; the reporting of qualitative data from one cohort only (as previously discussed); and the short time frame of the analysis. The survey instrument did not trace students' responses. Tracing would have produced more reliable quantitative results but was not pursued because of the reduced sample size arising from the requirement to have the same students respond to the pre- and post- assessment survey. In the absence of tracing, the quantitative study does not incorporate a true longitudinal survey design, which would have enabled the authors to draw stronger conclusions about the impact of the assessment. Rather, the survey results produce a snapshot of different student populations in each cohort who experienced different online resources, different assessment design and practices (including the reflective exercise in C4), and different criteria as the elevator pitch activity evolved from cohort to cohort. For example, the significant change in skills and self-efficacy in C2 possibly may not be attributable to the assessment item itself but to the higher proportion of female students compared to C3 and C4. It may be that female students possess a greater awareness of their skill level and/or are less confident about their skills than their male counterparts, as evidenced by the lower average self-reported 'before' scores in C2. Furthermore, the domestic students of C3 who participate in the PDP cannot be compared to the mix of domestic and international student respondents in C2 and C4, who are not exposed to the PDP experience.

This study reports students' perceptions of their generic skills. This is a subjective measurement and therefore does not necessarily correspond with students' actual skill levels. Whilst there is some support that students can make meaningful judgements about their capabilities, Lizzio and Wilson (2004, p. 112) warn that there are 'perhaps more objective approaches to assessing capability' than employing a normative formula to measure students' capabilities. For example, the authors could have tested the students' communication skills at the start of the teaching period using the rubric in Table 1 and compared these results with the actual assessment results. This would have facilitated the tracing of students and provided a more objective basis for measuring the impact of the elevator pitch assessment on skill levels. Nevertheless, the use of semi-structured interviews to ascertain how the assessment affected students' communication skills did introduce a measure of objectivity to the study with respect to C4. The authors also posit that the video technology improved the accuracy of the self-reported 'after' scores in the quantitative study by enabling students to view their presentations after completing the assessment.

Further research could involve follow-up interviews with the students in the final year of their degree and/or after graduation to evaluate their later perceptions of the three communication dimensions. Accounting educators could apply all or part of the survey instrument and/or interview protocol to assess the influence of other authentic learning activities on oral communication skills and self-efficacy. With a larger sample size and tracing, researchers could also measure correlations amongst the three dimensions of communication in this study (e.g. the impact of relevance on self-efficacy and skills), as well as their relationships to academic performance and student demographics.

Conclusion

Accounting educators must not only equip their students with context-specific oral communication skills, but must also convey to those students the importance of such skills in terms of their employability. Both of these objectives can be achieved through the elevator pitch assessment. This paper provides preliminary evidence, using students' self-reporting measures and interviews, that the assessment positively influences three dimensions of communication: skills, self-efficacy, and relevance. Scores for all 10 self-reported elements increased during the evaluation period for each cohort, with the exceptions of visual aid use (C2) and relevance (C3). During follow-up interviews, the value of video technology was the dominant theme in students' responses to questions about skills and self-efficacy development. The students' viewing of their presentations using video technology fostered greater self-awareness of their skill levels, in particular with respect to voice, pace, body language, and the conclusion. The video technology enhanced students' self-efficacy through the mastery experience of the assessment itself; through self-modelling associated with reviewing the presentation; and through the correction of the students' assumption that their physiological state of nervousness was evident to group members and the teacher assessing the student. Students' responses also revealed that the contextualised learning experience of the elevator pitch enabled them to better appreciate the relevance of oral communication to their future employment, most notably regarding how the skills developed by the elevator pitch could be applied to a variety of business contexts.

The most significant result concerning oral communication in the quantitative study, as reported by the students, involved the structure or organisation of the presentation. The double digit increase in the score for the skills element *I know how to design a presentation to facilitate people's learning* and the highest reported 'after' score for the self-efficacy element *Present your ideas in a logical way which the audience can easily follow*, across all cohorts, support the positive student feedback about the online resources, which were designed to assist students with the organisation of their presentation. The results for these skill elements may also suggest that accounting educators need to provide more teaching and learning activities addressing oral communication skills. Based on the authors' experiences, the potential reasons for this include a lack of resources, academic capability, and time, in an already crowded curriculum, to teach generic skills such as oral communication. A 'gap' in the learning and teaching of generic skills has important implications for university administrators. Accreditation bodies require universities to demonstrate not only the assessment but the teaching and learning of generic skills. At the same time, administrators are facing growing concerns from industry and employers about the work-readiness of accounting graduates. The elevator pitch represents an authentic activity that can assist in bridging the skills-expectation gap in accounting education and meet the assurance of learning requirements of accreditation bodies with regard to oral communication.

References

Anderson, J. S. and Mohrweis, L. C. (2008) Using rubrics to assess accounting students' writing, oral presentations, and ethics skills, *American Journal of Business Education*, 1(2), pp. 85–93.

Bandura, A. (1977) Self-efficacy: toward a unifying theory of behavioral change, *Psychological Review*, 84, pp. 191–215.

Bandura, A. (1982) Self-efficacy mechanism in human agency, *American Psychologist*, 37(2), pp. 122–147.

Bandura, A. (1997) *Self-Efficacy: The Exercise of Control* (New York: Freeman).

Bandura, A. (2001) Social cognitive theory: an agentic perspective, *Annual Review of Psychology*, 52, pp. 1–26.

Bui, B. and Porter, B. (2010) The expectation-performance gap in accounting education: an exploratory study, *Accounting Education: An International Journal*, 19(1), pp. 23–50.

Creswell, J. W. (2008) *Educational Research: Planning, Conducting, and Evaluating Quantitative and Qualitative Research* (Upper Saddle River, NJ: Pearson Education).

Dallimore, E. J., Hertenstein, J. H. and Platt, M. B. (2004) Classroom participation and discussion effectiveness: student-generated strategies, *Communication Education*, 53(1), pp. 103–115.

Dickfos, J., Cameron, C. and Hodgson, C. (forthcoming) Blended learning: making an impact on assessment and self-reflection in accounting education, *Education + Training*, 56(2).

Freudenberg, B., Brimble, M. and Cameron, C. (2010) Where there is a WIL there is a way, *Higher Education Research & Development*, 29(5), pp. 575–588.

Freudenberg, B., Brimble, M. and Cameron, C. (2011) WIL and generic skill development: the development of business students' generic skills through work-integrated learning, *Asia-Pacific Journal of Cooperative Education*, 12(2), pp. 79–93.

Gist, M. E. and Mitchell, T. R. (1992) Self-efficacy: a theoretical analysis of its determinants and malleability, *Academy of Management Review*, 17(2), pp. 183–211.

Grace, D. M. and Gilsdorf, J. W. (2004) Classroom strategies for improving students' oral communication skills, *Journal of Accounting Education*, 22, pp. 165–172.

Gray, F. E. (2010) Specific oral communication skills desired in new accountancy graduates, *Business Communication Quarterly*, 73(1), pp. 40–67.

Gray, F. E. and Murray, N. (2011) 'A distinguishing factor': oral communication skills in new accountancy graduates, *Accounting Education: An International Journal*, 20(3), pp. 275–294.

Gulikers, J. T. M., Bastiaens, T. J. and Kirschner, P. A. (2004) A five-dimensional framework for authentic assessment, *Educational Technology, Research and Development*, 52(3), pp. 67–86.

Herrington, J. and Oliver, R. (2000) An instructional design framework for authentic learning environments, *Educational Technology, Research and Development*, 48(3), pp. 23–48.

Institute of Chartered Accountants (ICAA) and CPA Australia (CPA). (2009) *Professional Accreditation Guidelines for Higher Education Programs*. Available at http://www.cpaaustralia.com.au (accessed 20 November 2012).

Jackling, B. and de Lange, P. (2009) Do accounting graduates' skills meet the expectations of employers? A matter of convergence and divergence, *Accounting Education: An International Journal*, 18(14/5), pp. 369–385.

Jackson, M., Watty, K., Yu, L. and Lowe, L. (2006) *Inclusive Assessment. Improving Learning for All. A Manual for Improving Assessment in Accounting Education* (Strawberry Hills: The Carrick Institute for Learning and Teaching in Higher Education).

Jones, A. (2010) Generic attributes in accounting: the significance of the disciplinary context, *Accounting Education: An International Journal*, 19(1/2), pp. 5–21.

Kavanagh, M. and Drennan, L. (2008) What skills and attributes does an accounting graduate need? Evidence from student perceptions and employer expectations, *Accounting and Finance*, 48, pp. 279–300.

Levenson, L. (2000) Disparities in perceptions of generic skills: academics and employer, *Industry and Higher Education*, 14(3), pp. 157–164.

Lizzio, A. and Wilson, K. (2004) First-year students' perceptions of capability, *Studies in Higher Education*, 29(1), pp. 109–128.

Pintrich, P. and Degroot, E. (1990) Motivational and self-regulated learning components of classroom academic performance, *Journal of Educational Psychology*, 82(1), pp. 33–40.

Schunk, D. H. and Hanson, A. R. (1985) Peer models: influence on children's self-efficacy and achievement behaviour, *Journal of Educational Psychology*, 77, pp. 313–322.

Smythe, M. and Nikolai, L. A. (2002) A thematic analysis of oral communication concerns with implications for curriculum design, *Journal of Accounting Education*, 20, pp. 163–181.

Tempone, I., Kavanagh, M., Segal, N., Hancock, P., Howieson, B. and Kent, J. (2012) Desirable generic attributes for accounting graduates into the twenty-first century: the views of employers, *Accounting Research Journal*, 25(1), pp. 41–55.

Wood, R. and Bandura, A. (1989) Effect of perceived controllability and performance standards on self-regulation of complex decision making, *Journal of Personality and Social Psychology*, 56(5), pp. 805–814.

Zimmerman, B. J. (2000) Self-efficacy: an essential motive to learn, *Contemporary Educational Psychology*, 25, pp. 82–91.

Appendix. Survey Form

This research project is designed to explore the effectiveness of the course in assisting students in oral communication skills. Participation in this research is voluntary, and you can discontinue participation at any stage without penalty or the need to provide an explanation. Your decision will in no way impact upon your relationship with Griffith University or the researchers. Please refer to the Consent Form for further information. Part 1 requests brief demographic details. Part 2 requires you to assess your beliefs and confidence levels on several issues. Part 3 requires you to assess your generic capabilities in oral communication.

Part One: Demographic Information

	Questions			
1	What is your Degree?			
	Bachelor of Commerce	☐		
	Bachelor of Business	☐		
	Other (please specify)	☐	_____	
2	Your gender is:	☐	Male	(tick appropriate
		☐	Female	box)
3	Your age is:	☐	<20 yrs	(tick appropriate
		☐	20–30 yrs	box)
		☐	31–40 yrs	
		☐	>40 yrs	
4	Nationality. Are you a …	☐	Domestic student	(tick appropriate box)
		☐	International student	
5	How many years have you been studying at Griffith University? (full-time equivalent years)	☐	<1 yr	(tick appropriate
		☐	1–2yrs	box)
		☐	3–4yrs	
		☐	>4 yrs	
6	How many years ago did you finish High School?		_____	(number of years)
7	Did either of your parents graduate from university?	☐	Yes	(tick appropriate
		☐	No	box)
8	Is either of your parents a member of a Professional body? (i.e. Chartered Accountants, CPA, Engineer Society, Law Society, Economics Society)	☐ ☐	Yes No	(tick appropriate box)
9	What was your rank to gain entry into University?		_____	
10	Do you have a prior Degree from a University?	☐	Yes	(tick appropriate
		☐	No	box)
11	Do you have professional work experience of greater than 500 hours? (approx. three months full-time equivalent)	☐	Yes	What type? _____
		☐	No	
		If no, have you had any type of work experience?		
		☐		Yes
		☐		No

(Continued)

Appendix. Continued

Questions		
12 How many oral assessment items have you completed during your current Degree (i.e. you received a mark for oral communication such as a presentation)?	☐ None ☐ 1–2 ☐ 3–4 ☐ >4	(tick appropriate box)
13 How many oral assessment items do you have (not counting Company Law) this semester?	☐ None ☐ 1 ☐ 2 ☐ >2	(tick appropriate box)

Part Two: Self Belief and Confidence

Below is a list of self-belief questions. Please indicate your confidence in your ability to perform each activity by circling the appropriate number using this scale:

How 'confident' are you in your ability to ...	Not confident at all	A little confident	Moderate amount of confidence	A lot confident	Very confident
1 ... be clear when presenting your ideas	1	2	3	4	5
2 ... present your ideas in a logical way which the audience can easily follow	1	2	3	4	5
3 ... present your ideas in a way which captures the audience's attention	1	2	3	4	5
4 ... use visual aids in a way which supports the presentation of your ideas	1	2	3	4	5
5 ... use appropriate eye contact and body language when presenting your ideas	1	2	3	4	5

Part Three: Self-assessment of Generic Capabilities

This is a self-assessment exercise; you are presented with a series of 'capability descriptions' and you are asked to rate them on a seven-point scale of how characteristic each is of you (**1 = not at all characteristic of you, 7 = very characteristic of you**).

Exercises like this are useful to the extent that they are based on **accurate information** – it is easy to inflate your ratings to 'look good' – but this is not an examination, there aren't any right or wrong answers. We invite you to make **a balanced assessment of your <u>current</u> capabilities**, being neither 'too hard' nor 'too soft' on yourself.

	Not at all			Moderately			Very
ORAL COMMUNICATION SKILLS	*(characteristic of me ...)*						
When I give verbal instructions or directions to people they usually clearly understand 'first time' what I mean	1	2	3	4	5	6	7
When I make a presentation it seems to stimulate a fair level of interest amongst the listeners	1	2	3	4	5	6	7
I know how to design a presentation to facilitate people's learning	1	2	3	4	5	6	7
I know that I can make a persuasive argument in a group for something that is important to me	1	2	3	4	5	6	7
How relevant do you consider 'Oral Communication Skills' will be to your future work or career?	1	2	3	4	5	6	7

A Business Communication Module for an MBA *Managerial Accounting* Course: A Teaching Note

DAVID E. STOUT

Youngstown State University, USA

ABSTRACT   *This Teaching Note describes a two-hour-and-40-minute* Business Communication *module developed and used by the author over the past six years in an MBA* Managerial Accounting *course at a university in the USA. The module has two modest but important goals: to sensitize graduate accounting students to the importance of communication skills for professional success; and to provide students with a set of writing-improvement resources. The students' component of the module consists of a set of five readings and two learning resources. For teachers, a comprehensive set of* PowerPoint *slides is available from the author. The module is flexible in two respects: it can be used in graduate-level accounting courses other than* Managerial Accounting; *and a reduced version of in-class presentation time is possible by using only a sub-set of the* PowerPoint *slides, based on teacher preferences. Student responses to the module have been consistently positive and have supported continued use of the module into the future.*

1. Introduction

The importance of developing student communication skills in graduate degree programmes, including business programmes, has been advanced for many years. This Teaching Note provides a detailed description of an in-class *Business Communication* module the author has developed and delivered to students in the MBA *Managerial Accounting* course which he teaches. The two-hour-and-40-minute module has two modest but important goals:

This paper was edited and accepted by Richard M. S. Wilson.

- to convince students of the validity of devoting class time in a graduate accounting class to the issue of communication skills, particularly the importance of written communication skills to professional success; and
- to provide students with resources (in the form of handouts) that they can use for reference purposes.

As preparation for the in-class session, students are assigned a set of five short readings. In class, the teacher uses a comprehensive set of self-developed *PowerPoint* slides to deliver the lecture.[1] These slides can be used in graduate accounting courses other than *Managerial Accounting* and can be amended or customized to meet differing educator objectives. The module's in-class presentation can be delivered by other accounting educators with a modest level of preparation time.

The rest of this Teaching Note is organized as follows. In the next section, the issue of the importance of communication skills to professional business practice is discussed (albeit briefly), selected resources as reflected in the literature of accounting education are referenced, and a personal statement regarding the involvement of the author in the area of communication skills and accounting education is offered. Next, the paper discusses the context for the module developed and used by the author. This discussion is followed by a detailed description of the module. Sample student feedback from the four most recent sections of the class taught by the author is then presented. The paper concludes with a short summary. An appendix to the paper contains a set of 50 multiple-choice items that teachers can use for assessment/evaluation purposes.

2. Background

2.1. *Importance of Developing Effective Communication Skills*

Many studies have been undertaken and pronouncements made over the past 25 years or so regarding the competencies needed for professional success in business and accounting. In summarizing this work as it relates to accounting, the Pathways Commission (2012a, pp. 131–132)[2] recently stated:

> Accountants (today) typically hold vital positions of trust with professional responsibilities to both internal and external users. Fulfilling those responsibilities requires technical competency and professional integrity. Competence entails more than technical knowledge. To be competent, an accountant must possess both technical knowledge and professional skills, such as the ability to apply knowledge in making reasoned judgments and to *communicate effectively*. (Emphasis added)

An online supplement (Pathways Commission, 2012b) to the Pathways Commission Report provides a summary of 'competencies needed by future accountants', based on an analysis of 27 sources. In this supplement, individual competencies are classified into three broad groups:

- Technical Knowledge, which includes five broad areas (Operational/Management Accounting, Financial Accounting and Reporting, etc.);
- Professional Skills, which includes eight broad areas (Communication/Collaboration, Leadership Skills, etc.); and
- Professional Integrity/Ethics includes five areas (Ethical Reasoning and Judgment, Professional and Legal Responsibilities, etc.).

It is interesting to note that, among the 18 broad areas, the two most-cited are 'Communi-cation/Collaboration' and 'Behaviour/Attitude Consistent with Core Values'. Each of these areas was cited in 11 of the 27 studied sources. 'Oral and Written Communication Skills' was the most highly-cited competency within the 'Communication/Collaboration' area, with nine of 27 citations.

Conrad and Newberry (2012, p. 112) assert that 'despite academia's best efforts there still remains a gap in communication skills desired by business practitioners and those delivered by new graduates'. The authors reference a study undertaken in the USA by the National Commission on Writing (NCW) (2004), which indicates that:

- a majority of respondent organizations assess writing skills when considering hiring and promotion decisions;
- writing skills of recent graduates are generally considered unsatisfactory; and
- writing skills are essential for those seeking managerial and promotion opportunities.

Thus, on the basis of many studies and pronouncements, and as summarized in the Path-ways Commission Report (2012b) and in the report prepared by the NCW (2004), devoting class time in accounting courses can be viewed a priori as a legitimate endeavour, the ulti-mate objective of which is to add to the professional skill set needed by future business professionals.

2.2. Selected Resources and Approaches: Accounting Education[3]

Ballantine and Larres (2009) provide evidence regarding the perceived effectiveness of cooperative learning (relative to simple group learning) in terms of developing both inter-personal and communication skills. Matherly and Burney (2009) present an intervention that can be used to improve the writing skills of accounting students. Their intervention builds on three primary approaches: *peer evaluation* (students evaluate the writing of fellow students), *repetition* (i.e. repeated effort), and *task-relevant topics*.[4] Craig and McKinney (2010) describe a semester-long programme that focuses on improving the fol-lowing writing skills of accounting students: organization, grammar, style, professional writing, and case writing.[5] Data obtained from a quasi-experimental design suggests that these writing interventions can improve accounting students' writing skills. Krom and Williams (2011) discuss the use of creative writing, in the form of three modes of storytelling (fairy tales, fables, and poetry), in *Introductory Accounting* courses. The authors discuss the application of these writing methods as an innovative way to enhance and assess student learning in accounting, as well as being a mechanism for improving student writing skills.

Each of the four publications described above provides a different method for integrat-ing writing skills into the accounting curriculum. Three of the papers (Matherly and Burney [2009]; Craig and McKinney [2010]; Krom and Williams [2011]) present evidence regarding writing-skill improvement, while the fourth (Ballantine and Larres [2009]) pro-vides evidence in the form of student perceptions. All four papers focus on undergraduate accounting education. In contrast, the present paper focuses on graduate-level accounting education.

2.3. Personal Reflection

From time to time, I have been queried as to what motivated my interest in and commitment to developing the writing skills of the students I teach, particularly graduate business students.

My interest in this area goes back to my initial faculty appointment at Rider College (now Rider University). I was one of several faculty members from the business school who participated in a college-wide 'writing-across-the-curriculum' programme. In the summer following this programme, I continued my involvement in the area through an appointment as a faculty fellow at a summer writing institute hosted by Rutgers University in the USA.

Very soon into my tenure as a full-time faculty member teaching accounting, I realized that, by and large, accounting educators in the USA were doing an excellent job in terms of conveying technical knowledge to students. Lacking, however, was attention to the development of professional (or 'soft') skills, such as writing. I made a personal commitment to do something to address this issue. Over the years, I have maintained an active publishing interest in the area,[6] an interest that was sparked initially by my experience at Rider College and then reignited during my tenure as editor of *Issues in Accounting Education*.[7]

3.   The Context: MBA *Managerial Accounting*

The instructional resource described in this paper was developed for use in the *Managerial Accounting* course required of all students in the MBA programme at the author's institution. The class meets one night per week over a 16-week term; each meeting is two hours and 40 minutes. The vast majority of students in the programme are part-time students. As indicated by information presented in Table 1, in addition to technical knowledge in the field of management accounting, my course embraces learning objectives related to ethics/social responsibility, communication skills development, and the honing of spreadsheet skills.

4.   Materials

An excerpt from the instructor's spring 2013 syllabus for the course pertaining to the communication skills module is presented in Table 2. The five assigned readings are posted to the *Blackboard* site designated for the course and are therefore readily accessible by students. In addition, two 'resource' files are posted to the site.[8] As indicated in the syllabus excerpt presented in Table 1, students are encouraged to use these resources in the present course, in other courses in the MBA programme, and in their day-to-day business writing.

For presenting the module in class, I use a set of self-constructed *PowerPoint* slides, available on request. Students do not receive these slides prior to class; however, the slides are made available to interested students after the presentation. The slides are divided into four parts, as follows.

1. *Introduction/Motivation/Justification: A Stakeholder Perspective* (slides 3 to 33). These slides address the issue of why development of communication skills matters for MBA students and why addressing this topic is a legitimate educational objective for a graduate-level 'accounting' course.
2. *Gap Analysis: How Are Educational Institutions Doing?* (slides 34 to 42, inclusive). These slides cover a single issue: whether there is an ability-expectations gap in the market regarding the communication skills of new hires.
3. *Writing-Related Resources* (slides 43 to 49). These slides first sensitize students to what businesses and educational institutions are doing to address the communication skills gap identified in part two of the presentation. The slides then provide an overview of the two writing-related resources (Word documents) I make available to my students. These slides conclude with reference to the work of Oppenheimer (2006) regarding the relationship between writing style and perceived intelligence.

Table 1. Learning objectives from MBA *Managerial Accounting* syllabus (ACC6902: Management Accounting Systems).

Educational Objectives

In addition to technical knowledge of managerial accounting, this course embraces the following educational objectives:

Communication Skills: Successful businesspeople possess strong communication skills. Thus, a goal of this course is to help hone these skills. I do this by:

(1) Delivering to you a class lecture on 'Improving Business Communication Skills'. As part of this lecture I will be posting to *Blackboard* five short background readings and two learning resource files ('tips' for improving business writing). You are encouraged to use these resources in this course, in other courses in your MBA programme, and in your day-to-day business writing.
(2) Providing some open-ended questions and short-essay questions on the in-class exams.

Computer Skills: As noted above, each week you will use *Excel* to complete one or more homework assignments. In addition, I've developed two instructional cases for this course, each of which has a heavy *Excel* component.

• The first case deals with the topic of *cost estimation* and has an extensive tutorial regarding the use of *Excel* for estimating and interpreting both linear and non-linear cost functions.
• The second case focuses on the development of a short-term profit-planning (i.e. cost-volume-profit, or CVP) model for a non-manufacturing business.

In short, weekly assignments plus coverage of the above two educational cases together should help hone your *Excel* skills.

Ethics and Social Responsibility: We will cover, as part of text Chapter 9 ('Behavioral and Organisational Issues in Management Accounting and Control Systems'), the IMA's *Code of Professional Conduct*, the WCBA *Code of Conduct*, and various ISO standards that relate to the management of environmental performance.

4. *Sample Grammatical Issue: The Problem of Faulty Modifiers* (slides 50 to 75). These slides are offered as a comprehensive set of examples of one of the 10 items discussed in the '10 tips' writing resource: the problem of 'faulty modifiers' (i.e. misplaced and dangling modifiers).

A detailed lesson plan based on the full set of slides is provided in Appendix A. This plan reflects the full complement of materials used by the author in a two-hour-and-40-minute session. Instructors can adapt the slides to fit their needs and preferences. The author has prepared a supplementary set of *PowerPoint* slides (available, on request) that provide additional examples of the grammar lesson covered in Part Four. Examples from this second set of slides can be used in lieu of, or in addition to, the slides contained in the primary deck. The author also has prepared slides covering grammar topics other than faulty modifiers, which also are available on request.[9] In addition, instructors may want to have students use the general guidelines presented in Gallo (2006) to rate the instructor's in-class presentation.[10]

5. Student Feedback

A short evaluation form developed by the author can capture student perceptions regarding the value of the presentation. The survey instrument consists of five closed-end questions,

Table 2. Communication skills module: excerpt from MBA *Managerial Accounting* syllabus (spring 2013).

Date	Topic	Learning resources/materials	Other
19 Feb.	Business Communication Skills	Read (prior to class): 1. Dillon (2004) 'What Corporate America Can't Build: A Sentence', *New York Times*, 7 December 2. Gallo (2006) 'Ten Worst Presentation Habits', *BusinessWeek Online*, 16 February 3. Associated Press (AP), 'Business Schools Take Aim at Bad Writing' (5 December, 2006) 4. Middleton (2011) 'Students Struggle for Words', *Wall Street Journal*, 3 March 5. Shallenbarger (2012) 'This Embarrasses You and I*', *Wall Street Journal Online*, 20 June Resources for improving your writing: 1. 'Ten Tips for Improving Business Writing' (Word document) 2. Excerpts from 'SEC Plain English Writing Handout' (Word document)	Instructor-prepared *PowerPoint* slides (in-class presentation by the instructor)

Note: SEC, Securities and Exchange Commission.

to which students respond using a five-point Likert-type scale (1 = 'Strongly agree' ... 5 = 'Strongly disagree'). The survey also asks the following two open-ended questions: What did you like most about the communication skills presentation? What, if anything, did you dislike about the presentation? Students are asked to respond anonymously to the survey.[11]

5.1. *Closed-end Questions*

Survey results for the five closed-end questions from the four most recent sections of the course taught by the author are reported in Table 3. As can be seen, student responses to the survey instrument indicate that they saw value in the module, that they agreed that it was appropriate to devote class time in an 'accounting' class to the material covered in the module, and that they recommended the continued use of the module in future offerings of the course.

5.2. *Open-ended Responses*

Across the four sections of the course (*n* = 64), 27 students offered comments on the two open-ended questions on the survey instrument. In this combined sample, there was only a single comment that could be construed as being negative:

Table 3. Student survey results (closed-end questions; scale: 1 = 'Strongly agree', 5 = 'Strongly disagree').

#	Question	Mean	Median	% 1 or 2	% 4 or 5
	Panel A: spring 2013 (*n* = 14)				
1	The communication skills module provided information that is likely to be useful for my professional career.	1.53	2.00	100	0
2	The communication skills module represented a good use of class time.	1.31	1.00	93	0
3	I found little incremental value in the assigned readings and in-class discussion (*PowerPoint* slides).	4.51	5.00	0	100
4	It was appropriate to devote accounting class time to covering the module.	1.40	1.00	100	0
5	I recommend continued use of the communication skills module in this course.	1.20	1.00	100	0
	Panel B: fall 2012 (*n* = 12)				
1	The communication skills module provided information that is likely to be useful for my professional career.	1.33	1.00	100%	0%
2	The communication skills module represented a good use of class time.	1.42	1.00	100%	0%
3	I found little incremental value in the assigned readings and in-class discussion (*PowerPoint* slides).	4.67	5.00	0%	100%
4	It was appropriate to devote accounting class time to covering the module.	1.17	1.00	100%	0%
5	I recommend continued use of the communication skills module in this course.	1.17	1.00	100%	0%
	Panel C: spring 2012 (*n* = 17)				
1	The communication skills module provided information that is likely to be useful for my professional career.	1.76	2.00	82.5%	0%
2	The communication skills module represented a good use of class time.	1.65	2.00	94.1%	5.9%
3	I found little incremental value in the assigned readings and in-class discussion (*PowerPoint* slides).	4.47	4.00	0.0%	100.0%
4	It was appropriate to devote accounting class time to covering the module.	1.47	1.00	100.0%	0%
5	I recommend continued use of the communication skills module in this course.	1.18	1.00	100.0%	0%
	Panel D: fall 2011 (*n* = 21)				
1	The communication skills module provided information that is likely to be useful for my professional career.	1.67	2.00	90.5%	0%
2	The communication skills module represented a good use of class time.	1.76	2.00	85.7%	4.8%
3	I found little incremental value in the assigned readings and in-class discussion (*PowerPoint* slides).	4.38	4.00	0.0%	100.0%
4	It was appropriate to devote accounting class time to covering the module.	1.57	1.00	100.0%	0%
5	I recommend continued use of the communication skills module in this course.	1.29	1.00	100.0%	0%

I took this course to learn about managerial accounting (which I don't know), not writing (which I do know).

The following comments are representative of the positive comments received.

It is refreshing to see that the professor cares more broadly about our education – beyond the subject matter at hand. I thought the communication module was very helpful.

Very convincing presentation. As a result of this presentation I've made a commitment to improve my writing skills.

I have an engineering background. I know I have certain deficiencies, including the area of writing ability. I entered the MBA program to address those deficiencies. Thank you for the module you've developed.

I wish other profs were as broad-minded and helpful in terms of skills and abilities beyond technical knowledge.

Your materials have convinced me of the need to hone my writing skills, as part of my professional development. Prior to your lecture, I thought the subject would be boring. It definitely was not! I enjoyed the presentation/discussion in class.

Thank you for taking the time to put together this lecture! It is greatly appreciated. I have an engineering background and your presentation is making me think about some 'gaps' in my education – gaps that I'll likely have to address (or that I should address). Thumbs up!

6. Assessment/Evaluation

When providing instruction on 'soft skills' such as writing skills, teachers commonly must grapple with the question of whether and how to assess the material covered in the module. Without assessment, it can be maintained, students will not take the material seriously and, as important, the instructor has no direct evidence as to whether related educational goals have been realized.[12]

The author is of two minds regarding this issue, at least as it pertains to the module discussed in this paper. On the one hand, there is validity to the argument that *some* students would take the material more seriously if it were 'covered in the exam'. On the other hand, over the past few years only a distinct minority of MBA students have asked that the module content be included on the course final exam.

After experimenting with the module for a number of years, I have decided not to test my students for material covered in this module for two reasons:

- the module is used within a graduate-level course offered as part of a professional degree programme (MBA). The presumption is that a majority of (though certainly not all) students will be inherently motivated to take seriously and use the material supplied to them; and
- as noted above, one of the primary goals of the module is to sensitize students to the importance of writing to their professional careers. The author is satisfied that the post-presentation survey administered to students provides sufficient feedback in this regard.

For teachers who, as a follow-up to the module, would like to include some test-related items on an in-class exam, Appendix B offers some relevant examples, all of which are in multiple-choice format. Alternatively, these items could be used informally to test student knowledge, either before the module, after the module, or both. For those programmes seeking accreditation (or reaffirmation of accreditation) the use of these items may be particularly useful.[13]

7. Summary

Communication skills development continues to be a key professional learning objective in professional business education, including accounting. This Teaching Note provides a detailed discussion and overview of a discrete business communication module in an MBA *Managerial Accounting* course. Student materials consist of seven files: five short readings (principally from the *Wall Street Journal*) regarding the importance of communication skills to professional success; and two resource files (which students are encouraged to use both in the course at hand, in other MBA-level courses, and in their professional lives). The comprehensive set of *PowerPoint* slides used as the basis for the author's in-class presentation is available for use by other teachers. These slides are divided roughly into four parts: introduction/motivation; the expectations gap ('how are we, as educational institutions, doing in terms of developing the communication skills of our students?'); institutional and business responses to the problem; and an in-depth exploration of the problem of 'faulty modifiers'. The *PowerPoint* slides are flexible and allow either for a reduced-time presentation or coverage of additional topics, based on the preference of the teacher. Two sets of supplementary slides are available from the author: the first contains additional examples of 'faulty modifiers'; the second addresses some additional writing-related problems. The module discussed in this paper has been used successfully by the author in an MBA *Managerial Accounting* course, but the material in the module can be used in other graduate accounting courses as well; it is not managerial accounting-specific.

Acknowledgements

The author thanks the guest editors (F. Elizabeth Gray and Lynn Hamilton) and the reviewers for their helpful (and supportive) comments, which improved both the content and flow of this manuscript. My special thanks, too, to Professor Joe DaCrema for our many chats, for his patience with me as I gained a renewed appreciation for the value of business communication skills, and for our earlier collaborations.

Notes

[1] These slides are available on request from the author.

[2] The Pathways Commission on Accounting Higher Education (www.pathwayscommission.org) was created by the American Accounting Association (AAA) and the American Institute of Certified Public Accountants (AICPA) in the USA to study the future structure of higher education for the accounting profession.

[3] The author reviewed writing-related articles published the past five years in *Accounting Education: an international journal*, *Issues in Accounting Education*, and the *Journal of Accounting Education*.

[4] In Exhibit 1 (p. 397) the authors present what they call 'Minimum Writing Rules', a handout which they provide to students at the beginning of the semester. These 'writing rules' are similar to those covered in my in-class presentation, either in the *PowerPoint* slides themselves or in the two learning resource files provided to students.

[5] The authors report (p. 258) that they chose this set of five writing competencies to address writing-related problems that they had observed in their accounting students over many years. Specific problem areas identified by the authors include: verb/subject agreement; confusion over the use of definite and indefinite articles, possessive case, and singular versus plural nouns; poor spelling; inattention to structure, argument

development, and paragraphing; and the use of inappropriate or imprecise words. The items in my own presentation cover many of the same topics as those listed by Craig and McKinney (2010).

[6]Papers in this regard include: Stout and Wygal (1989), Stout and Hoff (1989/90), Stout, Wygal and Hoff (1990), Stout, Sumutka and Wygal (1991), Stout and DaCrema (2004), and Stout and DaCrema (2005).

[7]During the three-year term of my editorship, Joe DaCrema, who had recently retired as an English professor from Villanova University, served as my administrative assistant. This close association rekindled my interest in the area of communication skills and accounting education. As indicated by the acknowledgement included at the end of this paper, I am very grateful to Professor DaCrema for his valuable insights, guidance, and motivation.

[8]An additional resource that can be used as a resource/handout to students – in particular, accounting students – is the article by Danziger (1997).

[9]These slides present various grammatical errors and corrections. As noted by an anonymous reviewer, 'teaching students by showing them slide after slide of all the mistakes they can make is not conducive to helping them learn to write well'. That reviewer points to Elbow (1998) and the work of Rose cited therein. The main argument here, as encapsulated by Elbow (1998, p. xix), is that 'getting rid of badness (in writing) doesn't lead to excellence'. Thus, a cautionary note needs to be raised in terms of the pedagogical practice embodied in the supplementary set of *PowerPoint* slides. The author maintains, however, that within the context in which he has used these slides, they have been well received by students. Further, this approach is, to varying degrees, used in popular writing handbooks (e.g. Alred, Brusaw and Oliu, 2000; Hult and Huckin, 2008). A recent book by Yagoda (2013), an obvious counter view to Zinsser (2006), provides support for this pedagogical approach. Yagoda's primary message is the need to teach individuals *how not to write bad* (or badly) and that the practice of 'directing students to the appropriate entry in the book [...] may actually help them learn what they are doing wrong and how to address the issue' (p. 4).

[10]On occasion, I use Gallo (2006) as a means for allaying student fears regarding the process (or 'journey') of developing communication skills, including presentation skills. After going through this assigned reading quickly, I ask students for honest feedback regarding my own presentation that evening. The goal is to reinforce in the minds of students that all of us make mistakes. Put another way, this is an attempt on my part to better connect with the students and to put a 'human face' on the presentation.

[11]Completed questionnaires are collected each term by the instructor's graduate assistant and returned to the instructor after the conclusion of the semester.

[12]The evidence presented in Table 3 is *indirect* in the sense that it reflects student *perceptions*, not actual performance.

[13]Note that the items included in Appendix B cover issues beyond the topic of faulty modifiers. These additional issues are addressed in the two hand-out resources made available to students. Also, several of the writing-related issues addressed in Appendix B are covered in the set of supplementary *PowerPoint* slides referred to in Section 4.

[14]The following ranking results can be conveyed to students: 2003 – Wharton School, University of Pennsylvania; Dartmouth College; University of Michigan; and Northwestern University; 2004 – University of Michigan; Carnegie Mellon University; Dartmouth College; Wharton School, University of Pennsylvania; 2005 – Dartmouth College; University of Michigan; Carnegie Mellon University; and Northwestern University; 2006 – University of Michigan; Dartmouth College; Carnegie Mellon University; and Columbia University; 2007 – Dartmouth College; University of California, Berkeley; Columbia University; and Massachusetts Institute of Technology.

[15] Frecka and Reckers (2010) surveyed practising auditors ($n > 500$) regarding the relevance of knowledge and skills needed in practice. In terms of required skills, 'high importance was attached to five (of the seven listed) skills, with critical thinking and problem analysis topping the list [...] followed closely by report writing and written communication' (p. 224). In terms of which of 21 listed knowledge and skills areas respondents thought should receive increased attention in the curriculum, 'report writing/written communication skills' garnered the number one spot.

[16]Bui and Porter (2010) provide survey results from students, employers, and accounting faculty members from a single university in New Zealand regarding the skills that accounting graduates should possess. All of the employer interviewees considered communication skills (oral, written, and interpersonal) to be *essential* (emphasis added). Chaffey, Van Peursem and Low (2011, p. 165) provide survey evidence – obtained from 130 practicing auditors in New Zealand – that 'the most preferred and agreed (audit) skill is [...] communication (ability)'. Even among (additional) 'disciplinary knowledge to which future auditors should be exposed', communication placed second – out of eight areas – in terms of perceived importance (p. 172). Finally, Crawford, Helliar and Monk (2011, p. 116) present survey responses from 124 UK academics and 321 practising chartered accountants regarding the importance of '16 generic

skills that may be important to the accounting and auditing profession'. Academic respondents indicated that analytical skills and written communication skills are the most important generic skills. Practitioner respondents 'thought that all 16 skills were important, but a ranking of their importance showed that analytical skills, presentation skills, and written communication skills were the most important' (p. 129).

[17]*Dangling modifiers* can be thought of as 'would-be' modifiers in the sense that they don't technically modify anything in a sentence. 'Passing the building, the vandalism became visible' and 'Although intact, graffiti covered every inch of walls and windows' are examples. By contrast a *misplaced modifier* falls in the wrong place in a sentence. 'He served steak to the men on paper plates' and 'According to police, many dogs are killed by automobiles and trucks roaming unleashed' are examples.

[18]A supplemental *PowerPoint* file containing additional examples, most taken from recent issues of the *Wall Street Journal*, is available, on request, from the author.

References

Alred, G. J., Brusaw, C. T. and Oliu, W. E. (2000) *The Business Writer's Handbook*, 6th edn (Boston, MA: Bedford/St Martin's).

Ansun, C. M., Schwegler, R. A. and Muth, M. F. (2007) *The Longman Concise Companion* (New York: Pearson Education).

Ballantine, J. and Larres, P. M. (2009) Accounting undergraduates' perceptions of cooperative learning as a model for enhancing their interpersonal and communication skills to interface successfully with professional accounting education and training, *Accounting Education: An International Journal*, 18(4–5), pp. 387–402.

Bui, B. and Porter, B. (2010) The expectation-performance gap in accounting education: an exploratory study, *Accounting Education: An International Journal*, 19(1–2), pp. 23–50.

Chaffey, J., Van Peursem, K. A. and Low, M. (2011) Audit education for future professionals: perceptions of New Zealand auditors, *Accounting Education: An International Journal*, 20(2), pp. 153–185.

Conrad, D. and Newberry, R. (2012) Identification and instruction of important business communication skills for graduate business education, *Journal of Education for Business*, 87(2), pp. 112–120.

Craig, R. C. and McKinney, C. N. (2010) A successful writing skills development programme: results of an experiment, *Accounting Education: An International Journal*, 19(3), pp. 257–278.

Crawford, L., Helliar, C. and Monk, E. A. (2011) Generic skills in audit education, *Accounting Education: An International Journal*, 20(2), pp. 115–131.

Danziger, E. (1997) Writing in plain English, *Journal of Accountancy*, July, pp. 71–74.

Elbow, P. (1998) *Writing with Power: Techniques for Mastering the Writing Process*, 2nd edn (Oxford: Oxford University Press).

Frecka, T. J. and Reckers, P. M. J. (2010) Rekindling the debate: what's right and what's wrong with masters of accountancy programs: the staff auditor's perspective, *Issues in Accounting Education*, 25(2), pp. 215–226.

Gallo, C. (2006) The 10 worst presentation habits – speakers can be their own worst enemies. Here are our expert's tips on how to make a presentation sing, *BusinessWeek Online*, 16 February. Available at http://images.businessweek.com/ss/06/02/mistakes/index_01.htm.

Hult, C. A. and Huckin, T. N. (2008) *The Brief New Century Handbook*, 4th edn (New York, NY: Pearson/Longman).

Krom, C. L. and Williams, S. V. (2011) Tell me a story: using creative writing in introductory accounting courses to enhance and assess student learning, *Journal of Accounting Education*, 29(2), pp. 234–249.

Matherly, M. and Burney, L. (2009) Using peer-reviewed writing in the accounting curriculum: a teaching note, *Issues in Accounting Education*, 24(3), pp. 393–414.

Milliron, V. C. (2012) CPAs explore a pre-certification pathway to excellence, *The Accounting Educators' Journal*, 22, pp. 43–71. Available at http://www.aejournal.com/ojs/index.php/aej/article/view/160/122.

National Commission on Writing (NCW) (2004) *Writing: A Ticket to Work . . . or a Ticket Out* (New York, NY: College Entrance Examination Board).

O'Conner, P. T. (1996) *Woe is I: The Grammarphobe's Guide to Better English in Plain English* (New York: Riverhead Books).

Oppenheimer, D. M. (2006) Consequences of erudite vernacular utilized irrespective of necessity: problems with using long words needlessly, *Applied Cognitive Psychology*, 20, pp. 139–156. Available at http://web.princeton.edu/sites/opplab/papers/Opp%20Consequences%20of%20Erudite%20Vernacular.pdf.

Pathways, Commission. (2012a) *The Pathways Commission: Charting a National Strategy for the Next Generation of Accountants*, American Accounting Association (AAA) and American Institute of Certified Public Accountants (AICPA). Available at www.pathwayscommission.org.

Pathways, Commission. (2012b) *The Pathways Commission: Charting a National Strategy for the Next Generation of Accountants. Chapter_7_Complete_with_detailed_tables*, American Accounting Association

(AAA) and American Institute of Certified Public Accountants (AICPA). Available at www. pathwayscommission.org.

Shallenbarger, S. (2012) This embarrasses you and I*, *Wall Street Journal Online*, 20 June. Available at http:// online.wsj.com/article/SB10001424052702303410404577466662919275448.html.

Stout, D. E. and DaCrema, J. (2004) A writing intervention for the accounting classroom: dealing with the problem of faulty modifiers, *Journal of Accounting Education*, 22(4), pp. 289–323.

Stout, D. E. and DaCrema, J. (2005) A writing-improvement module for accounting education, *Advances in Accounting Education*, 7, pp. 307–328.

Stout, D. E. and Hoff, K. (1989/90) Practical accounting/English collaboration to improve student writing skills: the use of informal journals and the diagnostic reading technique, *The Accounting Educators' Journal*, (Winter), pp. 83–96.

Stout, D. E. and Wygal, D. E. (1989) Incorporating writing techniques in the accounting classroom: evidence in financial, managerial, and cost accounting, *Journal of Accounting Education*, (Fall), pp. 245–252.

Stout, D. E., Wygal, D. E. and Hoff, K. (1990) Writing across the disciplines: applications to the accounting class-room, *The Bulletin of the Association for Business Communication*, (December), pp. 10–16.

Stout, D. E., Sumutka, A. and Wygal, D. E. (1991) Experiential evidence on the use of writing assignments in upper-level accounting courses, *Advances in Accounting*, 9, pp. 125–141.

Ulrich, T. A., Mchenzi, A. R. and Blouch, W. E. (2003) CPAs assess the development of professional skills of recent accounting graduates, *Journal of the Academy of Business Education*, 4, pp. 126–137.

Wayne Calloway School of Business and Accountancy (2004) *A Report on Recruiters' Perceptions of Under-graduate Business Schools and Students* (Winston-Salem, NC: Wake Forest University).

Yagoda, B. (2013) *How to Not Write Bad: The Most Common Writing Problems and the Best Ways to Avoid Them* (New York, NY: Riverhead Books).

Zinsser, W. (2006) *On Writing Well: The Classic Guide to Writing Nonfiction*, 30th anniversary edn (New York, NY: Collins).

Appendix A. Recommended Four-Part Lesson Plan (In-Class Use of *PowerPoint* Slides)

Part One. Introduction/Motivation/Justification: A Stakeholders' Approach

I generally begin the two-hour-and-40-minute presentation by discussing with students the importance of communication skills, and in particular writing skills, to my own work, as an author, textbook writer and editor. My intention here is to establish in the minds of my students the connection between such skills and professional success. I then tell students that most individuals are not innately gifted writers (or oral communicators). For most individuals, improvements in communication skills come with practise and dedicated effort. I then recount for my students the history of my involvement in the area of com-munication skills and accounting. I do this principally to convey to students my sincere (and continuing) interest in this area as well as my sincere interest in the professional success of my students. I typically conclude my introduction by making a simple state-ment: If, in fact, communication skills are important for success in business and that a gap between demonstrated and desired ability is observed, then I as an educator would be remiss in my duties if I did not help address this issue in the courses I teach. I then tran-sition to the set of *PowerPoint* slides, which are used as explained below.

After the title slide, I present slide 2, which contains the goals of my presentation. I then use slides 3–34 to make the argument that (a) communication skills development is important to students' professional development, and (b) that it is appropriate to devote time in an MBA 'accounting' class to the development of these skills. In short, these slides contain both an introduction to and motivation for my communication presentation. The general approach is to present evidence from stakeholders, including practitioners and recruiters. Put another way, I allow the underlying rationale for the presentation to be delivered by someone other than myself. (This point is made cogently on slide 3.) Experi-ence suggests that the slides devoted to this task are effective in terms of the above two arguments. Graduate students seem to react well to the evidentiary support contained in the slides.

Slide 4, which is hidden and therefore meant only for the instructor, provides an overview of the evidence presented in the slides comprising the rest of part one; the four items listed on the slide in red represent four of the five required readings for class (see Table 2). Slides 5–18 provide information regarding factors used by national recruiters in the USA to assess the quality of MBA programmes and their graduates. This information was, until 2007, presented annually in the *Wall Street Journal's Ranking of MBA Programs*. While this information is no longer reported by the *WSJ*, students realize that the message from earlier rankings (and referenced in the *PowerPoint* slides) is compelling and not likely to be obsolete or irrelevant.[14] Slides 19 and 20 provide some interesting information regarding a study conducted in the USA by Wake Forest University (Wayne Calloway School of Business and Accountancy, 2004) regarding recruiters' (i.e. stakeholders') perceptions of undergraduate business schools and students. This study provides confirmatory evidence regarding the importance of communication skills, as seen through the eyes of national recruiters.

Slides 21–25 attempt to get students to think about the *cost* of the problem of poor communication skills, as viewed by 'corporate America'. The example offered on slide 23 is designed as an attention-getter for students. In some sense, this example is more powerful than the ranking-criteria results presented earlier in the deck: the comment is meant to bring the discussion down to a more personal level.

Slides 26–32, inclusive, relate to a recent article in accounting education (Milliron, 2012) that presents survey evidence regarding the relative importance of technical knowledge (i.e. subject matter) versus professional (or generic) skills. Though limited to responses from accounting practitioners, the data make a compelling case for devoting class time in an 'accounting' course to the issue of communication skills. This summary point for part one of the presentation is conveyed in slide 33.

Part Two. The Expectations Gap: How Are We Doing?

The purpose of slides 34–45, inclusive, is two-fold:

- to provide evidence regarding the existence of an *expectations gap* (i.e. gap between demonstrated and desired characteristics of entry-level hires in terms of communication skills ability); and
- to preview what selected educational institutions in the USA are doing to address this expectations-gap problem.

This two-fold purpose is listed on slide 34.

Slides 35 and 36 provide relevant quotations from the 2004 report by the US National Commission on Writing. Together, these slides raise the issue of the existence of the above-referenced expectations gap. Slides 37 and 38 provide evidence regarding the relative importance of communication skills versus technical knowledge, in the form of survey responses obtained from accounting alumni; another stakeholder group. Though related specifically to accounting graduates from a single programme in New Zealand, the message reflected in slide 38 is very powerful, particularly for MBA students: many of such students may have formed the impression that accountants are individuals who deal principally with 'numbers' and 'quantitative stuff'. Slide 38 is designed to dispel this notion. Should the instructor desire, this slide can be supplemented by referencing and discussing with students a portion of the survey results from Master of Accountancy students in the USA, as reported in Frecka and Reckers (2010).[15]

Slides 39 and 40 continue the argument by presenting direct evidence of an ability-expectations gap: what businesses value (or desire) versus what they are receiving in terms of communication skills demonstrated by new hires. Data in this regard were obtained from a sample of accounting practitioners outside the USA. Teachers who at this point feel the need to supplement the gap-analysis results presented on these two slides can consult any of the following references: Bui and Porter (2010), Chaffey, Van Peursem and Low (2011), or Crawford, Helliar and Monk (2011).[16] Instructors of courses offered specifically for accounting majors, including those outside the USA, may find these alternative references of particular interest.

Slide 41 contains a statement regarding the relative importance of grammatical issues, based on survey responses obtained in Ulrich, Mchenzi and Blouch (2003). This slide provides a springboard to part four of the slides: dealing with the grammatical issue of 'faulty modifiers'. The quotation reflected in slide 42 is used to close part two of the presentation.

Part Three. Writing-Related Resources

By way of introduction to part three of the presentation, slide 43 is used to pose three questions that are designed to have students think about the (or a) solution to the problem identified in part two of the presentation. Slides 44 and 45 are meant to expose students to recent initiatives, at both the corporate level and by a handful of premier MBA programmes in the USA, associated with the problem. At this point I generally pause and ask, rhetorically, whether the students now feel it is appropriate to devote time in their MBA programme to the issue of communication skills development. More specifically, I ask them whether in the accounting course they are taking it is appropriate to devote class time to this subject.

Assuming a positive response to the question raised above, I then go on to slide 46, on which I list the two resources ('takeaways') that I make available to students as part of the presentation. As a follow-up to slide 46, the instructor can use slides 47 and 48 to raise yet another potential benefit of writing ability and professional success. Specifically, these two slides relate to the psychological studies by Oppenheimer (2006), who provides experimental evidence that writing style (which is, at least partially, under the control of the individual) is related to perceptions formed regarding the intelligence of the individual. Slide 49 concludes part three of the slides by providing an overview of the 10 topics covered in *Ten Tips for Improving Business Writing*, the second of two resources made available to students. The term 'Faulty Modifiers' is highlighted on this slide because this is the subject of part four of the slides, as explained below.

Part Four. Identifying and Dealing with the Problem of 'Faulty Modifiers'

Slides 50–75 address a grammatical problem that is a personal favourite of the author: the problem of *faulty modifiers* (both 'dangling modifiers' and 'misplaced modifiers').[17,18] These slides contain many examples, across various media, collected by the author over the past 10 years. Some of the examples are humorous; some are more serious. The primary point of these examples is two-fold:

- the problem of faulty modifiers is, unfortunately, a pervasive one; and
- these problems are typically easy to remedy: much of the task is associated with the ability to spot these grammatical errors.

The volume and diversity of examples given in these slides should be beneficial in this regard. If there is a time constraint, the instructor is free to use a reduced number of these examples.

Appendix B. Sample Assessment Questions (Answers Listed in Bold-face Type)*

1. The CFO, as well as the VP of Operations and the VP of Marketing, _____ chiefly responsible for the progress we've made thus far this year.
   A is
   B are

2. Neither the CEO nor the CFO _____ willing to attest the most recent set of financial statements.
   A was
   B were

3. Neither the CFO nor his subordinates _____ willing to attest to the financial statements.
   A was
   B were

4. _____ some pretty good reasons for embracing a just-in-time (JIT) philosophy.
   A They're
   B There are
   C There's

5. _____ the two budget reports you requested, sir.
   A Here's
   B Here are
   C Here is

6. There _____, as best as I can tell – and others have confirmed this – two glaring errors in her final report.
   A are
   B is

7. 'Wearing a broad smile, he applauded the speaker, who offered an intelligent solution to the problem before us'. The preceding sentence is:
   A grammatically incorrect, because _____
   B grammatically correct

8. 'Rolling down the highway, the bus had to swerve to avoid what could have been a horrible accident'. The preceding sentence is:
   A grammatically incorrect, because _____
   B grammatically correct

9. The Empire State Building _____ is 1,454 feet high.
   A that is at Fifth and 34th
   B , which is at Fifth and 34th,

10. Assume that Mary had but one son, Michael. Complete the following: 'Mary's _____ made dinner for us'.
    A son, Michael,
    B son Michael

11. Our high school _____ often told us: the _____ way to a virtuous life is to follow your _____.
    A principal, principle, principles
    B principal, principal, principles
    C principle, principal, principals
    D principal, principal, principles

12. The plant controller _____ her on her ability to reduce the _____ of inventory items.
   - **A complimented, complement**
   - B complimented, compliment
   - C complemented, complement
   - D complemented, compliment

13. The United States _____ fifty states.
   - A comprises
   - B is comprised of
   - C consists of
   - **D both (A) and (C) are correct**

14. A gallon _____ four quarts.
   - A is comprised of
   - B consists of
   - C comprises
   - **D both (B) and (C) are correct**

15. To _____ real change in the company, we've concluded that the whole board needs to be replaced.
   - **A effect**
   - B affect

16. The termites had a startling _____ on the piano.
   - **A effect**
   - B affect

17. This chicken dish is _____.
   - A well-done
   - **B well done**

18. Our former CFO was a _____ individual.
   - A strong willed
   - **B strong-willed**

19. The fine suit that I am wearing came from _____ finest men's shop.
   - A Arkansas'
   - **B Arkansas's**

20. The _____ rest room was recently renovated.
   - A womans
   - B womens'
   - **C women's**

21. After the successful IPO, the company was able to provide all ___ employees some needed time off.
   - **A its**
   - B it's

22. To better accommodate the needs of working parents, the company provided a _____ play area near the cafeteria.
   - A childrens'
   - **B children's**

23. I really believed the company CEO when she said the _____ first priority was for them to ensure a safe and pleasant working environment for all employees.
   - A managers
   - B manager's
   - **C managers'**

24. The draft copy of the employment contract was, oddly enough, vague regarding _____ effective date.

    A   it's

    B   its

25. Our team of internal auditors _____ at creating value-added reports on a timely basis.

    A   excels

    B   excel

26. Floodwaters during the recent hurricane damaged three buildings. Consequently, all the _____ records were lost.

    A   buildings'

    B   building's

    C   Neither is correct

27. Pressure exerted by management _____ the morale of employees.

    A   affects

    B   effects

28. Recent scientific evidence suggests that cinnamon has a positive _____ on blood cholesterol levels.

    A   affect

    B   effect

29. One of the few things I recall from my statistics class is the admonition that correlation does not imply a cause and _____ relationship.

    A   affect

    B   effect

30. The auditor asked Jeff and _____ to provide additional support for the adjusting journal entries in question.

    A   me

    B   I

31. Ramone, our supervisor, was checking whether Jeff, Nadeem, and _____ had completed and turned in our travel-expense reports.

    A   I

    B   me

32. Please forward the signed contract to Harry and _____.

    A   I

    B   me

33. Maria was the _____ author of the report.

    A   principal

    B   principle

34. That Marsha was a woman of _____ was beyond dispute.

    A   principal

    B   principle

35. The recent reaccreditation was a special source of pride for the school's _____.

    A   principal

    B   principle

36. Areas _____ are designated as 'contaminated' are to be avoided at all cost.

    A   that

    B   which

37. The GAAS Guide is a comprehensive reference _____ can be consulted as we develop our audit plan.

    A   that

    B   which

38. The new software provides detailed student reports, _____ students can access almost effortlessly.
   A   that
   B   which
39. It seemed as if the CFO only hesitatingly solicited _____ advice.
   A   their
   B   they're
   C   there
40. Marketers, I thought! It seems as if ____ always trying to purchase things we don't need with money we don't have!
   A   they're
   B   there
   C   their
41. A consensus had not yet been reached _____ the four internal auditors.
   A   among
   B   between
42. The recount confirmed that Jane, in fact, received 25 _____ votes than the winning opponent.
   A   less
   B   fewer
43. 'After overeating, the hammock looked pretty good to Archie'. This is an example of which of the following grammatical problems?
   A   comma splice
   B   run-on sentence
   C   faulty modifier
   D   restrictive vs. non-restrictive clauses
44. We were surprised to learn that the _____ producer of apples in the USA is New York.
   A   second-largest
   B   second largest
45. Many cancer treatments are, unfortunately, _____.
   A   nausea inducing
   B   nausea-inducing
46. Both of the following sentences are valid, though they differ in meaning: 'The charts drawn by hand were hard to read'. 'The charts, drawn by hand, were hard to read'. The grammatical issue associated with these sentences is:
   A   use of comma splices
   B   restrictive vs. non-restrictive clauses/modifiers
   C   run-on sentences
   D   active vs. passive voice
47. 'The wife believes she sees a living figure behind the wallpaper in the story by Charlotte Perkins Gilman, which adds to her sense of entrapment'. This construction:
   A   is grammatically correct
   B   reflects the problem of a misplaced modifier
   C   illustrates the problem of a comma splice
   D   illustrates the difference between restrictive and non-restrictive clauses
48. 'Our cleanup crew found a container behind the building that was leaking toxic wastes'. This construction:
   A   Is grammatically correct
   B   reflects the problem of a misplaced modifier

    C   illustrates the problem of a comma splice
    D   illustrates the problem of active vs. passive voice
    E   illustrates the problem of a dangling modifier

49. 'Marsha and her crew served dinner to the visitors standing around the room on flimsy paper plates'. This construction:

    A   is grammatically correct
    B   reflects the problem of a misplaced modifier
    C   illustrates the problem of a comma splice
    D   illustrates the problem of active vs. passive voice
    E   can be corrected through the use of a compound adjective or a restrictive clause

50. 'The newly hired research assistant, unfamiliar with chimpanzees, was surprised when they undermined the experimental results'. This construction:

    A   is grammatically correct
    B   reflects the problem of a misplaced modifier
    C   illustrates the problem of a comma splice
    D   illustrates the problem of active vs. passive voice
    E   can be corrected through the use of a compound adjective or a restrictive clause

*Notes: Items 21–42, inclusive, are adaptions of examples presented in Shallenbarger (2012). Item 43 is adapted from O'Conner (1996, p. 162). Item 46 is adapted from Ansun, Schwegler and Muth (2007, p. 435), while items 47–50, inclusive, are adapted from Ansun, Schwegler and Muth (2007, p. 374, 375).

Effects of Interspersed versus Summary Feedback on the Quality of Students' Case Report Revisions

FRED PHILLIPS* and SUSAN WOLCOTT**

*University of Saskatchewan, Canada; **CA School of Business, Canada

ABSTRACT *This study examines whether students show greater improvement in written case analyses when given feedback that is either interspersed throughout their written case analyses or presented only as a summary, and whether the benefits of these placements vary across differing levels of student performance in the course. Results from an exploratory field experiment conducted with Canadian accounting students who revised and resubmitted case analyses indicate that the effectiveness of feedback depended on an interaction between its placement and the course performance of students to which it was provided. Lowest-performing students increased the quality of their case responses most when provided with interspersed rather than summary feedback, mid-level students improved more when given summary rather than interspersed feedback, and highest-performing students improved significantly regardless of feedback placement. The primary conclusion from this study is that feedback placement influences how well students at different levels respond, suggesting that teachers should consider students' relative course performance when determining the most appropriate placement for their feedback. We also present evidence of the factors that affect the initial quality of case analyses and which influence students' decisions to revise and resubmit their case analyses.*

Introduction

An important goal for accounting educators is to help students to develop the ability to analyze accounting information and express their analyses in writing. To create opportunities for students to develop this ability, we ask them to prepare written case reports, business memoranda, and essays, and we provide feedback that directs their development.

This paper was edited and accepted by Richard M. S. Wilson.

This feedback usually provides both an assessment of the quality of the written work and advice about improving writing and analysis in future submissions. The primary purpose of the current study is to determine whether a variation in the placement of feedback from teachers affects how well students revise their written case reports. Specifically, we examine whether students generate greater improvement in their reports when given feedback that is either interspersed throughout their reports or presented only as a summary, and whether the benefits of these feedback placements vary across students exhibiting different levels of course performance. A secondary goal is to identify factors associated with the initial quality of students' written case reports and with their decision to take advantage of an option to revise their initial case submission. By identifying these factors, we aim to support accounting educators in better engaging students in writing assignments.

Prior accounting education research provides little guidance to indicate how teachers should present their feedback on students' written work. Most of the prior studies have focused on developing writing skills through initiatives that can be embedded within courses or used in curriculum-wide writing programs (for a review, see Stout and DaCrema, 2004). Few studies in accounting provide teachers with guidance on the characteristics of feedback that will most help students in improving their ability to express technical analyses in writing (cf. Marriott and Teoh, 2012). Outside of accounting, researchers are studying how improvements in written reports and essays may depend on various feedback characteristics including its source (peer versus teacher), tone (positive versus negative), quantity (targeted versus exhaustive), scope (macro versus micro), and clarity (e.g. Nelson and Schunn, 2009; Orsmond and Merry, 2011; Vardi 2009). Although the primary focus of these studies has been technical writing components such as spelling, grammar, and word choice (Stern and Solomon, 2006), some researchers have begun to examine how feedback features affect students' written expression of disciplinary knowledge (e.g. Cho, Schunn and Charney, 2006; Patchan, Charney and Schunn, 2009; Vardi 2009). Our goal is to extend that research to accounting by providing evidence that indicates whether the placement of feedback (interspersed versus summary) affects how well accounting students respond to feedback when revising written case analyses.

In the next section, we review prior studies in and outside of accounting to develop expectations about the effects of assessment feedback on improvements in students' written case analyses. This research is premised on the belief that feedback on written work is an indispensable part of an effective teaching-learning environment (Hounsell *et al.*, 2008) and can produce substantial learning gains by helping students to actively construct their understanding of topics in their discipline (Nicol and Macfarlane-Dick, 2006).

Review of Prior Research

Accounting educators and practitioners have long recognized that written expression of technical analyses is vital to success in accounting, and they urge teachers to help students develop this aspect of professional communication (e.g. Addams, 1981; AECC, 1990; AICPA, 1999, 2002; American Accounting Association, 1986; Estes, 1979; IAESB, 2012; Ingram and Frazier, 1980; Maupin and May, 1993; Ng *et al.*, 1999; Sriram and Coppage, 1992). In response, several accounting studies have examined the effect of broad writing initiatives on students' written work. Johnstone, Ashbaugh and Warfield (2002) conducted a field study in the USA, using a quasi-experimental design, to determine the effects of a comprehensive writing initiative to instruct students and provide practice and feedback on writing. Their study demonstrated that accounting students developed knowledge of grammar, punctuation, and exposition, and generated better written accounting reports when exposed to the writing initiative. Stone and Shelley (1997) documented similar improvements in accounting students' writing and analysis skills in the USA after participating in a cognitive skills development program. Most recently, Craig and McKinney (2010) presented a semester-length writing skills development program at a Canadian university, which improved *Intermediate Accounting* students' ability to express their accounting knowledge in writing. Although these and other studies indicate that accounting students can become better at expressing their written analyses through practice and feedback (for a more complete review, see Stout and DaCrema, 2004), few accounting education studies have examined the characteristics of feedback that help students become better writers (Watson *et al.*, 2007). Marriott and Teoh (2012) provide one exception, in a study undertaken in the UK, in which they used screencast feedback as an alternative to traditional written feedback on students' case reports. Although they do not attempt to measure how effectively students were able to use this feedback, they did find that students responded positively to the blended audio/visual form of feedback.

Research conducted outside the field of accounting recognizes the general benefits of providing students with feedback and creating opportunities for students to reflect on and revise their written work (e.g. Beach, 1979; Beach and Friedrich, 2006; Fitzgerald, 1987; Hayes *et al.*, 1987; McCutchen, Hull and Smith, 1987; Sommers, 1980). One stream of this research addresses practical implementation matters such as students' views on the attributes that make assessment feedback effective, teachers' divergent views on its purposes, and teachers' divergent styles and practices when providing feedback (for a recent review, see Li and De Luca, 2012). Another stream of research, which we review below, develops theoretical models to explain factors that contribute to effective assessment feedback. Some of these models describe macro-level constructs, whereas others depict concrete, operational variables.

At the macro level, Hattie and Timperley (2007) distinguish among four targets for feedback:

- the task;
- the processing of the task;
- self-regulation while processing; and
- the learner as a person.

Building on empirical research, Hattie and Timperly argue that assessment feedback is most effective when it focuses learners on better understanding the task and how it is best processed, and then moves learners from processing to regulation. Their model emphasizes that, although feedback about the learner as a person is common ('good try'), it is usually ineffective because it deflects attention from the task, it does not inform the learner about processing the task, and it is too shallow to penetrate learners' existing self-conceptions so as to influence their regulatory actions. Other macro-level models similarly conclude that feedback is most effective when it directs attention to appropriate goals (Kluger and DeNisi, 1996), encourages reflective processing (Bangert-Drowns *et al.*, 1991), and facilitates self-regulation (Nicol and Macfarlane-Dick, 2006).

At a concrete operational level, Nelson and Schunn (2009) propose that specific attributes of assessment feedback can generate improvements in performance and learning, but the effectiveness of these attributes depends on the extent to which learners understand, agree with, and effectively respond to the feedback. Influential attributes of assessment feedback involve both affective and cognitive dimensions, and can be categorized by function (evaluative versus formative) (Orsmond and Merry, 2011), scope (local versus global) (Stern and Solomon, 2006; Vardi, 2009), and focus (mechanics, organization, or content) (Patchan, Schunn and Clark, 2011).

Most closely related to our study of interspersed and summary feedback is a study of concrete feedback characteristics conducted by Cho and MacArthur (2010). In this research, undergraduate psychology students received written comments from a subject-matter expert and from the students themselves, as part of a blind peer-review process. The expert and peer comments were subsequently coded and classified as either directive feedback, which included units of feedback that recommended specific changes for each student's paper, or non-directive feedback, which included more general and reflective comments such that they could apply to nearly any part of a student's response. Revisions in the students' essays also were examined to determine the number of simple repairs, complex repairs in meaning, elaboration of content, or other more significant changes to content. Subsequent analysis showed that directive feedback was associated with students making simple mechanical repairs related to spelling and grammar, which yielded only modest improvements in the quality of students' written reports. In contrast, non-directive feedback was associated with students making more complex revisions to clarify and elaborate content, which were associated with significantly greater improvements in report quality. One limitation of Cho and MacArthur's analysis was that they did not directly distinguish directive and non-directive comments as relating to exposition versus content, although it is likely that the directive comments related to exposition issues and the non-directive feedback focused on content (Cho, Schunn and Charney, 2006). Nonetheless, this research shows that variations in the specificity of feedback influenced the extent of improvement in student revisions.

We speculate that the placement of feedback (interspersed versus summary) is likely to affect student revisions in written accounting reports in a manner similar to how directive and non-directive comments influenced students in the Cho and MacArthur (2010) study. Because interspersed comments are embedded within a student's written report (for an illustration, see Exhibit 1 Panel A), they may be perceived as applying to only isolated

Exhibit 1. Illustrations of interspersed and summary feedback.[a]

Panel A: interspersed feedback	Panel B: summary feedback
The company used declining balance depreciation, which is appropriate because it will use up the benefits of computer equipment quickly during the asset's useful life.	The company used declining balance depreciation, which is appropriate because it will use up the benefits of computer equipment quickly during the asset's useful life.
You concluded that the depreciation method is appropriate, but you did so before presenting and evaluating alternative accounting methods.	It should be considered how this affects the company's net income and share value.
It should be considered how this affects the company's net income and share value.	*Before concluding on any issues, always present and evaluate alternative accounting methods. For a more professional tone, use active rather than passive writing.*
Avoid starting sentences with 'it', which comes across in this sentence as passive rather than active.	

Note: [a]An illustrative students' response appears in regular text and teachers' feedback appears in italics.

parts of a student's response and are likely to elicit isolated simple repairs. In contrast, as suggested in Exhibit 1 Panel B, summary comments are presented at the end of a student's report so they may be perceived as relating to the entire work and are likely to lead students to contemplate more comprehensive revisions. Given these perceptions and responses, the overall quality of revisions is potentially greater when students are given summary rather than interspersed feedback. However, whether students are able to fully exploit the potential value of summary feedback is likely to depend on how well they are performing in the course, as discussed in the following section.

Student Course Performance

In a review of higher education writing research, Fitzgerald (1987) noted a developmental pattern in students' writing: more successful students tended to make broader, more extensive revisions, including greater changes to meaning. Generally, high-performing students were better able to coordinate the presentation and content of their writing, take on a reader's perspective when making revisions, and know how to make appropriate changes. In contrast, lower-performing students were less likely to understand and effectively use feedback. More recently, McCutchen, Francis and Kerr (1997) have made similar observations.

Based on this prior research, we anticipate that a student's level of course performance will interact with feedback placement to influence revision effectiveness. Specifically, the lowest-performing students may have greater difficulty understanding and using summary feedback, but benefit from the directive nature of interspersed feedback. For example, when these students encounter interspersed feedback, such as presented in Panel A of Exhibit 1, they can easily identify the specific contexts to which the feedback applies. But when confronted with summary feedback presented at the end of a report, as shown in Panel B, these students will struggle to identify the specific contexts to which the feedback applies because their underdeveloped knowledge structures limit their ability to generalize to multiple contexts. In contrast, students exhibiting stronger course performance are expected to take better advantage of summary feedback because they can use it to direct revisions throughout their reports rather than make only the isolated revisions suggested by interspersed feedback. Whether these differences in responding to feedback extend to the highest-performing students is an open question. It is possible that the highest performers will react like the mid-level students and benefit more from summary feedback. But it is also possible that highest-performing students will see that interspersed feedback does not apply only to isolated instances but also generalizes to other aspects of their reports. In this latter instance, highest-performing students will benefit equally from interspersed and summary feedback. In the light of these equally plausible outcomes, we present the anticipated effects for the highest-performing students in null form.

Taken together, the preceding reasoning suggests the following expectation: lowest-performing students will benefit more from interspersed than summary feedback, mid-level performers will benefit more from summary than interspersed feedback, and the highest-performing students will benefit equally from interspersed and summary feedback. We expect these differences will be evident in the extent of improvement between initial and revised case submissions.

Other Factors Influencing the Quality of Written Analyses

Beyond our primary goal of determining whether feedback placement and course performance interact to affect improvement in written case analyses, we are interested in identifying factors that are associated with the initial quality of students' case submissions. Prior research suggests that initial quality will vary as a function of academic performance, time spent preparing initial submissions, and the extent to which students consider grading criteria that indicate how their analyses will be evaluated (Andrade, 2001; Fitzgerald, 1987; Saddler and Graham, 2007). To confirm the prior research and to improve our ability to detect the incremental interactive effects of feedback placement and students' course performance, we include these factors as covariates in our analyses. We also are interested in identifying factors that influence accounting students' decisions to revise initial case submissions. Prior research suggests these decisions will be associated with the following factors:

- students' self-efficacy beliefs in identifying and executing appropriate revisions (Klassen, 2002);
- initial performance scores and motivation to develop communications skills (Sommers, 1982); and
- perceptions about the adequacy of time available to complete revisions (Porte, 1996).

By gathering data from students on the extent to which these factors affected their decisions, we are able to advise teachers on how to motivate students to reflect on their feedback and revise their initial submissions.

Method

Data Collection

During the fall 2010 semester, 209 students from four sections of *Introductory Financial Accounting* taught by two instructors at a large Canadian university submitted written analyses of an integrative case (Phillips and Mackintosh, 2011). The case described a small private company that was to be sold by one of two founding owners to the other owner, based on the company's net income. Seeded throughout the case were nine accounting issues, all of which involved matters of accounting judgment and choice. The assigned task for students was to prepare a written report for the purchaser which analyzed the judgments and choices that affected the company's net income and which could influence the price at which the purchase-and-sale would occur.

To promote consistency in students' reports, a 1250-word limit was imposed and a detailed grading rubric was distributed with the case. The grading rubric indicated that students' reports would be assessed for overall writing quality, professional awareness, and adequacy of technical accounting analyses. Within each of these categories, the rubric indicated three possible levels of performance (i.e. poor, fair, excellent) and described each level of performance with respect to particular elements of the students' reports (e.g. spelling, report structure, sensitivity to clients' needs, identification and evaluation of accounting issues, and alternative choices or judgments).

Using the detailed grading rubric in Phillips and Mackintosh (2011), the two teachers involved in this course graded the responses and provided written feedback on each student's response. The rubric and responses with feedback were returned to students for revision and resubmission. Ten per cent of the course grade was allocated to the case analysis; the final case grade was computed as the student's score on the initial submission plus 90% of the grade improvement on an optional revised submission. At the conclusion of the course, a post-case survey was administered to gather information about factors that led students to revise (or not revise) their reports and to learn how students used the feedback to guide their revisions. Of the 209 students in the four course sections, 143 (68.4%) submitted responses to the post-case survey. Of these respondents, 107 chose to revise and resubmit their case analyses.[1]

Research Design

The design followed traditional program evaluation research, which was approved by the university's research ethics office. Such a design involves comparing students exposed to different methods of instructional programming. Specifically, in our case, students were exposed to one of two different feedback placements: *interspersed* comments, which were presented inline within the body of each student's submission that was returned for revision, or *summary* comments, which were presented in a paragraph after the end of each student's submission. Because the interspersed and summary feedback was intended to help students improve their written submissions, it had the potential to influence students' grades on the case report and in the course. Thus, precautions were taken to ensure that students receiving one feedback placement were not advantaged more than students receiving the other placement of feedback. For example, we ensured that all students received the feedback at the same time, so that some students did not have more opportunity to revise than others. Also, we provided the same grading rubric to all students, so that they shared the same basic grading structure and were able to identify their individual scores within the grading dimensions specified in the rubric. Finally, we assured the research ethics board that, should the different feedback placements lead to significantly different overall performance gains between the two feedback groups, we would 'curve' (i.e. adjust) the assigned grades to produce similar mean scores between groups.

Several steps also were taken to ensure that students' participation in the study was voluntary. These steps were particularly important in this study because one of the researchers was also a teacher of the course. Students were asked to participate in the research only after final course grades had been entered into the university's grade system. Thus, at the time the case reports were graded and re-graded, the teacher/researcher could not know which students would later decide to participate in the study. 'Participation' was defined as merely giving consent for the researchers to access and use course submissions and data in their analyses. We also assured students that any scores used in the analyses would be aggregated with that of other students so that no individual could be identified in the reported findings. Students were further assured that their decision to participate or not participate in the research would not affect their academic or social standing in the university; the researchers did not teach other undergraduate courses at the university.

We chose to manipulate feedback placement by varying the teacher who used that placement of feedback. To control for selection threats that arise from comparing different sections of the course, which may systematically differ in composition, we randomly assigned students from all four course sections to one of the two feedback groups. In the *interspersed* group, one course teacher presented feedback in an interspersed manner throughout each written submission in that condition. In the *summary* group, a different teacher presented feedback as a written summary at the conclusion of each submission. This design assured that approximately one-half of students' submissions were graded by their own teacher and one-half were graded by a different teacher, thereby counterbalancing the risk that a student's identity might inadvertently bias teacher grading. With one grader for each experimental group, this design also promoted consistency in grading within each experimental group, and the variation in feedback placement presented in an ecologically valid way differences in teacher feedback that exist in practice

(Li and De Luca, 2012). To promote consistency in grading across experimental groups, both teachers completed the same grading rubric for each student's submission.[2] Analyses of case report scores indicate that teachers did not favor their own students; case scores did not vary by course section ($F = 3.22$, $p = 0.32$) or the interaction between course section and feedback placement ($F = 1.54$, $p = 0.22$). Also, as reported below, the average improvement in case scores did not vary by feedback placement ($F = 0.03$, $p = 0.882$), suggesting that one teacher did not provide better overall feedback than the other.[3]

Participant Demographics

Of the 209 students who initially submitted a case report, 60 women and 83 men submitted responses to the post-case survey which asked about their decisions and experiences involving the case revisions. Students who responded to the survey did not differ significantly from non-respondents with regard to performance on homework assignments ($F = 0.53$, $p = 0.469$) or the final examination ($F = 0.89$, $p = 0.346$). However, the average case report score of survey respondents (55% of the maximum available case mark) was greater than that of non-respondents (44%) ($F = 13.92$, $p < 0.001$). Thus, the following analyses are representative of students with somewhat stronger case performance, but were otherwise similar to the general population of students.

On average, participants were 20 years old (SD = 1.6) and had already completed 1.6 years of university education (SD = 1.3). The majority of participants were registered in the School of Business (88.8%) or College of Agriculture (9.1%). More than one-quarter of students had not chosen a major area of study (25.2%), but others indicated an intention to major in accounting (19.6%), management (14.0%), finance (12.6%), human resources (9.1%), marketing (8.4%), or other areas (11.2%).

Results

The independent variables of primary interest in this study are feedback placement and the relative levels of students' performance in the course. Before testing the effects of these factors on the primary dependent variable (improvement in case report scores), we conducted exploratory analyses to better understand the factors that affect students' initial case submissions and their decisions to revise (or not).

Factors that Affect the Quality of Students' Initial Case Report Submissions

Based on the literature review, we anticipated that the scores which students earn on their initial case submissions would vary as a function of:

• prior course performance, the time spent preparing initial case submissions; and
• the extent to which students used the grading rubric as guidance when preparing their initial case submissions.

As a measure of prior course performance, we obtained the grades that students earned on 10 weekly, online homework assignments, which were common to all sections of the course.[4] Measures of time spent and extent of rubric use were obtained from the post-case survey. Specifically, students self-reported the number of hours they spent preparing their initial submissions and they rated, on a scale from 1 (not at all) to 10 (all the time), the extent to which they referred to the grading rubric when preparing their initial case submission. Descriptive statistics for these measures, along with other metrics analyzed later in the paper, are presented in Table 1.

A regression of homework scores, time spent preparing the initial case submission, and extent of rubric use on the initial case submission score found that homework scores and use of the grading rubric were significant ($\beta = 0.387$, $t = 4.25$ and $\beta = 0.214$, $t = 2.37$, respectively, both with $p < 0.001$), but self-reported hours spent analyzing the case was not ($\beta = -0.030$, $t = -0.32$, $p = 0.746$). Thus, it appears that initial case performance did not depend on the time spent in preparing the written case analysis, but rather on the students' prior course performance and the extent to which they attempted to align their report with grading expectations.

Factors that Students Identify as Influencing their Revision Decision

In the post-case survey, students rated five factors that could affect the decision to revise and resubmit their case reports.[5] Ratings were indicated on a scale from 1 (low importance) to 10 (high importance). Table 2 presents the mean ratings of each factor influencing students' decisions to revise and resubmit, for all students (first column of data) and for students who chose to revise (second column) or not (third column). Using Bonferroni-adjusted comparisons of the ratings given by all students, we found that one reason stood out as being significantly more important than others: the score which students received on the initial submission (mean = 8.7). Students who chose to revise their responses had earned initial case report scores which, on average, were significantly lower (52.5%) than those of students who chose to not revise (64.5%) ($F = 10.18$, $p = 0.002$). Three other reasons of lesser importance to students were:

- the extent to which they understood what they needed to revise (7.6);
- their confidence in being able to successfully execute revisions (7.2); and
- the time available for revising (7.1).

Sadly, the one reason that was least important in deciding whether to revise was the amount that students thought they would learn from revising (6.2). This latter finding reveals a disparity between teachers and students: whereas teachers offered the revision opportunity as a pathway to greater learning, students did not consider potential learning to be particularly important in deciding whether to revise.

Table 1. Measures relating to students' case report submissions.

Factor	Mean	Standard deviation
Initial case submission score[a]	55.3	19.8
Extent of rubric use when preparing initial submission[b]	7.5	1.9
Hours spent preparing initial submission	9.2	5.5
Average weekly homework score[a]	85.9	12.8
Case score improvement[a]	19.3	14.1
Extent of rubric use when preparing revised submission[b]	9.1	1.2
Hours spent preparing revised submission	4.4	3.6

Notes: [a]Expressed as percentages of maximum available score on the case report. [b]In response to a question 'to what extent did you **use** the grading rubric in preparing your initial (or revised) response', students indicated a rating on a scale anchored by 1 = not at all and 10 = all the time.

Table 2. Factors influencing students' decisions to revise or not revise case report submissions.[a]

	Revision decision		
Factor[b]	All students ($n = 138$)	Revise ($n = 106^c$)	Not revise ($n = 32$)
Score received on initial submission	8.7 (2.1)[d]	8.7 (2.2)[e]	8.6 (1.6)[f]
Ability to understand what needed to be revised	7.6 (2.1)[g]	7.8 (1.9)[h]	6.6 (2.6)[i]
Confidence in being able to effectively revise	7.2 (2.1)[g]	7.4 (1.9)[h]	6.6 (2.6)[i]
Time available to complete a revision	7.1 (2.5)[g]	6.6 (2.4)[j]	8.6 (2.2)[f]
Amount to be learned from revising	6.2 (2.6)[k]	6.5 (2.5)[j]	5.1 (2.9)[l]

Notes: [a]Cell entries include mean rating (from 1 to 10), and standard deviation (in parentheses). [b]Students were asked the following: 'In deciding whether to revise your case analysis, how important were each of the following factors? For each factor, indicate its importance by choosing a number from 1 to 10, where $1 =$ not at all important and $10 =$ extremely important.' [c]One respondent did not complete this portion of the survey. [d, e, f, g, h, i, j, k, l]Within each column of data, cell means with different superscripts differ at statistically significant levels in Bonferroni-adjusted within-subject repeated contrasts ($\alpha = 0.0125$). Ratings differed between revisers and non-revisers (i.e. the last two columns) for all factors ($p < 0.013$) except the score received on the initial submission.

To determine whether the relative importance of revision factors differed between students who decided to revise and those who decided not to revise, we conducted a repeated-measures analysis of variance (ANOVA), with the revision factor ratings as the repeated dependent measure and the revision decision as the independent variable. The revision factor ratings interacted with the revision decisions at a statistically significant level (Wilks' $\lambda = 0.772$, $F = 9.75$, $p < 0.001$), suggesting that the relative importance of the revision factors varied between revisers and non-revisers. Consequently, we reran the analyses of factor revision ratings separately for revisers and non-revisers. As shown by the superscripted letters in the middle data column of Table 2, students who revised their reports continued to indicate that the most important factor to them was their (lower-than-average) score on their initial submission. Their only departure from the overall results was that they were less concerned with the time available to revise. In contrast, students who decided not to revise reported being significantly influenced by their perceptions of the time available to revise. As reported in the final column of Table 2, this factor was just as important in their decision not to revise as the score they received on the initial submission.[6]

Factors that Affect the Quality of Students' Revisions

The factors of primary interest in this study are feedback placement and students' relative level of course performance. We anticipated that interspersed feedback would lead to more effective revisions than summary feedback for low-performing students, because the interspersed feedback would better support these students by directing them to specific areas in their reports where revision was required. We expected that mid-level students would benefit more from summary feedback because it would invite these students to carry revisions throughout their reports. Finally, we posited that highest-performing students might not benefit from one placement over the other because they would be able to generalize interspersed feedback as well as summary feedback. We measured the improvement in submission quality arising from the revision by subtracting the initial case report score from the revised case report score. We conducted the following analyses using all the data from the students who had submitted a revised case and completed the post-case survey questions that provided data for the covariates ($n = 107$).

Figure 1 and Table 3 present the average improvement in case report scores, and Table 2 also presents the related cell sizes and standard deviations in brackets and parentheses. The first row of Table 3 suggests that interspersed feedback provided its greatest benefits to students in the lowest quartile (23.1 percentage points average improvement) but those benefits declined for students in higher quartiles (15.0 and 11.6 percentage points improvement for quartiles 2 and 3). However, interspersed feedback did not impede the highest-performing students (quartile 4), who improved their case scores by 21.1 percentage points. The second row of Table 3 suggests that summary feedback, in contrast, yielded a different pattern of improvement. The lowest-performing students benefited the least from summary feedback (15.4 percentage points improvement) whereas the highest-performing students benefited the most (25.5 percentage points). Taken together, these descriptive data suggest that lowest-performing students benefit from interspersed feedback whereas summary feedback best benefits the highest-performing students. However, this conclusion is somewhat tentative because these analyses have not controlled for other explanatory variables related to case performance, such as the score earned on the initial submission and the extent to which students used the grading rubric to guide revisions. The following analysis of covariance (ANCOVA) provides these additional controls.

Panel A of Table 4 presents the ANCOVA summary table and Panel B presents the estimated marginal means, which indicate the case score improvement after controlling for the effects of initial case scores and rubric use. The ANCOVA indicates that both initial case score and extent of rubric use are significantly and positively related to the improvement in case scores. Students who had scored higher on the initial submission improved the most on resubmission ($F = 36.25$, $p < 0.001$), and those who reported greater rubric use improved more ($F = 11.44, p = 0.001$). Also, the ANCOVA indicates a significant interaction between feedback placement and course performance level ($F = 2.78, p = 0.045$), consistent with results reported earlier in Table 3. The estimated marginal means in Table

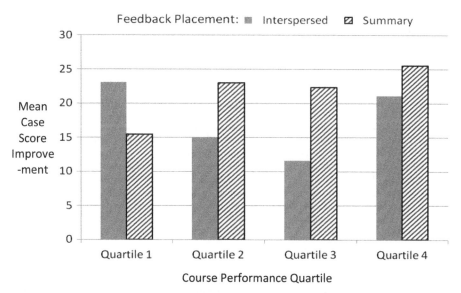

Figure 1. Mean case score improvements by feedback placement and course performance quartile[a]
[a]See Table 3 for descriptions of case report score improvement, feedback placement, and course performance.

Table 3. Case report score improvements by feedback placement and students' course performance.[a]

Feedback placement[c]	Students' course performance[b]			
	Quartile 1	Quartile 2	Quartile 3	Quartile 4
Interspersed	23.1 (17.9) [11]	15.0 (11.6) [14]	11.6 (13.3) [16]	21.1 (10.7) [14]
Summary	15.4 (15.0) [12]	23.0 (15.5) [14]	22.3 (11.3) [15]	25.5 (15.2) [11]

Notes: [a]Case report score improvement is calculated as the difference in percentage scores earned on the initial and revised submissions. Cell entries include mean improvement, standard deviation (in parentheses), and number of participants [in brackets]. [b]Students' course performance is determined using the average scores earned on weekly homework assignments. [c]Students were randomly assigned to receive either interspersed feedback (distributed throughout each student's initial case submission) or summary feedback (presented after the conclusion of each student's initial case submission).

Table 4. Analysis of covariance of case report score improvements.[a]

	Sum of squares	df	Mean square	F-statistic	p-value
Panel A: ANCOVA summary table					
Intercept	226.30	1	226.30	1.73	0.192
Students' course performance[b]	1305.39	3	435.13	1.26	0.421
Feedback placement[c]	9.05	1	9.05	0.03	0.882
Performance × placement	1091.63	3	363.88	2.78	0.045
Covariates					
Initial case score	4750.96	1	4750.96	36.25	0.000
Extent of rubric use	1499.33	1	1499.33	11.44	0.001
Error	12713.88	97	131.07		
Total	21596.54	107			

Feedback placement[c]	Students' course performance[b]			
	Quartile 1	Quartile 2	Quartile 3	Quartile 4
Panel B: estimated marginal means				
Interspersed	19.0 (3.5) [11]	14.4 (3.1) [14]	18.4 (3.0) [16]	23.9 (3.1) [14]
Summary	8.6 (3.5) [12]	20.3 (3.1) [14]	24.2 (3.0) [15]	25.2 (3.5) [11]
F-statistic (p-value)[d]	3.09 (0.048)	2.58 (0.061)	2.86 (0.051)	0.28 (0.604)

Notes: Significance values for quartiles 1, 2, and 3 are one-tailed and two-tailed for quartile 4. [a]Case report score improvement is calculated as the difference in percentage scores earned on the initial and revised submissions. Panel B cell entries include the mean improvement, standard deviation (in parentheses), and number of participants [in brackets]. [b]Students' course performance is determined using the average scores earned on weekly homework assignments. [c]Students were randomly assigned to receive either interspersed feedback (distributed throughout each student's initial case submission) or summary feedback (presented after the conclusion of each student's initial case submission). [d]Differences between groups are tested with between-subject ANCOVAs within each quartile.

4 confirm that the lowest-performing students benefited more from interspersed feedback (19.0 percentage points improvement) than from summary feedback (8.6 percentage points improvement) ($F = 3.09$, $p = 0.048$). In contrast, mid-level students in the second and third quartiles benefited more from summary feedback (20.3 and 24.2

percentage points, respectively) than from interspersed feedback (14.4 and 18.4 percentage points, respectively) ($F > 2.58$, $p < 0.061$). The amount of improvement among the highest-performing students did not depend on whether they received interspersed feedback (23.9 percentage points) or summary feedback (25.2 percentage points) ($F = 0.28$, $p = 0.604$).[7]

Exploratory Analyses of Writing versus Accounting Content

Having shown that interspersed and summary feedback led to different improvements in students' case report scores, we undertook further exploratory analyses to determine whether these improvements in case scores were driven primarily by improvements in writing execution or technical accounting content. The grading rubric had allocated 25% of the case grade to writing execution and 75% to technical accounting content, and had tracked the grades by each of these dimensions, so we analyzed these two distinct dimensions. Specifically, we entered these two dimensions as dependent variables in a repeated-measures model with independent variables and covariates identical to those shown in Table 4. The results of this analysis (not tabulated) showed that the effects of feedback placement and students' course performance did not differ across improvements in writing and technical accounting scores ($p > 0.320$), suggesting that the overall effects were not driven exclusively by improvements in either writing or technical accounting content.

We also explored whether the different feedback placements may have inadvertently manipulated different feedback qualities pertaining to writing versus technical accounting issues. To conduct this analysis, we trained an independent research assistant, who was not aware of the hypotheses being examined in this study, to code the teachers' feedback in each group as relating to writing execution or technical accounting content. This analysis proceeded by first separating the feedback into individual units that represented distinct observations, and then categorizing each feedback unit as relating to writing execution or technical accounting content. The results of this analysis found that, on average, each student was given 3.6 units of writing feedback and 12.8 units of feedback pertaining to accounting content; the proportions of writing versus accounting feedback (22% vs. 78%) were similar to the 25/75% split in marks in the grading rubric. Importantly, the total number of units of writing feedback in the *interspersed* and *summary* groups (3.5 and 3.7, respectively) did not differ significantly ($p = 0.683$). Likewise, the total number of units of accounting-focused feedback in the *interspersed* and *summary* groups (13.0 and 12.6, respectively) did not differ significantly ($p = 0.625$).

Taken together, these additional exploratory analyses suggest that students were given feedback of a similar nature in the *interspersed* and *summary* conditions and, consequently, the overall improvements in their case analyses were not isolated solely in either writing execution or technical accounting analyses. These additional analyses extend the prior study by Cho and MacArthur (2010), which did not rule out the possibility that their directive and non-directive feedback led to differences in students' revisions because the former focused on writing execution and the latter focused on technical content.

Discussion, Limitations, and Implications

The purpose of this study was to determine the feedback placement that would contribute most to improving students' written analyses in an accounting course. Through an exploratory field experiment in which students were randomly assigned to different feedback groups, we determined that the placement of feedback does affect the quality of revisions students made to written case analyses. However, the nature of the relationship between feedback and writing was not a simple one in which one placement always dominated the other. Instead, we found a contingent relationship in which lower-performing students benefited more from interspersed feedback than from summary feedback, mid-level students benefited more from summary feedback than interspersed feedback, and the highest-performing students benefited equally from summary and interspersed feedback. These findings are consistent with the idea that higher-performing students more clearly see where and how feedback applies throughout their written work. In contrast, low-performing students benefit from the additional direction that comes from using interspersed comments to show where revisions are needed most.

As with all research, our study is limited in several ways, each of which provides a direction for future research. First, we examined improvements in the written responses of students registered in an introductory-level accounting course at one university. Although introductory students are amendable to writing initiatives (Webb, English and Bonanno, 1995), future research could extend the scope of these findings by examining a broader cross-section of students or courses and by studying the impact of feedback in one course assignment across other assignments, courses, or subsequent semesters. Second, we examined only the quantitative scores earned on the case analyses. Although we considered whether the overall improvements in case report scores were driven solely by writing execution or technical accounting content, future research could adopt a more qualitative approach when characterizing the nature of students' revisions. Third, we examined two extremes in feedback placement as implemented by two course instructors. Although steps were taken to ensure consistency in grading (e.g. use of a common rubric, random assignment of students from different course sections) and post-hoc analyses suggest that the quality and nature of feedback (i.e. extent of writing versus technical accounting comments) did not differ significantly across teachers, the possibility exists that the observed interaction between feedback placement and students' prior performance arose not from the placement of interspersed versus summary feedback but instead from other unmeasured differences in the feedback given by the two teachers. This limitation could be avoided in future research designs either by having interspersed and summary feedback generated by the same individual, or by having each teacher generate comments for both the interspersed and summary feedback groups.

Notwithstanding these limitations, the primary implication of this study is that the placement of feedback provided to students does exert a measurable effect on the quality of the revisions which they make to their written work. Moreover, this effect varies across different groups of students. Teachers are advised to consider the prior performance of students when giving feedback, such that they identify specific locations and give prescriptive directions for improvement to the lowest-performing students. But, just as importantly, teachers will assist higher-performing students most by encouraging them to look beyond isolated repairs, instead leading them to generalize feedback to the multiple instances in which it applies.

Our advice to avoid using a singular feedback placement and instead to tailor it to students' demonstrated abilities will likely require a subtle but significant change in the way in which many instructors provide feedback. Rather than exhaustively cataloging all areas for improvement in students' submissions, teachers are advised to be attentive to patterns of recurring writing deficiencies and recurring strengths within each individual student's submission. These patterns are significant because they reveal each student's writing customs or 'habits', which likely reside in most of his or her writings, not just in the present assignment. By correcting recurring deficiencies and reinforcing recurring strengths, teachers are likely to help improve students' writing on current reports and possibly future assignments that resemble the projects they will complete in the workplace, resulting in what others refer to as 'authentic assessment' (Banta, 2002).

In addition to recommending pattern-based assessment, we also underscore the value in involving students in revising their initial submissions. Initially, we included the opportunity for students' revisions so that we could measure the improvement in written case quality solely for research purposes. And now that these benefits have been identified, other teachers can implement interspersed versus summary feedback without providing opportunities for revising and resubmitting. However, having seen the vast improvements that students were able to achieve through revisions, we must reiterate one of the principles for effective feedback expressed in the general education research literature: build writing assignments that require students to revise their papers (Stern and Solomon, 2006) and thereby help them to continue to close the gap between current and desired performance (Nicol and Macfarlane-Dick, 2006). Our data indicate that students initially focus on how revisions will affect their course grade and do not immediately appreciate the learning and skill development that arises through rewriting. By helping students to see that revisions involve re-visioning, rather than mere 'fixing', teachers may more successfully engage students in this important stage of writing.

Acknowledgements

The authors thank Brandy Mackintosh for research assistance, and Don Bacon, Darius Fatemi, Sarah Guina, Barbara Phillips, Fred Pries, Regan Schmidt, participants at the Canadian Academic Accounting Association annual conference, anonymous reviewers, and the two guest editors – Elizabeth Gray and Lynn Hamilton – for comments on a prior version of this paper. The authors also gratefully acknowledge the CAAA/CMA-Canada Scholarship of Teaching and Learning funding program.

Notes

[1]One student completed only a portion of the survey. This student provided data relevant to the main analyses of case writing improvement but did not provide data relevant to the factors that affected the revision decision. Reported results are based on all available data, but results do not change if data from this student are excluded.

[2]In retrospect, a stronger design to promote consistency across experimental groups would have been for each teacher to provide summary feedback to one-half of the randomly allocated submissions and interspersed feedback to the other half of the submissions.

[3]Because the average improvement across feedback groups did not differ at statistically significant levels, we did not 'curve' (i.e. adjust) students' final case scores.

[4]Grade point average (GPA) is often used as an alternative measure of prior performance, but we did not collect GPA in this study.

[5]Five respondents did not provide ratings of these factors, so the sample size for the analyses of revision factors is reduced from 143 to 138.

[6]A multivariate ANOVA conducted using the five revision factor ratings as the dependent measures and the revision decision as the independent variable finds the following levels of statistical significance between revisers and non-revisers (all tests two-tailed): score on initial submission ($p = 0.730$), understand what to revise ($p = 0.004$), confidence in being able to revise ($p = 0.064$), time available ($p < 0.001$), and amount to be learned ($p = 0.013$).

[7]We also ran the ANCOVA including the number of self-reported hours spent revising as a covariate, but it was not significant and did not change the reported results. We also ran an ANCOVA to explore whether the extent of rubric use might depend on initial case score, feedback placement, or time spent revising, but these variables were not associated through main or interactive effects ($p > 0.170$).

References

Accounting Education Change Commission (AECC). (1990) Objectives of education for accountants: position statement number one, *Issues in Accounting Education*, 5(2), pp. 307–312.

Addams, H. L. (1981) Should the Big 8 teach communication skills?, *Management Accounting*, 5, pp. 37–40.

American Accounting Association (AAA). (1986) Future accounting education: preparing for the expanding profession, *Issues in Accounting Education*, 1(1), pp. 168–195.

American Institute of Certified Public Accountants (AICPA). (1999; 2002) *Core Competency Framework for Entry into the Accounting Profession* (New York, NY: AICPA). Available at www.aicpa-eca.org.

Andrade, H. G. (2001) The effects of instructional rubrics on learning to write, *Current Issues in Education*, 4(4). Available at http://cie.ed.asu.edu/volume4/number4/.

Bangert-Drowns, R. L., Kulik, C. L., Kulik, J. A. and Morgan, M. T. (1991) The instructional effect of feedback in test-like events, *Review of Educational Research*, 61(2), pp. 213–237.

Banta, T. W. (2002) *Building a Scholarship of Assessment* (San Francisco: Jossey-Boss).

Beach, R. (1979) The effects of between-draft teacher evaluation versus student self-evaluation on high school students' revising of rough drafts, *Research in the Teaching of English*, 13, pp. 111–119.

Beach, R., and Friedrich, R. (2006) Response to writing, in: C. A. MacArthur, S. Graham, and J. Fitzgerald (Eds) *Handbook of Writing Research*, pp. 222–234 (New York: The Guilford Press).

Cho, K. and MacArthur, C. (2010) Student revision with peer and expert reviewing, *Learning and Instruction*, 20, pp. 328–338.

Cho, K., Schunn, C. D. and Charney, D. (2006) Comment on writing: typology and perceived helpfulness of comments from novice peer reviewers and subject matter experts, *Written Communication*, 23(3), pp. 160–294.

Craig, R. and McKinney, C. N. (2010) A successful competency-based writing skills development programme: results of an experiment, *Accounting Education: An International Journal*, 19(3), pp. 257–278.

Estes, R. (1979) The profession's changing horizons: a survey of practitioners on the present and future importance of selected knowledge and skills, *The International Journal of Accounting Education and Research*, 14(1), pp. 47–70.

Fitzgerald, J. (1987) Research on revision in writing, *Review of Educational Research*, 57, pp. 481–506.

Hattie, J. and Timperley, H. (2007) The power of feedback, *Review of Educational Research*, 77(1), pp. 81–112.

Hayes, J. R., Flower, L., Schriver, K. A., Stratman, J. and Carey, L. (1987) Cognitive processes in revision, in: S. Rosenberg (Ed.) *Reading, Writing, and Language Processing: Advances in Applied Psycholinguistics*, pp. 176–240 (Cambridge, UK: Cambridge University Press).

Hounsell, D., McCune, V., Hounsell, J. and Litjens, J. (2008) The quality of guidance and feedback to students, *Higher Education Research & Development*, 27(1), pp. 55–67.

Ingram, R. W. and Frazier, C. R. (1980) *Developing Communications Skills for the Accounting Profession* (Sarasota, FL: American Accounting Association).

International Accounting Education Standards Board (IAESB). (2012) *International Education Standard 3 (IES 3): Initial Professional Judgment: Professional Skills*. Available at http://www.ifac.org/publications-resources/ies-3-initial-professional-development-professional-skills.

Johnstone, K. M., Ashbaugh, H. and Warfield, T. D. (2002) Effects of repeated practice and contextual-writing experiences on college students' writing skills, *Journal of Educational Psychology*, 94(2), pp. 305–315.

Klassen, R. (2002) Writing in early adolescence: a review of the role of self-efficacy beliefs, *Educational Psychology Review*, 14(2), pp. 173–203.

Kluger, A. N. and DeNisi, A. (1996) The effects of feedback interventions on performance: a historical review, a meta-analysis, and a preliminary feedback intervention theory, *Psychological Bulletin*, 119(2), pp. 254–284.

Li, J. and De Luca, R. (2012) Review of assessment feedback, *Studies in Higher Education*, DOI:10.1080/03075079.2012.709494.

Marriott, P. and Teoh, L. K. (2012) Using screencasts to enhance assessment feedback: students' perceptions and preferences, *Accounting Education: an international journal*, 21(6), pp. 583–598.

Maupin, R. J. and May, C. A. (1993) Communication for accounting students, *International Journal of Educational Management*, 7(3), pp. 30–38.

McCutchen, D., Hull, G. A. and Smith, W. L. (1987) Editing strategies and error correction in basic writing, *Written Communication*, 4, pp. 139–154.

McCutchen, D., Francis, M. and Kerr, S. (1997) Revising for meaning: effects of knowledge and strategy, *Journal of Educational Psychology*, 89(4), pp. 667–676.

Nelson, M. M. and Schunn, C. D. (2009) The nature of feedback: how different types of peer feedback affect writing performance, *Instructional Science*, 37, pp. 375–401.

Ng, J., Lloyd, P., Kober, R. and Robinson, P. (1999) Developing writing skills; a large class experience: a teaching note, *Accounting Education: An International Journal*, 8(1), pp. 47–55.

Nicol, D. J. and Macfarlane-Dick, D. (2006) Formative assessment and self-regulated learning: a model and seven principles of good feedback practice, *Studies in Higher Education*, 31(2), pp. 199–218.

Orsmond, P. and Merry, S. (2011) Feedback alignment: effective and ineffective links between tutors' and students' understanding of coursework feedback, *Assessment & Evaluation in Higher Education*, 36(2), pp. 125–136.

Patchan, M. M., Charney, D. and Schunn, C. D. (2009) A validation study of students' end comments: comparing comments by students, a writing instructor, and a content instructor, *Journal of Writing Research*, 1(2), pp. 124–152.

Patchan, M. M., Schunn, C. D. and Clark, R. J. (2011) Writing in the natural sciences: understanding the effects of different types of reviewers on the writing process, *Journal of Writing Research*, 2(3), pp. 365–393.

Phillips, F. and Mackintosh, B. (2011) Wiki Art Gallery, Inc.: a case for critical thinking, *Issues in Accounting Education*, 25(3), pp. 593–608.

Porte, G. (1996) When writing fails: how academic context and past learning experiences shape revision, *System*, 24(1), pp. 107–116.

Saddler, B. and Graham, S. (2007) The relationship between writing knowledge and writing performance among more and less skilled writers, *Reading & Writing Quarterly*, 23(3), pp. 231–247.

Sommers, N. I. (1980) Revision strategies of student writers and experienced writers, *College Composition and Communication*, 31(4), pp. 378–388.

Sommers, N. I. (1982) Responding to student writing, *College Composition and Communication*, 33(2), pp. 148–156.

Sriram, R. S. and Coppage, R. E. (1992) A comparison of educators' and CPA practitioners' views on communication training in the accounting curriculum, *Journal of Applied Business Research*, 8(3), pp. 1–11.

Stern, L. A. and Solomon, A. (2006) Effective faculty feedback: the road less traveled, *Assessing Writing*, 11, pp. 22–41.

Stone, D. N. and Shelley, M. K. (1997) Educating for accounting expertise: a field study, *Journal of Accounting Research*, 35, pp. 35–61.

Stout, D. E. and DaCrema, J. J. (2004) A writing intervention for the accounting classroom: dealing with the problem of faulty modifiers, *Journal of Accounting Education*, 22, pp. 289–323.

Vardi, I. (2009) The relationship between feedback and change in tertiary student writing in the disciplines, *International Journal of Teaching and Learning in Higher Education*, 20(3), pp. 350–361.

Watson, S. F., Apostolou, B., Hassell, J. M. and Webber, S. A. (2007) Accounting education literature review (2003–2005), *Journal of Accounting Education*, 25(1-2), pp. 1–58.

Webb, C., English, L. and Bonanno, H. (1995) Collaboration in subject design: integration of the teaching and assessment of literacy skills into a first year accounting course, *Accounting Education: An International Journal*, 4(4), pp. 335–350.

A Successful Competency-Based Writing Skills Development Programme: Results of an Experiment[1]

RUSSELL CRAIG* and C. NICHOLAS McKINNEY**

*Department of Accounting and Information Systems, University of Canterbury, Christchurch, New Zealand, **Rhodes College, Memphis, USA

ABSTRACT   *We describe a successful, semester-length writing skills development programme conducted at the University of Toronto Mississauga (UTM) with intermediate level undergraduate financial accounting students. The programme focused on improving students' writing in five competency areas: organization, grammar, style, professional writing and case writing. Effectiveness was assessed by means of a quasi-experiment involving a pre-test, post-test design with a treatment group and a control group. Comparison of entry and exit test scores of students in the treatment group with those in the control group revealed a highly statistically significant increase in the writing skills of the treatment group. The programme outlined is not presented as a template for emulation, but rather to prompt educators to ponder how they might address the challenge of improving (and assessing) the writing skills of students.*

Background, Purpose, Objectives

Universities face strong community and media criticism for producing graduates who possess poor written communication skill. *BusinessWeek* journalist Gordon (2006, n.p.), for example, has claimed that 'too often undergraduates enter—and leave—B [Business] school without the basic knowledge to write effectively.' In the realm of accounting education, Reinstein and Houston (2004, p. 53) claim that 'accounting education reform has long emphasized the need to improve graduates' writing.'

The source and nature of much criticism, and of the calls to develop accounting students' writing skills, is captured in the opening paragraphs of prior articles on writing enhancement programmes for accounting students (see, for example, Ashbaugh,

Johnstone and Warfield, 2002, p. 123; Ng, Lloyd, Kober and Robinson, 1999, p. 47; Mohrweis 1991, p. 309). While debate on this general issue has continued without relent in recent years, we do not re-visit that debate. Rather, we presume readers accept the need for educators to improve the writing abilities of accounting students. Thus, we focus on reporting the features and effectiveness of a writing intervention initiative that was successful in improving the writing skills of undergraduate accounting students.

We present the results of a pre-test, post-test quasi-experiment (with control group), conducted by a team led by the first author, that assessed the effectiveness of a writing skills development programme for a treatment group of 176 intermediate financial under-graduate accounting students at the University of Toronto Mississauga (UTM) in 2006. The programme was implemented with strong support from UTM's Academic Skills Centre (ASC). The ASC's writing specialist gave technical instruction in aspects of writing and compiled most of the testing instruments used.

A strong motivating impetus for the programme arose from some language and writing difficulties that were a natural consequence of the demographic profile of UTM students. UTM is located at Erindale in Mississauga (Canada's sixth largest city, with a population of 670,000). It is about 15 km west of the main downtown campus of the University of Toronto, but within the Greater Toronto Area. UTM students are preponderantly commuters who live in the Mississauga region. UTM's interest in developing students' writing ability was prompted partly by the very high proportion of UTM students whose first language is not English. In the 2006 Canadian Census, 51% of Mississauga's population reported a 'mother tongue' other than English or French (the national average is 25%). Forty-nine per cent of the population in Mississauga is deemed by census authorities to be a 'visible minority' (the national average is approximately 15%). The principal minorities in Mississauga were South Asian (comprising 20% of the total population) and Chinese (7% of the total population) (*Statistics Canada*, 2006).

The general intent of the writing skills development programme was to enhance five areas of students' writing competency:

Organization (competency 1),
Grammar (competency 2),
Style (competency 3),
Professional writing (competency 4) and
Case writing (competency 5).

The programme was similar, in very broad nature, to the writing skills initiative reported by Ashbaugh et al. (2002). We develop, as they did, *direct* writing skills (e.g. writing a memorandum) and *indirect* skills (e.g. grammar, punctuation and organization).[2]

The five chosen competencies address the principal problems of expression that we had experienced over many years in reading and assessing students' writing. These were mainly lack of verb/subject agreement; confusion over the use of definite and indefinite articles, possessive tense, and singular and plural; poor spelling; inattention to structure, argument development, and paragraphing; and use of inappropriate or imprecise words. We wanted to help students overcome these problems and encourage them to reflect newly acquired skills in two subsequent writing tasks. Another strong motivator was the finding of Webb et al. (1995) that first year accounting students are most in need of help with organizing and developing written text (our competency 1) and writing in academic style (our competencies 2 and 3). We implemented a structured programme of competency enhancement interventions that yielded highly significant improvements in students' writing skills.

We begin by briefly reviewing literature reporting results of programmes that have aimed to enhance accounting students' writing skills. We discuss how the present study contributes to understanding the corpus of knowledge about student writing improvement programmes. We then describe the writing skills development programme and outline how its effectiveness was tested experimentally. The results of our experimentation are presented, including statistical support for our claim that the programme was effective. We then present results of a survey of students' opinion of the programme, engage in some discussion, and draw conclusions.

Literature Review

This paper has similarities and dissimilarities with prior studies of writing skills improvement programmes for accounting students. For a summary of studies conducted before 1992, see Mohrweis (1991, p. 311). The principal studies conducted since 1992 have had a stronger influence on the nature and composition of the writing skills programme we devised. They are referred to elsewhere in this paper. For a summary of the accounting education literature on writing skills development 1987–2004, see Stout and DaCrema (2004, pp. 292–298).

Whereas many reported writing enhancement initiatives (such as those of May and Arevalo 1983; Hirsch and Collins 1988; Mohrweis 1991; and Ashbaugh et al., 2002) took place over several semesters of a student's undergraduate experience in accounting, our focus is applied to a *semester-length* writing development programme. *Some* features of our study are shared with *some* prior studies. These include pre-test post-test design (e.g. Mohrweis 1991); collaboration with a writing specialist (e.g. McIsaac and Sepe 1996; Ng et al., 1999); an intervention approach (Graham, Hampton and Willett, 2008); reporting of student opinion (e.g. English et al., 1999); focus on intermediate level financial accounting students (e.g. Jack and McCartney, 2006); and direct emphasis on grammar (e.g. Stout and DaCrema 2004). However, no prior study shares *all* of our study's features. We also believe our study is the first to use a control group in a pre-test post-test design to assess the results of experimentation with a writing skills improvement programme for undergraduate accounting students; the first to report results for Canadian accounting students; and the first study of an overtly competency-based approach to writing skills enhancement of accounting students. Our evaluation method seems to have stronger internal validity and reliability than prior studies. Many prior studies seem to have been conducted in 'quasi primitive conditions' (Reinstein and Houston 2004, p. 62), rendering them susceptible to sampling, attrition and experimenter biases, and jaundiced conclusions.

Our selection of competencies 1, 2 and 3 was influenced by the weaknesses Webb et al. (1995) reported in the writing of first year accounting students at the University of Sydney. These weaknesses, when categorized in terms of the linguistic explanations of Halliday (1985), provided strong input to our choice of writing competencies 1, 2, and 3 (see Table 1).

Our focus on grammar (competency 2) was motivated in part also by Stout and DaCrema's (2004, p. 289) study on 'dealing with the problem of faulty modifiers,' which contends that grammatical problems 'can inhibit accounting students and professionals from achieving the clarity and conciseness widely regarded as essential in the accounting profession' (p. 289).

Influential in our choice of competency 4 (professional writing) and competency 5 (case writing) was the review by Ashbaugh et al. (2002, 124) of the theories and literature pertaining to the 'theoretical underpinnings for ... writing-skill improvement initiative[s].' Specifically, we were motivated to select competencies 4 and 5 by Ashbaugh et al.'s conclusion (2002, p. 125) that:

Table 1. Competencies and linguistic explanation of writing weaknesses (adapted from by Webb et al., 1995, and English et al., 1999)

Type of weakness	Linguistic category (Halliday 1985)	Competency in the present study
Lack of appreciation of the purpose of the writing task Lack of awareness of how to structure and develop writing that serves different purposes Inability to present ideas analytically	Structure and development of text	Organization: Competency 1
Lack of control over the grammatical resources of language, with a tendency toward grammatical errors that obscure meaning	Grammatical correctness	Grammar: Competency 2
Lack of control over the wording of writing, with a tendency towards writing that is not appropriate for an academic context	Academic style	Style: Competency 3

... [T]hese theories suggest it is important to provide professionally relevant writing experiences to students in order to improve their writing skills. Professional writing experiences (e.g. writing a business memorandum summarizing a technical analysis) are more likely to improve students' writing skills than general writing experiences (e.g., a term paper) because professional business writing experiences require students to adhere to strict business conventions and supply professionally relevant content. Furthermore, these theories suggest that a close matching between educational writing experiences and professional writing demands can facilitate subsequent recall and application of writing skills.

To facilitate such recall and application of writing skills, we required students to write a short memorandum on an accounting topic (competency 4), and an answer to a case study question (competency 5).

Method

Participation in the writing skills development programme was compulsory for all students enrolled in the intermediate financial accounting course. We believed that students most in need of writing skills enhancement would be more likely to disengage if the programme was voluntary.

There were five tests (one for each competency) worth 2.5% each of the overall assessment in the course. Thus, 12.5% of total marks for the course were available for performance in the writing skills development programme. However, to be awarded *any* course mark of 12.5% (5 × 2.5%) for the writing programme, students were required to completed an *entry point* benchmark test of writing in their first tutorial, *and* an *exit point* benchmark test of writing in their last lecture class. This requirement was introduced to encourage students to engage fully with the complete programme and to avoid problems of attrition that were likely to compromise statistical and experimental validity. A diagrammatic overview of the experimental design is provided in Figure 1.

In the week prior to the commencement of the semester we provided teaching assistants (TAs) with pre-course training to ensure they understood the features of the writing programme and adopted common procedural and assessing protocols. In the same week, we sent each student an e-mail and a formal letter advising them of their obligation to participate in the programme and outlining how it would operate. Students were advised that they would receive a *Certificate of Writing Competency Achievement* upon completion of the programme, signed by the Chair of the Department of Management, and stating the competencies they had passed satisfactorily.

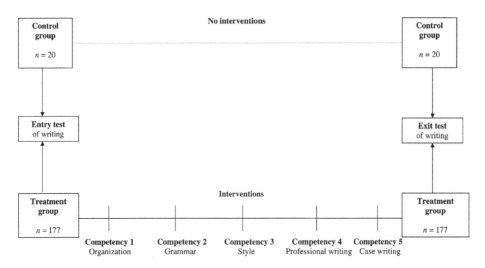

Figure 1. Experimental Design: Writing skills development programme

We conducted a pre-test and a post-test of writing-related skills for all treatment group students ($n = 176$); and identical tests for a control group of students enrolled in an inter-mediate management course ($n = 20$). Students in the control group were not exposed to any writing competency development initiatives during the semester. Students in both groups were preponderantly from the same entry cohort, but pursued different majors. Selection of the control group was based on advice of senior academic staff at UTM that the intermediate management class provided the closest match, in terms of student profile, to the students in the treatment group.[3] Indeed, admission to the respective majors was based on an identical minimum grade point average and on an identical minimum mathematics requirement. A quasi-experimental design was adopted in prefer-ence to a true experimental design because of the infeasibility of randomizing the selection of students in the control and treatment groups (Campbell and Stanley, 1963).

Pre-test

Students' writing ability was measured in the first tutorial of the semester by a test comprising 36 multiple choice questions. This test was devised in close collaboration with the writing specialist. To facilitate comparison, this type of test was used for the exit test also. An example of the type of test used (in this case the exit test) is provided in Appendix A. The answer key is in footnote 4 for readers who wish to benchmark their writing skills (at least as assessed in this study) against the mean correct score of the treatment group (28.27 out of 35) on the exit test.[4] One beneficial aspect of the pre-test was that it allowed the writing specialist to diagnose the principal areas of writing difficulty experienced by the treatment group. These were in areas of punctuation, verb/subject agreement, and dangling modifiers. (For an understanding of dangling modifiers, see Stout and DaCrema, 2004.)

Interventions

Thereafter, during most weeks of the semester, one writing-related 'intervention' lesson of one hour's duration supplemented the three hours of instruction in financial accounting. Attendance was voluntary. On average, about 50% of students attended. Registers of attendance were not kept. The lessons were delivered using a variety of teaching approaches (including PowerPoint® presentation). They focused on explaining (with examples) the writing skills inadequacies highlighted in the entry test of writing and in unsuccessful attempts to pass tests of competencies 1, 2 and 3. For reinforcement, the lessons drew upon the content of a writing skills development textbook that was prescribed for student purchase: Troyka, Hesse and Strom (2006).[5]

Competencies 1, 2, and 3

In the first six weeks of the semester students were instructed in some important features of good writing: organization (competency 1), grammar (competency 2), and style (competency 3). Some details of the matters addressed in each competency are detailed in Table 2.

Table 2. Matters addressed in competencies 1, 2 and 3.

Competency	Prescribed reading	Principal focus
1. Organization	TH & S, Part 1	Planning, drafting, revising, paragraphs, argument.
2. Grammar	TH & S, Parts 2 & 7	Parts of speech, sentence structures, tense, subject-verb agreement, singulars and plurals, articles, word order, dangling modifiers.
3. Style	TH & S, Parts 3 & 4	Conciseness, preciseness, punctuation, word choice, abbreviations, numbers.

Students were required to complete on-line mastery tests of competencies 1, 2 and 3. The tests were marked automatically and results and model answers were available to each student soon afterwards. The test for Competency 1 (Organization) is reproduced in Appendix B. The answer key is given in footnote 6.[6] These tests were compiled from a bank of questions provided with the instructor's copy of the prescribed text. If a student's initial test attempt was 'unsuccessful' (i.e. <80%) he/she could attend a remedial writing tutorial of one hour's duration and then attempt the test a second time. Four versions of each competency test (each with randomized answers) were available. Students could not re-take the same version of the test that they had completed earlier. For course assessment purposes, students who attained mastery in the competency were awarded the full 2.5% of course marks available; those who did not were awarded a course mark of 0% for that competency.

Competencies 4 and 5

In the rest of the programme, students had opportunities to develop writing skills that would be important in a professional career in accounting (professional writing), and for them as continuing university students in subsequent subjects (writing case answers). Two guest lecturers helped in this task. One was a senior business executive (with responsibility in Human Resources and Communication) who was a UTM commerce degree alumnus. The other was a faculty member of UTM who was a highly experienced assessor of students' case writing responses. The test of professional writing required students to compose a memo to a senior non-accountant manager about a simple accounting matter. Students also completed a case writing test (competency 5). Both tests were completed in class. They were marked by the TAs based on criteria established at a meeting between them and the writing specialist. Requirements for the test of professional writing are reproduced in Appendix C. Unlike competencies 1, 2 and 3, students had only one chance to demonstrate mastery of competency 4 and competency 5—a score of 70% in each. For assessment purposes, marks allotted for each of the competencies 4 and 5 ranged between 0 and 2.5%.

Examples of good and bad professional writing and case writing (including evaluation guides) were discussed with students. Additional reading and in-class guidance was provided on these writing tasks.[7] All students received a marked-up copy of their professional writing test as formative feedback prior to their case writing test. In the case writing test students were required to analyse an accounting scenario, exercise professional judgment, and write a report. Some generic criticisms of the professional (memorandum) writing test and case writing test were related to inappropriate tone and style, poor structure, ambiguity, and the inclusion of irrelevant material (the latter seemingly based on the false assumption of students that length and quality of writing were correlated highly).

Post-test and Student Opinion

To gauge the programme's effectiveness, each student completed a test of writing ability (involving 35 multiple-choice questions selected by the writing specialist) in the semester's last lecture class. The questions used were taken from the publishers' test bank accompanying the prescribed writing textbook. They were matched, in form and content, to questions on the entry test of writing. (The exit test is reproduced in Appendix A.) Additionally, students were asked to complete a brief questionnaire-based assessment of the writing programme.

Statistical Analysis

Results of the entry test, the five competency tests, the exit test, and the survey of students' opinions were analysed statistically in terms of means, variances, and distributions. A range of demographic data about students in the treatment group was obtained from the Repository of Student Information (ROSI) system at UTM. ROSI comprises information on gender, degree enrolled in, whether undertaking honours, citizenship status, home address, number of degree credit points attained, and whether a student is enrolled on a part-time or full-time basis. No students' names or numbers were provided. These data were used with the university's permission in multiple regression analyses of results of the treatment group.

Results

On average, the 176 students in the treatment group scored 10.12 out of the 12.5 marks available for the writing component in their course assessment.[8] Table 3 reveals the best student performance was in competency 2 (grammar: 81% successful). The worst performance was in competency 4 (professional writing: 47% successful). The mean

Table 3. Students' performance in the five competencies ($n = 176$)

	Successful: first attempt %	Successful: re-take %	Total successful	Not successful %	Average mark %
1. Organization[a]	44	32	76	24	NA
2. Grammar[a]	70	11	81	19	NA
3. Style[a]	57	20	77	23	NA
4. Professional writing[b]	47	NA	47	53	73
5. Case writing[b]	68	NA	68	32	77

[a]Success in competencies 1, 2 and 3 was a score $\geq 80\%$ on each competency.
[b]Success in competencies 4 and 5 was a score $\geq 70\%$ on each competency.

number of competencies passed (maximum $= 5$) was 3.88, with a mode of 4. A pleasing aspect was the apparent effect of the remediation (revision lessons and students' self-learning) in helping a sizable cohort of students (32% in the case of competency 1) to master competencies 1, 2 or 3 at a second attempt.

Pre-test versus Post-test Performance

Table 4 reports summary statistics and *t*-tests of the pre-test and post-test results for the treatment group and control group.

Table 4(a) reports descriptive statistics (e.g. mean and standard deviation) of both groups' tests. On the entry test, the control group ($M = 74.9$) performed slightly better than the treatment group ($M = 72.4$). However, the results were reversed on the exit test: the treatment group ($M = 80.9$) performed much better than the control group ($M = 72.4$).

Table 4(b) reports the between-group comparisons. There are no statistically significant differences between the two groups on the pre-test (*P* value $= 0.348$). However, there is a weak difference between the two groups on the post-test (*P* value $= 0.055$). The key result in Table 4(b) is the highly significant statistical evidence that the pre-test and post-test scores differ by almost a full standard deviation between the two groups (*P* value $= 0.007$).

Table 4(c) reports the within-group *t*-tests. The 1.3 point increase in the mean score of the control group is not statistically significant (*P* value $= 0.557$). However, the 8.4-point increase in the treatment group is highly significant (*P* value <0.001). These results point to the success of the five interventions in improving the writing skills of students in the treatment group.

Table 4. Comparison of entry and exit test scores.

		Entry test	Exit test	Exit − entry test	Per cent change
(a) Summary statistics					
Control group	Means	74.86	76.14	1.28	2%
$n = 20$	Standard deviations	10.83	9.78	10.11	
Treatment	Mean	72.41	80.78	8.37	12%
group	Standard Deviations	9.05	10.73	10.94	
$n = 176$					

	Entry test	Exit test	Entry − exit test
(b) Between groups comparisons (unpaired *t*-test: control group versus treatment group)			
Control group means	74.86	76.14	1.28
Treatment group means	72.41	80.78	8.37
t (df)	−0.96 (23)	2.02 (23)	2.95 (24)
Significance (two-tailed)	0.348	0.055	0.007

	Control group	Treatment group
(c) Within group comparisons (paired *t*-test: entry test versus exit test)		
Entry test	74.86	72.41
Exit test	76.14	80.78
Difference	1.28	8.37
t (df)	−0.57 (19)	−10.15 (175)
Significance (two-tailed)	0.577	<0.001

The improved results should be evaluated cautiously. We maintain that they are attributable to the effects of the writing interventions. However, it is conceivable that they might be influenced by at least five other factors. First, there is a potential maturation effect. Students' writing skills might have improved as they aged during the three months of the analysis period – but this effect seems likely to be negligible. Second, is the possible effect of communication between students in the treatment group and students in the control group. Based on discussions with UTM faculty who observed the patterns of social behaviour of students in the two groups, we consider this effect to be negligible. Indeed, any such effect most likely would result in higher exit scores for the control group than otherwise, which strengthens our conclusion about the effectiveness of the writing programme for the treatment group. Third, an instrumentation effect would arise if the entry test and exit test were not identical in scope and standard. Since the entry test and exit test questions were selected randomly (but with regard for matching form and content) from the same bank of test questions, we believe this effect is negligible. Fourth, the improved performance of students in both groups in the exit test might have been affected by 'learning' from having taken one or more similar tests in the three months since the entry test. Fifth, we are unaware of any intervening external factors (such as a university-wide or community-sponsored literacy programme) which might have affected students' performance in either group.

Of these five possible confounding factors, it is likely that testing effects would have had the strongest impact. Although we do not believe that 'testing' had a major impact, we cannot be certain about this. If we assume that two points of the 8.4 point improvement between the mean entry and exit scores in the treatment group (that is, from 78.8 to 80.8) was caused by any, or all, of the five factors just mentioned (holding all other factors constant), there would still be a significant improvement ($P < 0.05$) between entry and exit test scores for the treatment group.

Multiple Regression Analysis

Analysis of the means for each demographic variable in the student demographic data (ROSI) revealed no strong evidence of associations with the various test scores. However, there is weak evidence that 'Canadian citizens and permanent residents' did better than 'non-residents' (students with study permits or other visas) in overall performance in the intermediate financial accounting course (*t*-test: P value $= 0.081$).

Multiple regression modelling was conducted of the level of improvement between entry and exit test scores for the treatment group for the ROSI demographic variables (gender, enrolled major, whether students were undertaking honours, citizenship status, stage of completion of degree, full time/part time status, and legal status in Canada). After addressing multicollinearity and heteroskedasticity issues, such modelling did not reveal any significant results for the difference in test scores.

Students' Opinions

Students' opinions in the treatment group regarding the writing programme (presented in Table 5) were elicited using seven point Likert-type scale responses in a short questionnaire survey (where 1 = very strongly disagree, 2 = strongly disagree, 3 = slightly disagree, 4 = neither disagree or agree, 5 = slightly agree, 6 = strongly agree, and 7 = very strongly agree). The student responses are very encouraging, especially after allowing for the impositions on students of the writing programme – an extra hour of instruction per week, the cost of the prescribed writing text, and additional testing and anxiety.

Table 5. Students' opinion of the writing skills development program ($n = 176$)

Statement	Mean[a]	Standard deviation
The writing skills development program was a good idea	5.13	1.33
The writing skills development program was well delivered	4.80	1.23
The degree of difficulty in the writing skills development programme was appropriate.	5.39	1.01

[a]The evaluations were marked on a seven-point Likert-type scale where 1 = 'very strongly disagree,' 4 = 'neither disagree or agree,' and 7 = 'very strongly agree'.

Table 6. Competency that students considered to be of greatest benefit

Competency	Responses (total = 261)	Per cent of responses
Professional writing	91	53
Case writing	79	46
Organization	39	22
Grammar	27	15
Style	25	15

Generally, students appeared to be well disposed to the programme. The mean scores reveal that they thought the programme was a good idea, was well delivered, and had an appropriate degree of difficulty. The slightly lower mean response on whether the programme was 'well-delivered' ($M = 4.8$) is likely to have been prompted by some timetabling and logistical problems in scheduling competency re-take tests.

Students were also asked to indicate the competency area in which they benefited most. Some students checked more than one competency. Table 6 reports responses for each category as a percentage of total responses, in descending order of perceived benefit.

Professional writing was the competency in which students were least successful in demonstrating mastery (47% were deemed successful), yet students regarded this competency as the one in which they benefited most. Indeed, the order of perceived benefit in Table 6 matches the order of difficulty reflected in the success rates for each competency in Table 3.

Generally, students felt that the writing skills programme had helped them. Such a conclusion is sustained not only by the students' opinions survey results, but also by anecdotal evidence (such as e-mail and personal correspondence). The following e-mail exemplifies much of this opinion. (The student e-mail quoted below is reproduced anonymously with their original grammar, spelling and punctuation preserved.)

Dear professor,

.....Actually i was not happy with the writing program at first because i failed for the first time, but i was benefited by the professional writing and case writing. I have not touched these kinds of writings before. Therefore, i learned a lot by this writing couse though I have not get really good mark in the writing. Anyways, thank you for your teaching me and I really hope that you enjoy the time being in Canada.

Conclusions and Discussion

The results point to the effectiveness of the five writing-related competency interventions. The model outlined should assist those who are devising similar writing improvement programmes. The detailed test information obtained for each student during the various testing phases has a strong empirical basis that helps identify, diagnose, and respond to the writing deficiencies of individual students. The programme described provides a structured way to improve and assess writing skills within a semester-length course. The professional writing and case writing components bring the writing and accounting aspects together in a way that relates closely to what students will subsequently face in professional examinations for CPA membership, and in their professional careers as accountants.

Mounting the writing programme required much commitment and administrative effort, and additional funding for tutorial support. Many difficulties arose in obtaining reliable quantitative results to use in assessing success. It is clear that much scope exists to improve students' writing. In particular, there is a strong need for educators to emphasize the importance of 'writing in context.' Using text messaging protocols is acceptable for text messages, but students should be reminded that those protocols and habits (e.g., avoidance of capitalization, absence of punctuation, omission of auxiliary verbs, and use of contracted words) are pernicious and non-acceptable when they infiltrate other writing contexts, such as essays and professional memos. Further, if the student's claim in the following e-mail is accurate ('I got full mark on grammar test on TOEFL') then the testing procedures for the Test of English as a Foreign Language (TOEFL) warrant review.

> This noon, I retook the test. I found there are always some new things on test after I finished reading all chpaters [name omitted] asked us to read. This is unfair becasue We can not have enough preparation to test, How can we get a good mark.We are international students in U of T. our english vocabulary is not enough to understand all things. Profesor, before I got in U of T, I took the TOEFL test, produced by princeton University. TOEFL test is to help student to enter English University to achieve university language level . I got full mark on grammar test on TOEFl. How can I not pass the test in U of T. This is strange.

The writing programme was repeated in modified format at UTM in 2007. An internal UTM report on the 2007 programme has described a 4% improvement in students' writing skills. However, this improvement was not quantified reliably. There was no control group. The exit test of writing was optional, and some students did not complete it. Of the students who attempted the exit test, some were alleged to have indulged in 'gaming' behaviour by not completing it conscientiously. For the effectiveness of a writing programme to be evaluated rigorously, there should be strong incentives to ensure students are conscientious in engaging with the programme.

UTM's commitment to improving students' writing is dynamic. Subsequent thinking, based on student feedback, is placing greater emphasis on *direct* writing skills (our competencies 4 and 5), rather than *indirect* ones. UTM is seeking to integrate and embed the writing programme into accounting content. It has also addressed timetabling and administrative problems by permitting students to re-take only one competency—and on one day only at the end of semester when scheduling is easier.

We see two major areas for future research. First, there is a need for comprehensive study to determine the characteristics of students who experience the greatest (and the least) improvement in writing from a writing development programme. Second, if we accept that much of the problem in improving accounting students' writing skills resides in accounting educators' under-developed writing skills,[9] further research should be directed to assess and remediate those areas of under-development.

Notes

[1]The experiment described in this paper was conducted in accord with guidelines provided by the Office of Research Ethics, University of Toronto.

[2]The plural pronouns 'we' and 'our', when used in the remainder of this section, and in the two following sections, refer to the group at UTM responsible for planning and implementing the program: the first author, CB and DF of the ASC, and MJ, Commerce Program Director at UTM. This group made decisions on operational policy and procedures collaboratively, based on collective experience and careful synthesis of relevant factors. Elsewhere in the paper, the pronouns 'we' and 'our' refer to the first and second authors.

[3]No tests were conducted for significant differences in student profile of the two groups (e.g. in terms of gender, or legal status in Canada). Because of privacy concerns, UTM was reluctant to disclose personal data, even anonymously, for the control group.

[4]The 'correct' answers are: 1B, 2B, 3C, 4A, 5D, 6A, 7A, 8B, 9A, 10A, 11C, 12A, 13C, 14A, 15D, 16B, 17B, 18A, 19C, 20C, 21D, 22C, 23C, 24C, 25C, 26C, 27A, 28B, 29D, 30A, 31C, 32C, 33B, 34D, 35B. We say 'correct' because several of the answers given in this (and similar) tests have been challenged, often on the grounds that the writing involved needs to be evaluated 'in context.'

[5]Non-Canadian editions of this book are available in other countries. In the USA, for example, the equivalent book is Troyka and Hesse (2006).

[6]1A, 2C, 3C, 4B, 5B, 6C, 7B, 8B, 9C, 10C, 11B, 12A, 13D, 14B, 15C, 16D, 17B, 18D, 19B, 20D, 21C, 22D, 23C, 24C, 25A.

[7]For example, 15 min of core class time was devoted to a PowerPoint®-assisted presentation titled 'Some Advice on Case Writing.' This provided advice on how to address, understand and analyse a case; steps in writing a case response; and some 'Dos and 'Don'ts' in case writing.

[8]191 students started the course, but 15 students dropped the course or otherwise did not complete it. All 176 students who finished the course completed both the entry and exit tests.

[9]The authors do not absolve themselves from the possibility that their writing skills could be improved.

References

Ashbaugh, H., Johnstone, K. M. and Warfield, T. D. (2002) Outcome assessment of a writing-skill improvement initiative: Results and methodological implications, *Issues in Accounting Education*, 17(2), pp. 123–148.

Campbell, D. T. and Stanley, J. C. (1963) *Experimental and Quasi-Experimental Designs for Research* (Chicago: Rand McNally).

English, L., Bonanno, H., Ihnatko, T., Webb, C. and Jones, J. (1999) Learning through writing in a first-year accounting course, *Journal of Accounting Education*, 17(2/3), pp. 221–254.

Gordon, J. (2006) Memo to students: Writing skills matter, *BusinessWeek*, 26 April. Available at http://www.businessweek.com/bschools/content/apr2006/bs20060426_682947.htm (accessed 1 May 2006).

Graham, A., Hampton, M. and Willett, C. (2008) What not to write: An intervention in written communication skills for accounting students. Paper presented to the British Accounting Association's Accounting Education SIG Annual Conference, Seville, May.

Halliday, M. A. K. (1985) *An Introduction to Functional Grammar* (London: Edward Arnold).

Hirsch, M. L. and Collins, J. D. (1998) An integrated approach to communication skills in an accounting curriculum, *Journal of Accounting Education*, 6(1), pp. 15–21.

Jack, L. and McCartney, S. (2006) The feeding (back) of the multitude: Practical issues arising when teaching writing skills to large groups. Working Paper No. 06/04, July (Colchester: University of Essex School of Accounting, Finance and Management).

May, G. S. and Arevalo, C. (1983) Integrating effective writing skills in the accounting curriculum, *Journal of Accounting Education*, 1(1), pp. 119–126.

McIsaac, C. M. and Sepe, J. F. (1996) Improving the writing of accounting students: A cooperative venture, *Journal of Accounting Education*, 14(4), pp. 515–533.

Mohrweis, L. C. (1991) The impact of writing assignments on accounting students' writing skills, *Journal of Accounting Education*, 9, pp. 309–325.

Ng, J., Lloyd, P., Kober, R. and Robinson, P. (1999) Developing writing skills; a large class experience: A teaching note, *Accounting Education: an international journal*, 8(1), pp. 47–55.

Reinstein, A. and Houston, M. (2004) Using the Securities and Exchange Commission's 'Plain English' guidelines to improve accounting students' writing skills, *Journal of Accounting Education*, 22(1), pp. 53–67.

Statistics Canada, 2006 Census of Population. Available at http://www.12.statcan.ca/english/census06/data/profiles/community/ (accessed 14 April 2008).

Stout, D. E. and DaCrema, J. J. (2004) A writing intervention for the accounting classroom: Dealing with faulty modifiers, *Journal of Accounting Education*, 22(4), pp. 289–323.

Troyka, L. Q., Hesse, D. and Strom, C. (2006) *Simon & Schuster Handbook for Writers, Fourth Canadian Edition* (Canada: Pearson Education).

Troyka, L. Q and Hesse, D. (2006) *The Simon and Schuster Handbook for Writers*, 8th edition (New York: Prentice Hall).

Webb, C., English, L. and Bonanno, H. (1995) Collaboration in subject design: Integration of the teaching and assessment of literacy skills into a first year accounting course, *Accounting Education: an international journal*, 4(4), pp. 335–350.

APPENDIX A

MGT 220 Exit Test

(The formatting of this test has been altered to save space. Some question options, which were listed vertically in the original, are shown here on the same line.)

MULTIPLE CHOICE

Choose the one alternative that best completes the statement or answers the question

You are about to take a test of English skills. The test contains 35 questions, each with four possible answers. Select the best answer and mark the appropriate place on your answer sheet.

I. Each of the following questions contains an error in one of the underlined sections. Select the answer corresponding to the section of the sentence containing the error.

1) Toronto is divided in to many communities including: Scarborough, North York, Mississauga_ Etobicoke, and the Danforth.
A) Toronto B) _ C), D) Danforth

2) During the Middle Ages, scribes copyed books carefully by hand using quill pens.
A) Middle Ages B) copyed C) carefully D) using

3) The newspaper reported_ that the supreme court of Canada would hear a case about suspects' rights next year.
A) newspaper B) _ C) supreme court D) suspects'

4) The mayors' decision to raise taxes rather than reduce personnel in government will cause her to lose the next election.
A) mayors' B) raise C) personnel D) lose

5) Employees were stunned when they were notified that the trainee got promoted to manager after only her 'fourth' week with the company.
A) stunned B) notified C) promoted D) 'fourth'

6) The detailed news report, about the advancing hurricane gave us good advice about how to protect our homes, and we were all ready when the storm arrived!
A), B) hurricane C) advice D) all ready

7) Spanish, like a number of other languages, <u>have</u> <u>its</u> roots in Latin, once spoken in <u>ancient</u> Rome.
A) have B) its C), D) ancient

8) 'Laughter,'said Victor Hugo,_ is the sun that drives <u>winter</u> from the human face.'
A), B) _ C) winter D) .

9) The <u>Senator</u> from Ohio spoke to the <u>governors</u> of Pennsylvania and New York about the serious pollution of <u>Lake</u> Erie, a body of water that borders on all three states.
A) Senator B) governors C) Lake D),

10) <u>Him and his</u> co-workers, the top bowling team in the tournament, will represent our <u>company</u> in the league finals.
A) Him and his B), C), D) company

11) We can <u>only</u> speculate about some of ancient <u>history's</u> <u>most strangest</u> mysteries, for example, how the heavy stones of the pyramids were put into place.
A) only B) history's C) most strangest D),

12) I want to tell <u>whomever</u> is in charge of the campaign to beautify our neighbourhood_ that my family and <u>I</u> are <u>extremely</u> grateful.
A) whomever B) _ C) I D) extremely

13) After <u>carefully</u> thinking through their plans, George and Kin are taking a course in <u>conversational</u> Spanish_ which makes a great deal of sense now that they <u>intend</u> to study in Mexico.
A) carefully B) conversational C) _ D) intend

14) Matt said that <u>their</u> not going to Vancouver, British Columbia, for the <u>summer</u>.
A) their B), C), D) summer

15) The vase, which was hand painted, slipped out of Joan's hands_ and <u>bursted</u> on the tile floor.
A), B), C) _ D) bursted

16) Often the reputation of an <u>entire</u> company <u>depend</u> on one employee who <u>officially</u> <u>represents</u> that company to the public.
A) entire B) depend C) officially D) represents

17) Realizing she was late for work, the accountant <u>drove</u> <u>quick</u> to get to the <u>board's</u> <u>annual</u> meeting.
A) drove B) quick C) board's D) annual

18) Yesterday when we <u>enter</u> the dimly lit card shop, the clerk <u>sternly</u> <u>asked</u> John and <u>me</u> to check our briefcases.
A) enter B) sternly C) asked D) me

19) The woman <u>who</u> was looking at suspects in the police lineup spoke up <u>loudly</u>, 'I think that is <u>he</u>, but I <u>am</u> not sure.'
A) who B) loudly C) he D) I am

20) <u>Generously</u>, my parents have offered to pay the <u>extraordinarily</u> high insurance on a car for my sister and <u>myself</u> for as long as we <u>maintain</u> B averages.
A) Generously B) extraordinarily C) myself D) maintain

II.   In the following questions, a section is underlined. Select the answer that shows the correct revision. Choice A repeats what is underlined; choose it if the original needs no revision.

21) <u>My mother telephoned my sister and told her she had won a trip to Ireland.</u>
A) My mother telephoned my sister and told her she had won a trip to Ireland.
B) My mother telephoned my sister and said she had won a trip to Ireland.
C) My mother telephoned my sister Ann and told her she had won a trip to Ireland.
D) My mother telephoned my sister and told her, 'I have won a trip to Ireland.'

22) <u>Many people own Turkish rugs who have never been there.</u>
A) Many people own Turkish rugs who have never been there.
B) Many people own Turkish rugs but have never been there.
C) Many people who own Turkish rugs have never been to Turkey.
D) Many people owning Turkish rugs have never been there.

23) <u>My college offers many interesting courses to first-year students. Therefore, I do not know. What electives to take.</u>
A) My college offers many interesting courses to first-year students. Therefore, I do not know. What electives to take.
B) My college offers many interesting courses. To first-year students. Therefore, I do not know. What electives to take.
C) My college offers many interesting courses to first-year students. Therefore, I do not know what electives to take.
D) My college offers many interesting courses to first-year students therefore, I do not know what electives to take.

24) <u>Many people apply to join the foreign service, however only a few are accepted.</u>
A) Many people apply to join the foreign service, however only a few are accepted.
B) Many people apply to join the foreign service however only a few are accepted.
C) Many people apply to join the foreign service; however, only a few are accepted.
D) Many people apply to join the foreign service, however; only a few are accepted.

25) Fad diets for weight reduction are <u>popular because many people like to look thin however unbalanced diets can harm people's health.</u>
A) popular because many people like to look thin however unbalanced diets can harm people's health.
B) popular, because many people like to look thin, however, unbalanced diets can harm people's health.
C) popular because many people like to look thin; however, unbalanced diets can harm people's health.
D) popular because many people like to look thin however; unbalanced diets can harm people's health.

26) <u>Massive traffic congestion will become common at all hours of the day. If our old highways and streets, riddled with potholes, are not repaired soon.</u>
A) Massive traffic congestion will become common at all hours of the day. If our old highways and streets, riddled with potholes, are not repaired soon.
B) Massive traffic congestion will become common at all hours of the day if our old highways and streets. Riddled with potholes are not repaired soon.

C) Massive traffic congestion will become common at all hours of the day if our old highways and streets, which are riddled with potholes, are not repaired soon.
D) Massive traffic congestion will become common. At all hours of the day if our old highways and streets riddled with potholes are not repaired soon.

27) Strongly arguing her case, the lawyer attempted to convince the skeptical jury.
A) Strongly arguing her case, the lawyer attempted to convince the skeptical jury.
B) Arguing her case strongly the lawyer attempted to convince the skeptical jury.
C) Arguing her case the lawyer attempted strongly to convince the skeptical jury.
D) Arguing her case, the lawyer attempted to convince strongly the skeptical jury.

28) Busy as a bee, the chef worked to prepare food that would melt in your mouth at the restaurant's anniversary party.
A) Busy as a bee, the chef worked to prepare food that would melt in your mouth at the restaurant's anniversary party.
B) The chef worked enthusiastically to prepare a splendid meal for the restaurant's anniversary party.
C) Without a minute to spare, the chef labored without a break to prepare edibles that would please the palates of everyone in attendance at the restaurant's anniversary party.
D) The chef cooked up a storm to get ready for the restaurant's anniversary party.

29) After she led a unit of 38 nurses for service in the Crimean War, Florence Nightingale became a legend. Someone who was a symbol of compassion and strength.
A) After she led a unit of 38 nurses for service in the Crimean War, Florence Nightingale became a legend. Someone who was a symbol of compassion and strength.
B) After she led a unit of 38 nurses for service in the Crimean War. Florence Nightingale became a legend. Someone who was a symbol of compassion and strength.
C) After she led a unit of 38 nurses. For service in the Crimean War. Florence Nightingale became a legend, someone who was a symbol of compassion and strength.
D) After she led a unit of 38 nurses for service in the Crimean War, Florence Nightingale became a legend, someone who was a symbol of compassion and strength.

30) After weeks of rehearsing their parts and making their costumes, the seniors' play was going to be a success.
A) After weeks of rehearsing their parts and making their costumes, the seniors' play was going to be a success.
B) After weeks of rehearsing their parts and making their costumes, the seniors' felt that their play was going to be a success.
C) The seniors' play, after weeks of rehearsing and making their costumes, was going to be a success.
D) It was going to be a success, the seniors' play felt, after weeks of rehearsing their parts and making their costumes.

31) Newspapers do more than report the news, they offer analyses of major trends, and they cover local events.
A) news, they offer analyses of major trends, and they cover local events.
B) news they offer analyses of major trends, and they cover local events.
C) news. They offer analyses of major trends, and they cover local events.
D) news. They offer analyses. Of major trends, and they cover local events.

32) It was necessary for the new employees to be given a lecture by the person who is director of the Confederated Health Insurance Plan.
A) It was necessary for the new employees to be given a lecture by the person who is director of the Confederated Health Insurance Plan.
B) The new employees were given a lecture, which they had to attend, by the person who is director of the Confederated Health Insurance Plan.
C) The director of the Confederated Health Insurance Plan gave the required lecture to the new employees.
D) The new employees had to give a lecture to the director of the Confederated Health Insurance Plan.

33) The newlyweds had many expenses. They needed to buy furniture for their apartment. On the contrary, they had to buy a car because public transportation was not available where they lived.
A) On the contrary, B) At the same time, C) At length, D) On the whole

III.   For each question, select the best answer.

34) In a paragraph, what is the best order for the five sentences below?
(1) He said that he heard something snap in his head when a train conductor pulled him by the ears onto a moving train he was trying to board in Michigan.
(2) Thomas Edison started to lose his hearing at the age of twelve.
(3) Despite his handicap, Edison obtained patents on over 1,000 inventions during his lifetime.
(4) When Edison met his wife-to-be, he was totally deaf.
(5) He taught her Morse code and proposed by tapping out his message on her hand.
A) 4, 5, 2, 1, 3 B) 3, 4, 5, 2, 1 C) 2, 4, 5, 1, 3 D) 2, 1, 4, 5, 3

35) Which of the following statements is suitable for an argumentative essay?
A) Last year's Christmas party was no ordinary event.
B) Parliament must allot an annual amount of money for restoration of our national parks.
C) Midst our sorrow and fear, the burning of our home had three positive effects.
D) Mexico City proved to be the opposite of all I had imagined.

APPENDIX B

Competency 1

Organization

MULTIPLE CHOICE

Choose the one alternative that best completes the statement or answers the question.

I. In the following questions, you will work on ordering sentences in paragraphs and narrowing topics for essays. For each question, select the best answer.

   Read the following paragraph. Some sentences contain errors. Answer the questions concerning the sentences in the paragraph. The sentences have been numbered for reference purposes.

Soccer Scores Big

(1) Soccer is a more practical sport for high school than football because it is less expensive, affords more opportunities for student participation, and causes fewer serious injuries. (2) With regard to equiptment, soccer is more economical than football. (3) Soccer players need shin guards, jerseys, shorts, and cleats. (4) However, the equipment list for football are longer and the items much more expensive. (5) Also, because there are fewer physical qualifications for playing the sport, soccer provides greater opportunity for student participation. (6) Size and strength are not as important, the soccer player does not have to be tall or weigh as much as the football player. (7) In addition, soccer is less dangerous than football for the player, who the audience applauds more for his speed than for his physical strength. (8) Injuries does occur in soccer, but they are usually bruises and sprains. (9) However, in football the injuries often include broken bones and permanent damage to joints. (10) These injuries require more time to heal. (11) Soccer will perhaps never surpass football in popularity, but its acceptance will increase. (12) Because soccer is a more practical sport than football.

1) The topic sentence for the paragraph is   1) _____
A) The first sentence   B) The second sentence   C) The last sentence   D) Is not stated

2) In mode the paragraph is   2) _____
A) Process   B) Comparison/Contrast   C) Argumentative   D) Descriptive

3) How many reasons does the paragraph state for soccer's being a more practical sport than football?   3) _____
A) One   B) Two   C) Three   D) Four

4) Identify the error in sentence two.   4) _____
A) An unnecessary comma   B) A misspelled word
C) A sentence fragment   D) Subject-verb agreement

5) Identify the error in sentence four.   5) _____
A) A misspelled word.   B) Subject-verb agreement
C) An omitted comma   D) An unnecessary comma

6) In sentence five the word also is   6) _____
A) An adjective   B) A conjunction   C) A transition word   D) A verb

7) Identify the error in sentence six.   7) _____
A) A sentence fragment   B) A comma splice
C) Subject-verb agreement   D) A misspelled word

8) Identify the error in sentence seven.   8) _____
A) Subject-verb agreement   B) Pronoun case   C) Fragment   D) Run-on sentence

9) Identify the error in sentence eight.   9) _____
A) Run-on sentence   B) Unnecessary comma   C) Subject-verb agreement   D) Pronoun case

10) Identify the error in sentence twelve.   10) _____
A) An omitted comma   B) Subject-verb agreement
C) A sentence fragment   D) A misspelled word

II. In the following questions, you will work on narrowing topics for essays. For each question, select the best answer.

11) Which of the following statements is suitable for a narrative essay?   11) _____
A) Parliament should enforce an eight percent national sales tax to replace our present tax system.
B) I never knew what fear meant until I realized that I was lost in the city of New York.
C) The beauty, atmosphere, and historical significance of Montreal were not soon forgotten.
D) Giving a home permanent proved to be temporary frustration as I followed the instructions.

12) Which of the following statements is suitable for a comparison/contrast essay?
    12) _____
A) Although news reports on both radio and television are informative, they differ in time allotment, visual impact, and the personal associations they arouse.
B) As a child my secret hideout was the old barn at the edge of the cornfield.
C) Every college should have an ESL programme for foreign students.
D) Failing my math class was devastating, but as a result I made three resolutions.

III.   Now you will work on correct sentence structure, sentence punctuation, and clarity. In the following questions, part of each item is underlined. Select the answer that shows the correct revision. Choice A repeats what is underlined; choose it if the original needs no revision.

Example: Air travel has become popular. When prices are low. Many people like to visit friends in distant cities. Therefore many flights are filled long in advance.

A) Air travel has become popular. When prices are low. Many people like to visit friends in distant cities.
B) Air travel has become popular when prices are low many people like to visit friends in distant cities.
C) Air travel has become popular. When prices are low, many people like to visit friends in distant cities.
D) Air travel has become popular, and when prices are low. Many people like to visit friends in distant cities.

Answer: C

13) Because most cars will break down sometime, all drivers should know how to change a flat tire. And how to signal for assistance.   13) _____
A) all drivers should know how to change a flat tire. And how to signal for assistance.
B) all drivers should know how to change a flat tire, and signal for assistance.
C) all drivers should know how to change a flat tire; and how to signal for assistance.
D) all drivers should know how to change a flat tire and how to signal for assistance.

14) Running thirty miles a week, the new jogging shoes quickly wore out.   14) _____
A) Running thirty miles a week, the new jogging shoes quickly wore out.
B) Running thirty miles a week, I quickly wore out my new jogging shoes.
C) Running thirty miles a week, the new jogging shoes were quickly worn out by me.
D) The new jogging shoes quickly wore out, running thirty miles a week.

15) <u>My friend's mother told me that she's not feeling well enough to receive visitors.</u>   15) _____

A) My friend's mother told me that she's not feeling well enough to receive visitors.

B) My friend's mother told me that 'she's not feeling well enough to receive visitors.'

C) My friend's mother told me that my friend wasn't feeling well enough to receive visitors.

D) My friend's mother told me that Elizabeth wasn't feeling well enough to receive visitors.

16) Many American colleges have long-standing <u>football rivalries, one of the most famous is the Army-Navy rivalry between West Point and Annapolis.</u>   16) _____

A) football rivalries, one of the most famous is the Army-Navy rivalry between West Point and Annapolis.

B) football rivalries, one of the most famous is the Army-Navy rivalry. Between West Point and Annapolis.

C) football rivalries; one of the most famous is the Army-Navy rivalry. Between West Point and Annapolis.

D) football rivalries; one of the most famous is the Army-Navy rivalry between West Point and Annapolis.

17) <u>Whoever parked a blue station wagon in front of the building. Must move it. The car is blocking traffic.</u> 17) _____

A) Whoever parked a blue station wagon in front of the building. Must move it. The car is blocking traffic.

B) Whoever parked a blue station wagon in front of the building must move it. The car is blocking traffic.

C) Whoever parked a blue station wagon in front of the building must move it the car is blocking traffic.

D) Whoever parked a blue station wagon in front of the building. Must move, the car is blocking traffic.

18) Campus parking is very limited. <u>People only with valid stickers will be allowed to park on campus.</u>   18) _____

A) People only with valid stickers will be allowed to park on campus.

B) People with valid stickers only will be allowed to park on campus.

C) People with valid stickers will be allowed to park only on campus.

D) Only people with valid stickers will be allowed to park on campus.

19) <u>My brother told my father that his car keys were on the desk.</u>   19) _____

A) My brother told my father that his car keys were on the desk.

B) My brother told my father, 'Your car keys are on the desk.'

C) My brother John told my father that his car keys were on the desk.

D) My brother spoke to my father and told him that his car keys were on the desk.

20) <u>Many people develop an interest in German movies without ever going there.</u>   20) _____

A) Many people develop an interest in German movies without ever going there.

B) Many of us are developing an interest in German movies even though we have never gone there.

C) Even though they like German movies, many people have never even gone on a visit there.

D) Many people develop an interest in German movies without ever going to Germany.

21) <u>Rebuilding the engine, our overalls were stained with grease.</u>   21) _____
A) Rebuilding the engine, our overalls were stained with grease.
B) Rebuilding the engine, with grease our overalls were stained.
C) Rebuilding the engine, we stained our overalls with grease.
D) With grease our overalls were stained, rebuilding the engine.

22) <u>Peering through my telescope, people twenty floors below were almost close enough to recognize.</u>   22) _____
A) Peering through my telescope, people twenty floors below were almost close enough to recognize.
B) People twenty floors below, peering through my telescope, were almost close enough to recognize.
C) People twenty floors below were almost close enough to recognize peering through my telescope.
D) Peering through my telescope, I saw that people twenty floors below were almost close enough to recognize.

23) <u>I plan to move off campus in the spring. If I can find a suitable apartment nearby.</u>   23) _____
A) I plan to move off campus in the spring. If I can find a suitable apartment nearby.
B) I plan to move off campus. In the spring. If I can find a suitable apartment nearby.
C) I plan to move off campus in the spring if I can find a suitable apartment nearby.
D) I plan to move off campus. In the spring, if I can find a suitable apartment nearby.

24) Because a babysitter may need to reach you in a hurry, <u>always leave a number where you can be reached. And a forwarding number</u> if you do not stay in that place.   24) _____
A) always leave a number where you can be reached. And a forwarding number
B) always leave a number where you can be reached, and a forwarding number
C) always leave a number where you can be reached, and leave a forwarding number
D) always leave a number where you can be reached; and a forwarding number

25) <u>Fishing can be relaxing and exciting at the same time. This is hard to explain to someone who has never gone fishing.</u>   25) _____
A) Fishing can be relaxing and exciting at the same time. This is hard to explain to someone who has never gone fishing.
B) Fishing can be relaxing and exciting at the same time. This is hard to explain. To someone who has never gone fishing.
C) Fishing can be relaxing and exciting at the same time, this is hard to explain to someone who has never gone fishing.
D) Fishing can be relaxing and exciting at the same time this is hard to explain to someone who has never gone fishing.

APPENDIX C

Competency 4

Test of 'Professional Writing'

Time Allowed: 22 minutes

Situation

You are Mark Ham, Chief Accountant of Mrs Saga Manufacturing (MSM) Inc.
MSM is contemplating reducing the estimated useful life of all of its Plant and Equipment from 10 years to 8 years. MSM currently amortizes Plant and Equipment using the straight line method. There have been no new acquisitions or disposals of Plant and Equipment by MSM during the year ended 31 December, 2009. All plant and equipment has been in service with MSM for less than seven years.

MSM's Balance Sheet as at 31 December, 2009 shows:

	$ million
Plant and Equipment	100
Less: Accumulated Amortization	50
	50

MSM's Income Statement for the year ended 31 December, 2009 shows:

	$ million
Amortization Expense: Plant and Equipment	10

Required

The newly-appointed CEO of MSM, Jane Islington, is an engineer. She has only a basic understanding of accounting and financial reporting matters.

Islington asks you to send her a memo detailing the effect the change in estimated life would have had on the company's cash flow and reported net income, if it had been applied during the financial year ended 31 December, 2009. Complete your memo on either or both of the following two pages.

Marking Guide

Your memo will be marked on format, content and style. Errors of grammar and spelling will be penalized. Accuracy of content, clarity and conciseness will also be graded.

'A distinguishing factor': Oral Communication Skills in New Accountancy Graduates

F. ELIZABETH GRAY and NIKI MURRAY

Massey University, New Zealand

ABSTRACT   *This study into the perceived importance of oral communication skills in accountancy included the collection and analysis of quantitative and qualitative data from a national survey of New Zealand accountants, followed by a series of semi-structured interviews. Survey and interview data reveal agreement with existing literature: New Zealand accountancy employers find all oral communication skills somewhat important and a number of specific skills extremely important, but employers also report seldom finding the required level of oral communication proficiency in new university graduates. The study produced an inventory of 27 individual oral communication skills that will be useful to similar investigations in different national contexts. Additionally, the findings of this study may be useful to curricular development both in the New Zealand and international contexts.*

1. Introduction

Academics and practitioners do not always concur but, in the case of communication skills in accountancy graduates, these two sets of stakeholders are in firm agreement: both written and oral communication skills are extremely important in the accountancy work-place (Albin and Crockett, 1991; Albrecht and Sack, 2000; Borzi and Mills, 2001; Hock, 1994; Johnson and Johnson, 1995; LaFrancois, 1992; McDonald, 2007; Morgan, 1997). This agreement extends across international boundaries, as a number of studies around the globe have reported the high value placed on communication skills, for example in the UK (Morgan, 1997), USA (Smythe and Nikolai, 2002), and Australia (Tempone and Martin, 2003). In New Zealand, the site of the present study, academic studies into the importance of communication skills in accountancy and the challenges of teaching those skills (Gardner, Milne, Stringer and Whiting, 2005; McLaren, 1990) have multiple corollaries in the workforce. Accountancy job advertisements regularly request both oral and written communication skills; competency in oral communication is emphasised on the website of the New Zealand Institute of Chartered Accountants (NZICA); and oral communication is an explicit component of the assessment structure of the PCE2 examination, which concludes the second (and final) stage of training towards becoming a Chartered Accountant in New Zealand. However, both formal studies and anecdotal evidence suggest that new accountancy graduates often do not possess communication skills sufficient to meet the demands of the workplace, particularly in the area of oral communication (Adler and Milne, 1994; Courtis and Zaid, 2002; Gray, 2010; McLaren, 1990; Zaid and Abraham, 1994).

Students in New Zealand may graduate with a university degree in accountancy after three years of full-time study. (Accountancy may also be studied in less rigorous programs at polytechnics and institutes of technology.) The intensity of the university programs of study, which are accredited by NZICA, means students have a challenging workload of technical study and very limited opportunity to take elective or 'liberal' courses. Of course, limited class time and the resultant curricular pressures and inadequate skill mastery are not unique to the New Zealand accountancy classroom (Pittenger, Miller and Mott, 2004; Wardrope and Bayless, 1999).

The globally-recognised problem of insufficient oral communication skill in accountancy graduates leads to a series of questions that need practical answers:

- How should university educators respond, strategically and pedagogically, to this reported lack of oral communication skills in new graduates?
- What approaches and assessments within university courses will best meet the needs of students aspiring to successful accountancy careers?
- To what extent is the development of such skills in students the responsibility of the university and what is the role of the workplace in developing oral communication skills?

Before university educators can make any meaningful decisions concerning pedagogy or curricula, and appropriately teach the oral communication skills needed for a successful accountancy career, they need concrete information regarding exactly which specific skills are most valued and most needed in accountancy. Thus a research question was formulated: to ascertain the value of specific oral communication skills in new graduates, as perceived by New Zealand accountancy employers. It was hoped that answers to this research question would provide educators with specific information with which to consider their optimal pedagogical responses.

The research question led to the construction and implementation of this longitudinal study. Initial research objectives were:

- To determine how much importance New Zealand accountancy employers place on oral communication skills in the new graduates they hire.
- To determine what specific kinds of oral communication skills are required by New Zealand accountancy employers in new graduates.
- To determine the degree to which accountancy employers are finding the required oral communication skills in newly-graduated accountancy students.

The study included the collection and analysis of quantitative and qualitative data, from a national survey of New Zealand accountants, followed by a series of semi-structured interviews. Initial findings from the first-phase survey have been reported elsewhere (Gray, 2010). Overall, survey and interview data revealed that accountancy employers find all oral communication skills somewhat important and a number of specific skills extremely important, but that the required level of overall oral communication skill was seldom found in new graduates. Accountancy employers agreed that the possession of strong oral communication skills improves a graduate's chance of succeeding in the hiring process and also of progressing in his or her career. The study produced an inventory of 27 individual oral communication skills, of which listening skills were most highly valued by accountancy employers, and formal presentation skills were considered least valuable, although there was disagreement on this point. It is hoped the oral communication skill inventory will be useful to similar investigations in different national contexts. Additionally, the findings of this study may be of use both in the New Zealand and international context in the long-term planning of curricular development.

2. Literature Review

Studies of communication in accountancy agree broadly on the importance of written and oral communication skills. Many formal and informal studies to this point have tended to use general terms such as 'communication skills,' or the even vaguer term 'generic skills';[1] it is difficult to ascertain the precise meaning of such all-encompassing terms as they apply to chartered accountancy. For example, Zaid and Abraham (1994) studied the problems encountered by accountancy graduates early in their employment careers, and reported a primary area of difficulty to be in 'communication with others.' Baker and McGregor (2000) compared the importance perceived in communication skills by a number of accountancy stakeholder groups; this study, too, only uses the broad term 'communication skills.' De Lange, Jackling, and Gut (2006) surveyed Australian accountancy graduates and found that students reported themselves to have a significant skill deficiency in the specific areas of 'interpersonal skills' and 'oral expression'; these two broad categories, however, were no more closely examined or defined.

Within the smaller number of studies that have examined a particular set of communication skills in accountancy, most have focussed on written communication skill (Albrecht and Sack, 2000; Ashbaugh, Johnstone and Warfield, 2002; English, Bonanno, Ihnatko, Webb and Jones, 1999; Hall, 1998; Ng, Lloyd, Kober and Robinson, 1999; Webb, English and Bonanno, 1995). Very few studies have examined oral communication specifically, or identified individual oral communication skills. Morgan (1997) is an exception: in a study of accountancy professionals in England and Wales he identifies 13 individual skill areas within oral communication activities in accountancy. There is no agreement on a classificatory inventory of such skills. One study into oral communication, by Maes, Weldy and Icenogle (1997), surveyed American business employers from a broad array of industries on graduates' possession of another 13 distinct oral communication skills. Maes et al. (1997) and McLaren (1990) both specifically list 'listening' as a desirable communication skill and, more recently, Goby and Lewis (2000) have examined listening as a specific business communication skill. Other research has variously investigated a number of individual oral communication skills across a range of business industries, including conveying expertise through spoken communication and giving intelligible explanations (Smythe and Nikolai, 2002), delivering formal presentations (Wardrope, 2002), and participating in a range of more informal presentations (Crosling and Ward, 2002). The first phase of this study drew together the foci and findings of previous studies in relation to the production of a comprehensive list of oral communication skills (Gray, 2010).

Ascertaining the particular requirements of accountancy employers in regard to specific communication skills should be of assistance to university educators planning the curricular content and assessments of university courses, as academics and practitioners agree that written and oral communication skills are two major areas needing more attention in the university accountancy curriculum (Albrecht and Sack, 2000; Henderson, 2001; Simons and Higgins, 1993). However, the relationship between workplace demand and classroom instruction is not necessarily simple. While a considerable body of scholarship has recommended a variety of curricular improvements for university level accounting education (see, for example, Henderson, 2001; Sin, Jones, and Petocz, 2007; and Usoff and Feldmann, 1998), the literature reflects a significant concern in relation to the transferability of taught communication skills from the university classroom environment to the 'real-world' environment of the accountancy workplace (Beaufort, 1999; Cooper, 1997; D'Aloisio, 2006; Davies and Birbili, 2000; Kemp and Seagraves, 1995; Thomas, 1995).

A number of academics and employers suggest that universities should not bear the entire responsibility for developing 'workplace-ready' communication skills in students. They argue that organisations employing new graduates—and graduates themselves—should share the responsibility for developing contextualised and discourse-specific communication competencies (Ford, 2009; Hayes and Kuseski, 2001; Muir and Davis, 2004; Triebel and Gurdjian, 2009). Such competencies, after all, are developed by means of a number of contributing factors, including age and maturity, as well as familiarity with and length of exposure to a specific discourse community. University training, however comprehensive, cannot encompass all these variables.

Research into accountancy education has also recognised the particular problems faced by English second language (ESL) speakers striving to develop written and oral communication competency as well as the technical proficiencies required in accountancy workplaces (Andrews, 2006; McGowan and Potter, 2008; Webb et al., 1995). Several studies in New Zealand and internationally report on the difficulties that ESL accountancy graduates face in a competitive hiring environment (Birrell, 2007; Jacobs, 2003; James and Otsuka, 2009; Kim, 2004).

With regard to the specific question of developing communication skills within university-level accountancy instruction, scholars have suggested an array of learning and assessment approaches (Adler and Milne, 1997; Milne, 1999; Milne and McConnell, 2001; Tempone and Martin, 2003). This study recognises that developers of curricula must balance data regarding workplace demand with institutional and accreditation-related demands and a number of other pedagogical considerations. Notwithstanding, educational responses to the challenges of developing oral communication skills in students may be usefully informed by empirical data identifying the particular skills most highly valued and most pressingly needed within accountancy, as perceived by employers themselves. This study provides such data.

3. Method

The project was conducted in two stages over the course of approximately six months. In phase one, a questionnaire was mailed to all New Zealand chartered accountancy firms, and this was followed in phase two by a series of telephone interviews with accountancy professionals. Prior to data collection, ethics approval was sought from and granted by the Ethics Committee of the authors' institution. Questionnaire and interview respondents were provided with a written description of the project, were assured of confidentiality, and granted permission before their responses were recorded.

3.1 *Questionnaire*

In the first stage, a questionnaire was sent to all New Zealand chartered accountancy firms, containing a series of questions concerning the quality of oral communication skills possessed by new accountancy graduates, the specific oral communication skills which employers desire, and the role of oral communication skills in the hiring process (Gray, 2010). The majority of the questions were designed to be answered on a five-point Likert scale, but the questionnaire also included several short-answer questions.

The questionnaire instrument was developed through a series of iterations. The findings and design of previous New Zealand and international research studies that had identified specific communication skills were consulted (including Gray, Emerson and MacKay, 2006; Maes *et al.*, 1997; McLaren, 1990; Morgan, 1997; Smythe and Nikolai 2002), and the individual oral communication skills collated. The catalogue of individual skills was further extended through conversations with university colleagues in the communication and accountancy departments, and then the input of New Zealand accounting practitioners was solicited from a pilot study. The aim of these iterations was to create the fullest possible inventory of oral communication skills, and to reflect the unique aspects of the New Zealand accountancy context.

A foundational study was McLaren's 1990 investigation into communication skill in New Zealand accountancy. One important construct borrowed from McLaren was the distinction between listening attentiveness and listening responsiveness. Constructs were also adapted from studies conducted by Morgan (1997), Zaid and Abraham (1994), and De Lange *et al.* (2006). Smythe and Nikolai's oral communication concerns model (1996, 2002) proved particularly useful in the construction of this questionnaire. This model identifies three categories of concern as a framework for grouping oral communication skills: self-concern, task-concern, and impact (or outcome) concern. Smythe and Nikolai postulate that a progression takes place from one category of concern to the next in line with a person's career progression and his/her growth in experience and confidence in communicating orally in the workplace. Since the target population for this study was a constituency at a mature career stage within chartered accountancy firms, Smythe and Nikolai's 'progressive' divisions were not retained (although a number of their questions were incorporated, particularly in the areas of task concern and impact concern). Instead, divisions between questions were created in relation to different audiences, building on the finding of a related study (Gray *et al.*, 2006) that New Zealand employers report new graduates to significantly lack audience awareness in their communications.

After a comprehensive list of specific oral communication skills was generated, the questionnaire draft was piloted on four accountancy professionals, and their feedback enabled questions to be refined. A number of skills that were initially individually identified were modified and condensed into a smaller number of broader and more inclusive skills: for example, 'Building audience confidence in recommendations' and 'Projecting an image of sincerity and commitment' (both 'impact concerns' from Smythe and Nikolai's taxonomy) were combined into the one, more inclusive skill category, 'Conveying a knowledgeable and confident demeanour.' Additionally, feedback from the pilot study led to the second of the two specified listening skills being more fully explicated, thus: 'Listening responsiveness: (that is, acting appropriately on messages received).'

Again building on feedback from the pilot regarding usability, the questionnaire as a whole was divided into three sections. Section A captured introductory information including the size of the organisation and the qualifications held by new graduates hired in the last three years. Section B listed the full, final inventory of 27 individual oral communication skills, collected into the following audience-related divisions: I. Listening skills; II. Collegial communication skills; III. Client communication skills; IV. Communication skills with management; and V. General Audience Analysis Skills. Respondents were asked to rate the importance of each skill, as well as the frequency with which this skill is found in new accountancy graduates. At the end of Section B respondents were invited to add to the questionnaire any other oral communication skills that they considered important for new accountancy graduates. Section C, Final Questions, asked respondents whether oral communication training was available in or through their organisation, whether oral communication training should be included in university accountancy education programmes, and finally to estimate the hours per working week a new accountancy graduate would be engaged in communicating orally. At the close of the questionnaire, respondents were given the option to volunteer for a follow-up interview.

3.1.2 *Respondents*. The questionnaire was sent to all chartered accountancy firms listed on the New Zealand online business directory, and was addressed to the Practice Manager as the individual most likely to have in-depth knowledge of the process of hiring new graduates. New Zealand's professional accountancy body, the New Zealand Institute of Chartered Accountants (NZICA) reports that 40.7% of its members work in the private sector, while the second largest percentage, 27.5%, are employed in Chartered Accountancy practices (*2008 annual report*). Working on the assumption that CA practices hire a percentage of new graduates proportionate to their sizeable percentage of NZICA members, CA practices were chosen as the focal population for this study as they represent (in contrast to the private sector) a readily identifiable and readily contactable group of employers.[2] While the New Zealand online business directory listed 1,111 chartered accountancy firms as of 1 April 2008, a number of listed organisations had ceased operations or were uncontactable, and the questionnaire was eventually mailed to 760 firms.

Of 760 mailings, 146 questionnaires were returned, producing a response rate of 19.2%. While this response rate was higher than the 15% usable response rate reported by McLaren in her 1990 study of New Zealand accountancy professionals, it remains marginally lower than the typical response rate for postal-based questionnaires (20–40%, as given in Frankfort-Nachmias and Nachmias, 1996). Possible reasons for this relatively low response rate include the fact that time and funding did not permit follow-up mailings, and also the fact that the target population is frequently time-poor and frequently surveyed. While non-response bias is an unavoidable concern when the response rate is less than 100 per cent, a low response rate does not necessarily equate to a non-response bias (Gendall, 2000). A degree of representativeness was observable in the geographical spread of respondents, the positions held by respondents (see below), and the types of businesses responding, suggesting generalisation across a range of accountancy business types is viable.

The questionnaire was mailed to separate groups of potential respondents in six postings, each approximately 10 days apart. The order in which responses were received generally mirrored the order in which postings were mailed: that is, the first group's responses were received before the second group's questionnaires began to be returned, and so on. As a record of receipt for each individual survey was not kept, early versus late response bias cannot be checked. As a single mail-out technique was used for each individual, it may be argued that differences in respondent type are not as applicable as may be seen in a survey where some participants responded early, whereas others received several reminders and mail-outs before responding.

Analyses were undertaken treating the six postings as separate groups to determine any potential differences by respondent type. All groups were similar in claiming that oral communication in general was either 'essential' or 'very important' in the accountancy profession. Furthermore, oral communication skill was 'always' important as a hiring factor for all mail-out groups. When comparing each group on importance and frequency of communication skills using a Kruskall-Wallis test, only one significant difference was found for frequency of listening skills seen in new graduates, $x^2 = 11.60$, $P < 0.05$. Post-hoc Mann-Whitney U tests subsequently revealed no significant differences in frequency of listening skills seen in new graduates between any of the six groups (using a Bonferroni correction).

While the questionnaires were addressed to the Practice Managers of each organisation, respondents revealed a degree of variability. The majority of completed questionnaires were anonymous, but the respondents who identified themselves ranged from partners in large firms, to senior employees in very small firms, to Human Resources directors.

3.2 Interviews

The second phase of the study involved employer interviews. Forty-five questionnaire respondents volunteered to be contacted for follow-up interviews, and 19 volunteers could subsequently be contacted by telephone for complete interviews. The interviewee sample size was considered adequate due to its purposive nature and the recent finding that, within such samples, data saturation (including metathemes and subthemes) occurs within the first 12 interviews (Guest, Bunce and Johnson, 2006). It was intended that the qualitative data from interviews would triangulate and extend conclusions arising from analysis of the quantitative data. The interview data incorporated into the study an ethnographic element, 'thick description, a rich, detailed description of specifics' (Neuman, 2003, p. 367), which helped produce more robust and credible conclusions.

Telephone interviews were conducted between October and December 2008. Interviewees ranged from accountancy practice managers to sole practitioners, to partners in large firms. The semi-structured interviews ranged in length from 15 to 45 minutes and sought clarification of a number of issues arising from the questionnaire data, including the implications of globalisation for oral communication in accountancy, the impact of new technologies and the importance of telephone skills, the centrality of listening skills, and the desirability of presentation skills for graduates new to the accountancy workplace.

3.3 Data Analysis

Once the data from the questionnaires was collated, statistical analysis was performed using SPSS. Mean and median scores were calculated with regard to the importance scores given to each individual oral communication skill, and to the frequency scores (how often each skill is observed in new graduate hires). Each mean was the product of the addition of all the individual importance or frequency scores for each communication skill, divided by the sample size. The standard deviation (SD) of each mean score, as well as the inter-quartile range for the median, was also calculated to indicate the relative spread of responses, with higher figures equating to wider ranges of scores. Owing to a number of missing responses, the denominator of responses to each question shows some variation. As the skill variables violated the assumption of normality (expected given the general level of agreement in employers' perceptions), non-parametric tests were used. Where relevant, all assumptions of the named tests below were met.

As mentioned in 3.1, Section B of the questionnaire invited respondents to write in any further oral communication skills which they felt were important for new accountancy graduates to possess, distinct from the 27 skills listed. Comments identifying additional skills were received from 36 respondents; these comments were recorded and analysed for thematic consistency.

Once the interviews were transcribed, themes were also identified and analysed. Grounded theory was applied to analyse these themes, that is, inductive analysis in which data produce meanings, rather than meanings being applied from exterior theory (Strauss and Corbin, 2000).

4. Findings

4.1 *Research Objective 1: How Much Importance do New Zealand Accountancy Employers Place on Oral Communication Skills in the New Graduates they Hire?*

The questionnaire data presented a clear answer to the first research question. Oral communication skill in general was considered to be 'essential' in a new graduate by 49.6% ($n = 133$) of respondents; a further 41.4% reported it to be 'very important'. On a rating scale from 1 to 5, where 1 was 'not important' and 5 was 'essential', the overall mean for oral communication skill in general was 4.39 ($Md = 4.00$). A Kruskal-Wallis test found no significant difference in the importance value assigned to oral communication skill depending on the size of the organisation, $x^2(4) = 5.48, p > 0.05$.

During the second phase of the study, interviewees strongly reiterated the perceived importance of oral communication skill: CL called oral communication 'a career divider,' meaning it was indispensable to success within accountancy, and EK labelled strong oral communication 'a distinguishing factor' setting good accountants apart from the mediocre. SWS stated: 'Being able to communicate is a number one priority … [and] it's going to get more and more important.' Interview data also supported the significance of a theme that emerged from written-in comments in the questionnaire: the importance of oral communication skills in accountancy is perceived to be increasing rapidly as a direct result of globalisation, and an increased speaking flexibility and cross-cultural adaptability are considered particularly important in this context.

Reporting that they 'always' take oral communication skill into account in hiring decisions were 64.1% ($n = 131$) of questionnaire respondents (a total of 90.8% reported this to be a hiring factor either 'always' or 'often'). RT stated that strong oral communication skills often proved the decisive factor in a hiring decision:

> The person who presents well … verbally, if you had to toss a coin between two of them, same grades and all that, the one who can communicate better, you'd give it to that person I think. […] It has to be one of the most powerful strengths or powerful weaknesses that people have.

No questionnaire respondents reported 'never' taking an applicant's oral communication skills into account in the hiring process, and several interviewees reported incorporating specific checks of a candidate's oral competency into their hiring process. For example, TB stated that he telephones all job applicants prior to an in-office interview, in order to gauge their skills in speaking on the telephone.

4.2 *Research Objective 2: What Specific Kinds of Oral Communication Skills are required by New Zealand Accountancy Employers?*

The questionnaire gathered specific data concerning the perceived importance of 27 individual oral communication skills. As an overview, Figure 1 outlines the perceived

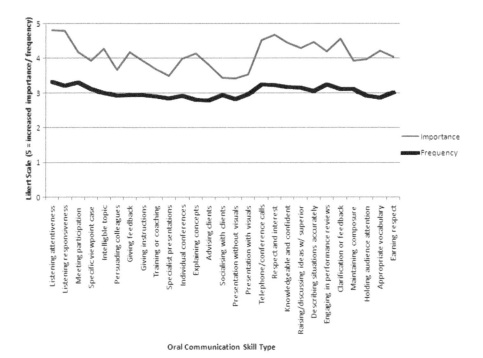

Figure 1. Perceived importance of communication skills by perceived frequency of new graduate ability

importance of the individual communication skills against the perceived frequency with which these skills are seen in new graduates. Figure 1 shows that the importance and frequency measures follow a similar pattern. This may reflect the influence of the workplace in focussing on developing certain communication competencies in new graduates, or hiring based on those competencies being present to a certain degree. However, there is still an obvious gap between the importance of each skill and the degree to which it is seen in new graduates.

4.2.1 *Listening skills.* On a rating scale from 1 to 5, where 1 was 'not important' and 5 was 'essential,' the two skills considered most important were those of listening attentiveness and listening responsiveness, valued respectively at 4.81 (*Md* = 5.00)—82% of respondents ranked listening attentiveness as 'essential'—and 4.80 (*Md* = 5.00)—a further 82% of respondents classifying listening responsiveness as 'essential'. In subsequent interviews, KC described listening to another person as being a more important skill than that of articulating one's own thoughts:

> Sometimes, speaking less is better than speaking more. Sometimes you have to have more listening ability. That listening ability will give you the timing of when to say things and when not to say things. ...

A number of interviewees linked listening skill to a related set of competencies concerning a speaker's ability to create rapport and adjust to audiences' needs. These interviewees spoke of the need for accountancy professionals to communicate with others (clients, colleagues, and managers) 'in their own language.'

> We learn to use sometimes slightly different language in order to be able to communicate to different people and that's certainly part of our job when we're in a service industry like

accountancy. We need to talk to people *in their language* and us[e] words and conduct that they are comfortable with (BR; emphasis added).

It's important to understand your client so that … *you're speaking almost in 'like language'* so that you know who you are talking to [and] you know they are understanding (SWS; emphasis added).

I think it's a horses for courses [principle], you've got to know… your clients or the people you're dealing with. If you happen to know someone didn't like a certain style or you could pick from their responses … [then] *you reply with like with like* (DW; emphasis added).

JC mentioned adjusting vocabulary and PW mentioned adjusting message channel, in relation to the particular needs of the audience. MT emphasised the importance for accountancy graduates to gauge appropriateness of language:

They've got to realise that when they're dealing with clients, or senior members of organis-ations, that they've got to communicate it appropriately and not in a manner that they may always communicate with their friends or colleagues.

Interviewees agreed that this kind of reflective adjustment to an audience's preferred register is dependent on a speaker's ability to listen and make appropriate communicative changes.

4.2.2 *Vocabulary and slang.* Several individual oral communication skills identified in the questionnaire concerned engaging in dialogue and using language and channels preferred by the communication partner. These included 'explaining or making a topic intelligible' to colleagues ($\bar{x} = 4.28$, $Md = 4.00$, ranked ninth); 'giving feedback' to clients: ($\bar{x} = 4.17$, $Md = 4.00$, ranked 13th); and 'using appropriate vocabulary for the audience', a general audience skill: ($\bar{x} = 4.21$, $Md = 4.00$, ranked 10th). Follow-up inter-view questions seeking more information concerning the importance of explanatory and vocabulary skills elicited a number of specific concerns with the use of slang by new accountancy graduates. TO stated: 'A lot of them have devolved into … use of a lot of colloquialisms that may not be acceptable to the older generation.' According to NM, overly casual language destroys credibility.

It's hard enough for a young person to break in and to be heard, I guess in a business sense when you're trying to sell to, I guess older people or experienced people. If you come out with schoolyard slang, you don't stand a chance.

Interviews emphasised the desirability in new graduates of a wide-ranging and flexible vocabulary (described by one interviewee as a mental 'drop-down menu' of words), oper-ating in tandem with the ability to access the correct level of spoken formality.

After listening attentiveness and listening responsiveness, questionnaire results ident-ified the next five most highly valued individual oral communication skills as being: 'Con-veying professional attitude of respect and interest in clients' ($\bar{x} = 4.68$, $Md = 5.00$); 'Asking for clarification or feedback from management' ($\bar{x} = 4.57$, $Md = 5.00$); 'Speaking on the telephone/making conference calls with clients' ($\bar{x} = 4.53$, $Md = 5.00$); 'Describ-ing situations accurately and precisely to superior(s)' ($\bar{x} = 4.47$, $Md = 5.00$); and 'Convey-ing a knowledgeable and confident demeanour to clients' ($\bar{x} = 4.45$, $Md = 5.00$). Please see Table 1 for a complete record of the average and median importance values accorded to each oral communication skill, as well as the reported mean and median frequency with which each skill was found in new accountancy graduates (see also, Gray, 2010).

Table 1. Importance and frequency values for specific oral communication skills ranked within communication skill grouping by importance

Oral communication skill	Importance Mean	SD	Frequency Mean	SD	Importance Median	IQR	Frequency Median	IQR
Listening skills								
Listening attentiveness	4.81	0.41	3.32	0.59	5.00	0	3.00	1
Listening responsiveness	4.80	0.47	3.21	0.56	5.00	0	3.00	1
Collegial communication skills								
Explaining or making a topic intelligible	4.28	0.75	3.00	0.65	4.00	1	3.00	0
Participating in meetings	4.18	0.72	3.31	0.64	4.00	1	3.00	1
Giving feedback	4.17	0.76	2.94	0.69	4.00	1	3.00	0
Making a case for a specific view	3.93	0.81	3.12	0.66	4.00	2	3.00	0
Giving instructions	3.93	0.95	2.95	0.61	4.00	2	3.00	0
Providing training or coaching	3.67	1.08	2.91	0.77	4.00	2	3.00	1
Persuading	3.65	0.81	2.92	0.57	4.00	1	3.00	0
Giving specialist presentations	3.48	1.07	2.85	0.82	3.00	1	3.00	1
Client communication skills								
Conveying attitude of respect and interest	4.68	0.51	3.23	0.68	5.00	1	3.00	1
Speaking on the telephone	4.53	0.64	3.24	0.67	5.00	1	3.00	1
Conveying knowledge/ confidence	4.45	0.62	3.17	0.63	5.00	1	3.00	0
Explaining concepts	4.13	1.04	2.80	0.67	4.00	2	3.00	1
Conducting individual conferences	3.99	1.03	2.93	0.70	4.00	2	3.00	1
Advising	3.82	1.18	2.79	0.68	4.00	2	3.00	1
Giving presentations with visuals	3.52	1.16	2.96	0.94	3.00	2	3.00	1
Socialising	3.43	1.00	2.94	0.80	3.00	1	3.00	1
Giving presentations without visuals	3.41	1.12	2.82	0.90	3.00	3	3.00	1
Communication skills with management								
Asking for clarification/ feedback	4.57	0.59	3.11	0.72	5.00	1	3.00	1
Describing situations accurately and precisely	4.47	0.59	3.05	0.66	5.00	1	3.00	0
Raising and discussing ideas	4.29	0.66	3.15	0.65	4.00	1	3.00	0
Engaging in performance reviews	4.20	0.87	3.25	0.82	4.00	1	3.00	1
General audience analysis skills								
Using appropriate vocabulary for audience	4.21	0.90	2.87	0.70	4.00	1	3.00	1

(Continued)

Table 1. Continued

Oral communication skill	Importance		Frequency		Importance		Frequency	
	Mean	SD	Mean	SD	Median	IQR	Median	IQR
Earning respect	4.05	0.91	3.01	0.66	4.00	1	3.00	0
Holding audience's attention/interest	3.97	1.02	2.92	0.79	4.00	2	3.00	1
Maintaining composure	3.92	0.96	3.12	0.73	4.00	2	3.00	0

NB: Importance ratings are based on a Likert scale from 1 to 5 where 1 is 'not important' and 5 is 'essential'.
  Frequency ratings are based on a Likert scale from 1 to 5 where 1 is 'never' and 5 is 'always'.

4.2.3 *Telephone skills.* Questionnaire data ranked skill at speaking on the telephone or on a conference call as the fifth most highly valued of the 27 oral communication skills. Interviewees voiced forceful support for the importance of telephone speaking skills in accountancy graduates. CL stated that speaking to a client on the telephone 'becomes the key contact point. It's the thing that kicks the whole job off.' DS agreed that excellent telephone skills are essential to client management: 'I think that's the most important of all communication skills, to be able to speak on the telephone because in most cases that's your first point of contact with a client.' Several interviewees noted that new graduates in their firms are held back from telephone contact with clients until they've had several months of experience in the workplace and/or until they've completed in-house telephone skills training (JS; MG; CL; SWS). While several interviewees noted that the importance of telephone communication has decreased somewhat in relation to the increasing use of e-mail (PW, NM), interviewees were united in agreeing telephone communication would never be eliminated from accountancy practice, and would remain an essential communication channel between accountant and client.

4.2.4 *Presentation skills.* Of the 27 individual oral communication skills identified in the questionnaire, three of the four lowest importance scores were awarded to skills concerning the giving of presentations. 'Giving presentations to non-accountants, without visuals,' was accorded the lowest mean importance score, 3.41 (*Md* = 3.00), and 'Giving specialist presentations to colleagues and/or other accountants' was the third lowest ranked skill, with a mean score of 3.48 (*Md* = 3.00). 'Giving presentations to non-accountants, with visuals (e.g. *PowerPoint*),' was the fourth lowest ranked skill, with a mean score of 3.52 (*Md* = 3.00). ('Socialising with clients' took the spot of second least important oral communication skill, with a mean score of 3.43, [*Md* = 3.00]).

While this raw quantitative data has been reported elsewhere (Gray, 2010), in the second phase of the study interviewees provided further insights into these findings regarding presentation skills. The majority agreed that while the ability to orally present to groups, including clients and management, was an important skill in accountancy, it was not of particular importance for new graduates, who would only be expected to present as they rose in seniority. 'Very, very rarely do we get young graduates actually presenting overheads and so forth, simply because that's a senior role' (NM). 'I think one-on-one communication for people at that level is far more important [than] that sort of presenting to a group, or whatever size that might be. I think conversation is more important than presentation at that level' (RT). 'For juniors, it [isn't] an important thing. But as you move up the ranks it becomes important' (MG).

However, a vocal minority of interviewees held the opposite view, that presentation skills were important for all accountancy employees, even junior ones, but these interviewees defined presentation skills quite broadly.

I think certainly in our particular area of work ... in some areas they're dealing with the clients quite early on, [so] it's a really important skill that they can have those presentations skills. Even if it's as simple as the confidence to be able to ask a question in a client meeting type thing, right through to actually being able to stand up and give a presentation (EK).

KC defined every meeting with a client as a kind of presentation: 'Every meeting you have ... is the presentation itself, or else what else can it be? You're presenting a set of accounts, you're delivering your opinion. So it is the presentation.' When asked to consider the particular parameters of a formal presentation, delivered with visual aids such as *PowerPoint*, all 19 interviewees conceded this was an oral communication skill less frequently needed on the part of new accountancy graduates.

4.2.5 *Oral communication skills with specific audiences*. Finally, the perceived importance of oral communication skills in relation to specific audiences (clients, colleagues, and managers) was compared. Means for the three audience-based skill-sets were compared using a Friedman test, which revealed a significant difference, $x^2(2) = 70.61$, $P < 0.05$. Post-hoc Wilcoxon Signed-rank tests with an applied Bonferroni correction subsequently revealed that while there was no statistically significant difference in the importance values accorded to collegial communication skills and client communication skills, ($z = -1.63$, $P > 0.02$), oral communication skills in relation to management were perceived to be significantly more important than both oral communication skills in relation to colleagues ($z = -7.64$, $P < 0.02$, $r = -0.68$) and oral communication skills in relation to clients ($z = -6.52$, $P < 0.02$, $r = -0.58$).

4.3 *Research Objective 3: To What Degree are Accountancy Employers Finding the Required Oral Communication Skills in Newly-graduated Accountancy Students?*

In general, questionnaire respondents and interviewees agreed that they are not finding the acceptable level of the oral communication skills which they require in new university graduates. A total of 54.3% of questionnaire respondents reported that accountancy graduates recognised the importance of oral communication skills only 'sometimes,' and a further 20.2% reported graduates 'seldom' recognised oral communication's importance. More specifically, the overall mean frequency with which new graduates were perceived to possess individual oral communication skills was relatively low, ranging from 2.79 to 3.32 on a five-point scale on which higher scores reflect greater frequency. Dispiritingly, interviewees not only confirmed the questionnaire data reporting a low level of skills on the part of new graduates, but also reported a high level of resistance to the suggestion they acquire them: 'It's hard to convince them [of] the necessity to learn how to speak well' (KC).

4.3.1 *Least frequently found skills*. Questionnaire data revealed those oral communication skills that accountancy employers found least frequently in the new graduates hired were the client-focused skills of 'Advising clients' ($\bar{x} = 2.79$, $Md = 3.00$), and 'Explaining concepts to clients' ($\bar{x} = 2.80$, $Md = 3.00$). The next four least frequently found individual oral communication skills in new graduates included two presentation-related skills but also two more diverse skills: 'Giving presentations to non-accountants, without visuals' ($\bar{x} = 2.82$, $Md = 3.00$); 'Giving specialist presentations to other accountants' ($\bar{x} = 2.85$, $Md = 3.00$); 'Using appropriate vocabulary for the audience' ($\bar{x} = 2.87$, $Md = 3.00$); and, 'Providing training or coaching to other accountants' ($\bar{x} = 2.91$, $Md = 3.00$). Interestingly, with the notable exception of 'using appropriate vocabulary,' these skills were also ranked among the least important by the employers.

4.3.2 *English second language difficulties.* Comments written into the questionnaire reflected a high level of employer concern with spoken English language competency on the part of non-native English speakers, which correlates with the concern reported in the literature. While using appropriate vocabulary and appropriate communication channels was mentioned a number of times in respondents' comments, the most frequently recurring theme in the comments (13 of 36) reflected concern that English second language speakers may have technical proficiency but inadequate oral language competency for entry-level accountancy employment. This view was queried in the follow-up interviews, and found strong support. TB, for example, reported clients who 'instantly switched off' upon hearing accented or halting English from an accountancy employee, and stated he has lost clients as a direct result.

While a number of interviewees noted similar client dissatisfaction over difficulties in understanding the speech of an ESL accountancy employee, SWS and CL both raised the issue of cosmopolitanism in relation to the perceived difficulty of such interactions. They noted that rural New Zealanders, and those from regional centres, generally had less exposure to accented English speakers, or to those born outside of New Zealand, and expressed significantly more discomfort with receiving their accountancy information from an ESL speaker than that reported by New Zealanders living in larger centres, particularly Auckland. DP felt very strongly both that large numbers of ESL accountancy graduates had inadequate oral communication skills and that the responsibility for ensuring all accountancy graduates could speak comprehensibly lay with the education system. She stated that New Zealand universities were irresponsible in graduating foreign accountancy students with inadequate oral communication skill: 'We are not teaching them the culture of business language ... by that [I] mean not just the terminology but also aspects of register and ability to talk to different kinds of people.'

4.3.3 *Acquisition of oral communication skills.* Finally, interviewees voiced some disagreement—and a degree of resignation—when questioned as to when and where new accountancy graduates should be acquiring the necessary oral communication skills. According to DP, these skills should be developed before a student is permitted to graduate with a university-level accountancy qualification. However, the majority of interviewees reported that they fully expect students often to graduate with inadequate oral communication skills, and have developed specific responses. CL, EK, MT, and MG reported that their organisations supply their own oral communication training after employing new graduates; in MD's firm, new graduates are placed in a 'hatchery' where they receive instruction in written and oral communication and are carefully mentored through a series of communication based tasks.

5. Discussion and Implications for Educators

This study's findings demonstrate that listening skills, concerning both attentiveness and responsiveness, are accorded the highest value by accountancy employers, which bears out the findings of several other studies (including James, 1992; Maes *et al.*, 1997; and McLaren, 1990). It is important to note, however, that on a five-point scale on which higher scores represent increased perceived importance, employers accorded none of the 27 oral communication skills an average value below three out of a possible five. This indicates that none of the oral communication skills identified in the questionnaire were considered to be truly unimportant.

However, the frequency with which the entire range of these skills is found in new graduates was generally low, with average frequency scores ranging from 2.79 to 3.32

on a five-point scale on which higher scores reflect greater frequency. Employers report that, while some accountancy students in New Zealand are graduating with an acceptable level of oral communication competency, many possess an inadequate mastery of the oral communication skills that will be of most value to them in an accountancy career. Employers are finding few new graduates either with the general level of oral communication skill, or with the particular specific skills, that they require.

Further, a large number of students seem to be, in the eyes of future employers, graduating with a misapprehension of how important oral communication skills will be in their accountancy career. Almost three quarters of questionnaire respondents, a total of 74.5%, reported that new accountancy graduates recognised the importance of oral communication skills only 'sometimes' or 'seldom.' Given the finding that oral communication skills in relation to management are perceived as being particularly important, and managers influence promotion decisions, graduates' poor skills may pose considerable barriers to their prospects of career success and progress. Interviews revealed that new graduates can be resistant to training in the area of oral communication, and this resistance may possibly be related to their under-estimation of the importance of oral communication skills. Data concerning employers' strong desire for these skills may be of marked use to accounting educators in the effort to improve students' attitudes towards acquiring oral communication skill during their university studies.

Findings also revealed the relatively frequent incidence of workplace programmes to develop graduates' oral communication skills after hiring. Forty-five questionnaire respondents reported having in place formal or informal communication training programmes within their own organisation, tailored for newly-hired graduates, with several interviewees reporting that they believe a certain amount of 'on-the-job' training is a practical necessity for most new graduates. While interviews elicited broadly expressed frustration with existing communication skill levels in new graduates, many employers were matter-of-fact about their own responsibility to help meet this skills gap. Further, most interviewees reported that new graduates' oral communication skills usually do improve to the required standard after a length of time in the workplace, although the length of time mentioned varied from three months to 'several years.' Three interviewees specifically reported that regular communication refresher courses were run in their firms. Interviewees confirmed that the complexity of communication tasks required of new graduates is initially low but grows over time. This change reflects an understanding of the communicative improvements that accompany increasing age, maturity, and familiarity with the discursive context of the industry and the particular workplace.

The information gathered from this study has potentially significant implications for university programs. The cynical view might suggest that no communication instruction need be included in a university accountancy programme, trusting that new graduates could simply 'learn on the job.' More pragmatically, communication instruction within university programmes might focus on the most highly valued specific oral communication skills, and be accompanied by assurance that on-the-job, contextualised communication development would be a necessary and ongoing part of a career in accountancy.

Questionnaire and interview data concerning the most highly valued oral communication skills in accountancy offer potential direction to educators wishing to better equip accountancy students. A significant finding was that, while individual oral presentations are often included in university curricula, presentation skills are not highly prized in new graduates by accountancy employers. In contrast, other specific skills, such as conveying respect and interest in a conversation with a client, asking a manager for feedback or clarification, and speaking on the telephone, were ranked by employers as being highly important skills, but are seldom targeted as skills to be developed in the instruction which accountancy students receive. Listening skills, perceived by employers as being most important, could potentially ground specific instructional modules in oral communication. Such modules would need to be specifically crafted around the development of listening, conversational, questioning and telephone skills, and might include the use of role-plays, group work, mentoring, and videotape for feedback and targeted reflection purposes. An array of oral communication training methods is used by educators in other disciplines, seeking to develop students' industry-specific communication skills: for example, via case-presentation training and standardised patient training in medicine (Islam and Zyphur, 2007; Spafford, Schryer, Mian and Lyngard, 2006); and via dialogue, conversational training, and mentored 'client presentations' in engineering (Freeman, 2003; Norback and Hardin, 2005). While pedagogical recommendations are beyond the scope of this paper, these examples are usefully illustrative of how accountancy educators may conceive of communication instruction in more specifically focussed terms.

From the interviews with accountancy employers emerged a particular and widespread concern in relation to the spoken language skills of non-native English language speakers. The communication learning needs of this group of learners pose another set of challenges for educators striving to strike a balance between inculcating technical and 'soft' skills in a university environment in which time is at a premium and individually-tailored instruction extremely difficult to incorporate. This conundrum sharpens rather than answers the question as to who should bear responsibility for students gaining the needed skills: should students themselves seek remedial help with their oral communication; should university educators compel them to seek it; and/or should employers simply expect to have to provide oral communication training to a large proportion of their new employees? More research needs to be undertaken concerning the particular needs of ESL accountancy students and the best strategies to help them develop their proficiency in communicating in English.

All interviewees were asked the same question at the close of the interview: 'Do you think that oral communication skills can be taught, or is a person simply naturally skilled (or unskilled) in this area?' Although there was general agreement that some individuals will always be stronger speakers and some will always be weaker, all interviewees agreed that oral communication skills can be taught and every individual can improve. Accountancy educators and students alike should take encouragement and motivation from this belief.

6. Limitations

This study, as with most research studies, is subject to some limitations. The first of these is its specifically New Zealand focus. While the literature review established that concern with accountancy students' oral communication skills was felt internationally, the scope of this investigation was limited to accountancy employers working in the researchers' home country. It is possible that New Zealand accountancy employers express preferences for oral communication skills that differ from employers in other countries. It is also possible that the chartered accountancy firms contacted in this research might conceivably have different requirements, with regard to oral communication skills in their new accountancy graduates, from other employers of accountancy graduates. The authors hope that similar quantitative and qualitative studies utilising the catalogue of 27 individual oral communication skills may be conducted in other countries and amongst broader samples of accountancy employers, to test the generalisability of the conclusions drawn here.

A second limitation concerns the relatively small proportion of employers who responded to the research (19.2% of questionnaires were returned). The findings from which conclusions were drawn may then not be as representative as desired. The questionnaire response rate and the number of interviews completed have been discussed and defended in section 3.1.2.

Amongst the 760 firms sent questionnaires were a number of sole practitioners. Because the questionnaire was anonymous, it is not possible to identify which respondents may have been sole practitioners, and because not all sole practitioners would employ accountancy graduates, their responses may be questionable. This factor must be recognised as a limitation of the findings. Finally, while the questionnaires were addressed in the first instance to Practice Managers at Chartered Accountancy practices, responses revealed a degree of variability in the positions held by respondents. While all respondents met the descriptor of 'accountancy employers,' they ranged from partners, to senior employees, to Human Resources directors. As such, responses concerning the oral communication skills possessed by new graduates may have been influenced by the varying degree of knowledge of graduate hiring processes possessed by the individual respondents.

7. Conclusion

This study produced findings that, at a broad level, agree with existing literature on the subject of communication in accountancy: New Zealand accountancy employers consider oral communication skill to be extremely important, but only sometimes find the required level of oral communication skill in new university graduates. More specifically, this study revealed that accountancy employers valued listening skills in new graduates extremely highly, and conveying an attitude of respect and interest to clients, speaking professionally with clients on the telephone, and asking managers for clarification or feedback were also considered among the most highly valued oral communication skills in new graduates. Although presentation-related skills were ranked lower than most others in the skills catalogue, no oral communication skills were perceived to be unimportant. While accountancy employers considered oral communication skills to be important in relation to a wide range of audiences, oral communication skills in regard to management were perceived to be the most important for new graduates to possess.

Employers agreed that university accountancy programmes did not always produce graduates with an adequate level of oral communication skill, but they also generally agreed that oral communication skill is also acquired in the workplace, over time, and many employers accept a particular responsibility in helping new graduates develop this competency. The degree to which a university environment can truly replicate that of business is questionable, and whether university educators should even strive to replicate that environment is a question which individual institutions must debate.

Ultimately, academics teaching accountancy juggle complex objectives: educating students for 'existing' careers in chartered accountancy or in broader accounting and business careers; and also educating students to learn how to learn, to adapt to a rapidly changing employment market. This study has produced a comprehensive inventory of 27 individual communication skills, which it is hoped will be useful for further studies into oral communication and accountancy education. While the aim of this research was not to supply a series of pedagogical suggestions for educators, it is hoped that the empirical data provided may be used by educators to inform their decisions on curricular content and assessments that may better prepare university students for the accountancy workplace which they hope to enter. In the light of this study's data on accountancy employers' specific needs, much more work is indicated to consider, pilot, and develop oral communication instruction modules at university level, ideally with input from employers as well as from educators. Further study into the particular needs of ESL accountancy students is also indicated.

Acknowledgements

The authors thank Maryann Groat, Aimee Gray, Catherine Parsons, and in particular thank Graham Crombie, 2008 President of the New Zealand Institute of Chartered Accountants.

Notes

[1] De Lange *et al.* (2006) make this point specifically (366, n.1). Bennett et al., (2000), discusses how the term "generic skill" continues to elude precise definition in the scholarly discourse.

[2] The age profile of Chartered Accountancy practice employees can only be logically assumed: while NZICA collects data on the age of its members, not every CA firm employee is a member of NZICA, and further, the data NZICA which collects and reports is provided by members on an optional basis, and therefore, may not be fully representative or accurate.

References

Adler, R. and Milne, M. (1994) Communication skills and attitude, *Chartered Accountants Journal of New Zealand*, 73(11), pp. 28–32.

Albin, M. J. and Crockett, J. R. (1991) Integrating necessary skills and concepts into the accounting curriculum, *Journal of Education for Business*, 66(6), pp. 325–327.

Albrecht, W. S. and Sack, R. J. (2000) *Accounting Education: Charting the Course Through a Perilous Future* (Sarasota, FL, American Accounting Association).

Andrews, B. (2006) The language barrier, *BRW*, 28(4), pp. 70–71.

Ashbaugh, H., Johnstone, K. and Warfield, T. (2002) Outcome assessment of a writing-skill improvement initiative: results and methodological implications, *Issues in Accounting Education*, 17(2), pp. 123–148.

Baker, W. M. and McGregor, C. C. (2000) Empirically assessing the importance of characteristics of accounting students, *Journal of Education for Business*, 75(3), pp. 149–157.

Beaufort, A. (1999) *Writing in the Real World: Making the Transition from School Work* (New York: Teachers College Press).

Birreli, B. (2007) Lack of English locks out migrant accountants, *In the Black*, 77(1), pp. 14.

Borzi, M. G. and Mills, T. H. (2001) Communication apprehension in upper level accounting students: an assessment of skill development, *Journal of Education for Business*, 76(4), pp. 193–198.

Cooper, L. (1997) Listening competency in the workplace: a model for training, *Business Communication Quarterly*, 60(4), pp. 75–84.

Courtis, J. K. and Zaid, O. A. (2002) Early employment problems of Australian accounting graduates: an exploratory study, *Accounting Forum*, 26(3), pp. 320–339.

Crosling, G. and Ward, I. (2002) Oral communication: the workplace needs and uses of business graduate employees, *English for Specific Purposes*, 21(1), pp. 41–57.

D'Aloisio, A. (2006) Motivating students through awareness of the natural correlation between college learning and corporate work settings, *College Teaching*, 54(2), pp. 225–229.

Davies, C. and Birbill, M. (2000) What do people need to know about writing in order to write in their jobs? *British Journal of Educational Studies*, 48(4), pp. 429–445.

De Lange, P., Jackling, B. and Gut, A. (2006) Accounting graduates' perceptions of skills emphasis in undergraduate courses: an investigation from two Victorian universities, *Accounting and Finance*, 46, pp. 365–386.

English, L., Bonanno, H., Ihnatko, T., Webb, C. and Jones, J. (1999) Learning through writing in a first-year accounting course, *Journal of Accounting Education*, 17(2–3), pp. 221–254.

Ford, L. (2009) Improving training transfer, *Industrial and Commercial Training*, 41(2), pp. 92–96.

Frankfort-Nachmias, C. and Nachmias, D. (1996) *Research Methods in the Social Sciences*. 5th ed. (New York: St Martin's Press).

Freeman, J. (2003) The science of conversation: training in dialogue for NNS in engineering, *IEEE Transactions on Professional Communication*, 46(3), pp. 157–167.

Gardner, C., Milne, M. J., Stringer, C. and Whiting, R. (2005) Oral and written communication apprehension in accounting students: curriculum impacts and impacts on academic performance, *Accounting Education: an international journal*, 14(3), pp. 313–336.

Gendall, P. (2000) Responding to the problem of nonresponse, *Australasian Journal of Market Research*, 8(1), pp. 3–18.

Goby, V. and Lewis, J. (2000) The key role of listening in business: a study of the Singapore insurance industry, *Business Communication Quarterly*, 63(2), pp. 41–51.

Gray, F. E. (2010) Specific oral communication skills desired in new accountancy graduates, *Business Communication Quarterly*, 73(1), pp. 40–67.

Gray, F. E., Emerson, L. and MacKay, B. (2006) 'They don't have much in their kitbags': equipping science students with communication skills for the workplace, *Australian Journal of Communication*, 33(1), pp. 105–122.

Guest, G., Bunce, A. and Johnson, L. (2006) 'How many interviews are enough?' An experiment with data saturation and variability, *Field Methods*, 18(1), pp. 59–82.

Hall, W. D. (1998) The education of an accountant, *Massachusetts CPA Review*, 62, pp. 34–38.

Hayes, J. and Kuseski, B. (2001) The corporate communication culture project: studying the real world of business, *Business Communication Quarterly*, 64(2), pp. 77–85.

Henderson, S. (2001) The education of accountants: a comment, *Accounting Forum*, 25(4), pp. 398–401.

Hock, S. (1994) The 100 most influential people in accounting: communication skills top list of student advice, *Accounting Today*, 8, pp. 27–30.

Islam, G. and Zyphur, M. (2007) Ways of interacting: the standardization of communication in medical training, *Human Relations*, 60(5), pp. 769–792.

Jacobs, K. (2003) Class reproduction in professional recruitment: examining the accounting profession, *Critical Perspectives on Accounting*, 14(5), pp. 569–596.

James, K. and Otsuka, S. (2009) Racial biases in recruitment by accounting firms: the case of international Chinese applicants in Australia. *Critical Perspectives in Accounting*, 20(4), pp. 469–491.

James, M. (1992) Essential topics and subtopics of business communication: are we teaching what employers want? *Business Education Forum*, 46(4), pp. 8–10.

Johnson, L. M. and Johnson, V. E. (1995) Help wanted—accountant: what the classifieds say about employers' expectations, *Journal of Education for Business*, 70(3), pp. 130–134.

Kemp, I. and Seagraves, L. (1995) Transferable skills—can higher education deliver? *Studies in Higher Education*, 20(3), pp. 315–328.

Kim, S. N. (2004) Racialized gendering of the accounting profession: toward an understanding of Chinese women's experiences in accountancy in New Zealand, *Critical Perspectives on Accounting*, 15(3), pp. 400–427.

LaFrancois, H. A. (1992) The marketing of an accounting graduate: characteristics most desired by CPA firms, *Journal of Education for Business*, 67(4), pp. 206–209.

Maes, J., Weldy, T. and Icenogle, M. (1997) A managerial perspective: oral communication competency is most important for business students in the workplace, *Journal of Business Communication*, 34(1), pp. 67–80.

McDonald, P. (2007) Preparing tomorrow's workforce, *Financial Executive*, 23(8), pp. 52–55.

McGowan, S. and Potter, L. (2008) The implications of the Chinese learner for the internationalization of the curriculum: an Australian perspective, *Critical Perspectives on Accounting*, 19(2), pp. 181–198.

McLaren, M. (1990) The place of communication skills in the training of accountants in New Zealand, *Accounting and Finance*, 30(1), pp. 83–94.

Milne, M. (1999) The promise of problem-based learning, *Chartered Accountants Journal of New Zealand*, 78(2), pp. 37–40.

Milne, M. and McConnell, P. (2001) Problem-based learning: a pedagogy for using case material in accounting education, *Accounting Education: an international journal*, 10(1), pp. 61–82.

Morgan, G. (1997) Communication skills required by accounting graduates: practitioner and academic perceptions, *Accounting Education: an international journal*, 6(2), pp. 93–107.

Muir, C. and Davis, B. (2004) Learning soft skills at work, *Business Communication Quarterly*, 67(1), pp. 95–101.

Neuman, W. L. (2003) *Social Research Methods: Qualitative and Quantitative Approaches,* 5th ed (United States: Allyn and Bacon).

Ng, J., Lloyd, P., Kober, R. and Robinson, P. (1999) Developing writing skills; a large class experience: a teaching note, *Journal of Accounting Education*, 8(1), pp. 47–55.

Norback, J. and Hardin, J. (2005) Integrating workforce communication into senior design, *IEEE Transactions on Professional Communication*, 48(4), pp. 413–426.

NZICA (2008) *2008 Annual Report of the New Zealand Institute of Chartered Accountants* (Wellington, NZ: NZICA).

Pittenger, K., Miller, M. and Mott, J. (2004) Using real-world standards to enhance students' presentation skills, *Business Communication Quarterly*, 67(3), pp. 327–336.

Simons, K. and Higgins, M. (1993) An examination of practitioners' and academicians' views on the content of the accounting curriculum, *The Accounting Educators' Journal*, 5(2), pp. 24–34.

Sin, S., Jones, A. and Petocz, P. (2007) Evaluating a method of integrating generic skills with accounting content based on a functional theory of meaning, *Accounting and Finance*, 47, pp. 143–163.

Smythe, M. and Nikolai, L. (1996) Communication concerns across different accounting constituencies, *Journal of Accounting Education*, 14(4), pp. 435–451.

Smythe, M. and Nikolai, L. (2002) A thematic analysis of oral communication concerns with implications for curriculum design, *Journal of Accounting Education*, 20(3), pp. 163–181.

Spafford, M., Schryer, C., Mian, M. and Lingard, L. (2006) Look who's talking: teaching and learning using the genre of medical case presentations, *Journal of Business and Technical Communication*, 20(2), pp. 121–158.

Strauss, A. and Corbin, J. (2000) *Basics of Qualitative Research: Grounded Theory Procedures and Techniques* (Newberry Park, CA: Sage).

Tempone, I. and Martin, E. (2003) Iteration between theory and practice as a pathway to developing generic skills in accounting, *Accounting Education: an international journal*, 12(3), pp. 227–244.

Thomas, S. (1995) Preparing business students more effectively for real-world communication, *Journal of Business and Technical Communication*, 9(4), pp. 461–474.

Triebel, O. and Gurdjian, P. (2009) Identifying employee skill gaps, *McKinsey Quarterly*, 2, pp. 18–19.

Usoff, C. and Feldmann, D. (1998) Accounting students' perceptions of important skills for career success, *Journal of Education for Business*, 73(4), pp. 215–220.

Wardrope, W. (2002) Department chairs' perceptions of the importance of business communication skills, *Business Communication Quarterly*, 65(4), pp. 60–72.

Wardrope, W. and Bayless, M. (1999) Content of the business communication course: an analysis of coverage, *Business Communication Quarterly*, 62(4), pp. 33–40.

Webb, C., English, L. and Bonanno, H. (1995) Collaboration in subject design: integration of the teaching and assessment of literacy skills into a first-year accounting course, *Accounting Education: an international journal*, 4(4), pp. 335–351.

Zaid, O. and Abraham, A. (1994) Communication skills in accounting education: perceptions of academics, employers, and graduate accountants, *Accounting Education: an international journal*, 3(3), pp. 205–221.

A Qualitative Exploration of Oral Communication Apprehension

MARANN BYRNE*, BARBARA FLOOD* and DAN SHANAHAN**

*Dublin City University, Ireland; **Dublin Institute of Technology, Ireland

ABSTRACT *Prior research has identified communication apprehension (CA), or fear of communicating, as a major factor which inhibits an individual's willingness to communicate and his/her capability to develop effective communication skills. While many prior studies have measured oral communication apprehension of students, there has been little qualitative exploration of the phenomenon. This study was conducted by interviewing first-year business and accounting students at a higher education institution in Ireland who were identified as encountering varying levels of oral communication apprehension. The experiences of the students in communicating in different contexts are analysed and the impact of factors, such as fear of peer evaluation, prior communication experiences, and preparation, are considered.*

Introduction

It is widely recognised that graduates entering the world of work require more than academic knowledge of their chosen discipline; they also need a diverse range of non-technical competencies and, in particular, they must be effective communicators (Cavanagh *et al.*, 2006; McDaniel and White, 1993; Mitchell, Skinner and White, 2010). The relationship between communication competence and job success has motivated many colleges and universities to introduce courses to enhance their students' skills (Ameen, Bruns and Jackson, 2010; Du-Babcock, 2006). In fact, many educators recognise that they must equip students with the communication skills desired by employers if their degree programmes are to be successful (Mitchell, Skinner and White, 2010; Plutsky, 1996). However, despite these developments, the communication capability of graduates across a range of disciplines has continued to attract considerable adverse criticism

This paper was edited and accepted by Richard M. S. Wilson.

(Graham, Hampton and Willett, 2009). Indeed, many employers remain dissatisfied with the communication competence of new graduates (Cavanagh *et al.*, 2006; Council for Industry and Higher Education, 2008; Gradireland, 2010; Hassall *et al.*, 1999; Quible and Griffin, 2007).

There is increasing recognition that students' failure to develop appropriate communication skills may not be due to the quality of relevant education and training programmes. Rather, an individual may experience a range of fears concerning oral and/or written communication tasks or situations (commonly referred to as 'communication apprehension' (CA)) which may inhibit the development of the requisite skills. Consequently, CA should be alleviated before focusing on the enhancement of communication skills. As a first step in this process, educators need to enhance their understanding of the concept and consequences of CA.

While there is quite a large body of research which has measured students' levels of CA, there has been little attention paid to exploring the phenomenon of CA using qualitative methods and through the lived experiences of students themselves. Thus, the aim of this paper is to address this research gap by qualitatively exploring the phenomenon of oral CA as experienced by business and accounting students. In so doing, the paper seeks to sensitise and enhance educators' awareness of the debilitating effects of high CA. This study focuses on oral CA, not because it is viewed as any more important than written CA, but simply because oral communication appears to prompt such fear among so many people and also because it crosses so many domains of an individual's life, from communicating on a one-to-one basis with friends or colleagues to communicating in a very public forum when making a presentation or a speech. It was considered most appropriate to focus on first-year students because it is important to understand the baseline of oral CA with which students commence their higher education study.

Oral Communication Apprehension (OCA)

The Nature of OCA

The issue of students' anxiety concerning communication was reported in the literature as far back as the early 1940s (see Gilkinson, 1942). McCroskey (1970, p. 270) labelled this communication-bound anxiety as 'communication apprehension' and described it as 'an individual's level of fear or anxiety associated with either real or anticipated communication with another person or persons' (McCroskey, 1977, p. 82). Each individual has a unique level of apprehension, which results in a number of individual differences, such as the effectiveness of, amount of, and desire for, communication (Richmond and McCroskey, 1998, p. 26). While all aspects of the CA phenomenon are still not fully understood, there is now a considerable body of research on CA. Indeed, from 1977 to 1997, CA became the single most researched concept in the field of communication studies (Wrench *et al.*, 2008). It is clear that a person may experience a different level of CA depending on whether he/she is communicating orally or in writing. OCA, which is the focus of the current study, is concerned with a fear of speaking or talking to other people in different contexts, such as on a one-to-one basis, in groups, in meetings, or public speaking.

Prior studies have shown that there are many negative consequences associated with high levels of OCA. When confronted with communication activities, individuals with high OCA report fear, tension, and physical symptoms, such as increased heart rate and sweating (Beatty and Dobos, 1997, p. 217). Many suffer in silence and are unaware that the complaint is so common. Indeed, Horwitz (2002, p. 1) refers to this fear as 'the hidden communication disorder because it is frequently not recognised, acknowledged or discussed'. In higher education, students suffering from high OCA often feel uncomfortable or unable to ask questions in class, they may skip classes or choose modules that exclude their feared type of communication, and they often achieve less than their aptitudes would justify (Bowers, 1986; O'Mara *et al.*, 1996).

Some students with high OCA may try to conceal their fear of communicating by over-communicating or talking all the time, but this is a rare and unusual response (Richmond and McCroskey, 1998, p. 53). A much more common reaction is to remain quiet. Kougl (1980) suggests that those with high OCA who remain quiet do so because of a feeling of inadequacy in handling communication situations. Some research has indicated that skills training may not reduce the fear (Allen and Bourhis, 1996). Thus, educators, no matter how well meaning, need to be very careful when designing OCA interventions and should seek guidance from communication psychologists.

Measuring OCA

An individual's level of OCA is commonly measured by using self-reporting survey instruments. The most widely-used instrument is the Personal Report of Communication Apprehension (PRCA-24) (McCroskey, 2006, p. 40). The PRCA-24 measures the overall construct of OCA, as well as four sub-constructs, which relate to different communication contexts (speaking one-to-one, in small groups, in meetings, and in public). McCroskey (1997a, p. 90), using data drawn from over 100,000 subjects in the USA, reports that the mean total score on the PRCA-24 was 65.60, with a standard deviation of 15.30. This mean and standard deviation are referred to by some researchers as a US national norm (Stanga and Ladd, 1990). McCroskey (1997b, p. 209) classifies those who score more than 80, which is approximately one standard deviation above the mean or US national norm, as highly apprehensive. Those who score less than 50, which is approximately one standard deviation below the US national norm, are considered to have low apprehension levels.

Studies measuring the levels of OCA experienced by business and accounting students have been conducted in many countries (e.g. USA: Fordham and Gabbin, 1996; Smith and Nelson, 1994; Stanga and Ladd, 1990;UK and Spain: Arquero *et al.*, 2007; Hassall *et al.*, 2000; Canada: Aly and Islam, 2003; New Zealand: Gardner *et al.*, 2005; Ireland: Byrne, Flood and Shanahan, 2009; Warnock and Curtis, 1997). Some consistent evidence has emerged from these studies. For example, as with students in other disciplines, business and accounting students have least anxiety concerning communicating orally on a one-to-one basis and most fear concerning public speaking. Several researchers have also explored variations in the levels of OCA experienced by students within different business specialisms (accounting, marketing, management, etc). In the USA, Simons, Higgins and Lowe (1995) found that accounting majors had higher OCA scores than other business majors and similar findings have been reported in the UK and Spain (Arquero *et al.*, 2007; Hassall *et al.*, 2000). In contrast, in a recent Irish study (Byrne, Flood and Shanahan, 2009) it was found that there were no significant differences between the OCA scores of accounting students and other business students, and Borzi and Mills (2001) found that accounting majors at two US universities had significantly lower levels of OCA than non-accounting majors.

It is somewhat surprising that no prior research with business and accounting students has explored the phenomenon of OCA using qualitative methods. Indeed, there is an absence of qualitative research of the topic with students in all disciplines. It would seem that, as educators struggle to cope with students experiencing high OCA, there would be considerable merit in analysing students' descriptions of their anxieties.

This would enable educators to develop a deeper and more holistic understanding of the OCA phenomenon, which may encourage them to reflect on various dimensions of their teaching and assessment practices.

Research Approach and Data Collection

The objective of the study is to qualitatively explore the phenomenon of OCA experienced by business and accounting students. To achieve this objective, interviews were conducted to develop an understanding of 'the world from the subjects' points of view, to unfold the meaning of people's experiences' (Kvale and Brinkmann, 2009, p. 1). Before the first interview took place, an interview guide was prepared, which, drawing from the literature, indicated the topics to be covered in the interview (see the Appendix).[1] More specifically, the emphasis in the literature on variation in CA levels in different contexts or situations shaped the construction of the interview guide, such that it sought to explore interviewees' experiences in the context of communicating on a one-to-one basis, in groups, in meetings, and when public speaking. One of the principal benefits of the semi-structured interview approach is that it offers flexibility and it is not necessary to stick rigidly to the guide. It has been found that this interview approach can yield rich and unexpected answers from participants (Kvale, 2007, p. 57).

The interview participants were selected from a cohort of 285 first-year business and accounting students at a higher education institution in Ireland,[2] who had completed the PRCA-24 earlier in the academic year (Byrne, Flood and Shanahan, 2009). Given the intention to gain rich insights and explore similarities and differences, the cohort was stratified by level of apprehension and students who had different levels of OCA were selected for interview. Thus, the interview sample includes students with high, average, and low OCA. If a selected student was unable to attend, another student with a similar OCA score was substituted. Each interviewee was given a pseudonym to protect his/her anonymity.

Seventeen students were selected to participate in the qualitative study. The details of the students interviewed and their OCA levels are outlined in Table 1.[3]

Table 1. Interview participants grouped by OCA category.

Apprehension category	OCA score	Student
Low: OCA < 50	24	Paul
	29	Eileen
	35	John
	40	Niall
	42	Ruth
	43	Tom
Average: OCA 50–80	51	Kate
	51	Ken
	60	Lisa
	63	David
	67	Anna
	70	Emma
	75	Colin
	80	Orla
High: OCA > 80	87	Cliona
	100	Mary
	106	Daniel

The interviews took place during the second semester of the students' first year of study. With the permission of the interviewees, each interview was recorded and all of the interviews were conducted by the same member of the research team. At the beginning of each interview the objective of the study was explained, the confidential nature of it was emphasised, and the anonymity of the interviewee was guaranteed. It was stressed that there was no compulsion to answer any question and that the interviewee could terminate the interview at any time if he/she so desired. The initial part of each interview was devoted to discussing the interviewee's family background, schooling, friends, and hobbies. When sufficient rapport had been built up and the interviewee appeared sufficiently relaxed, the conversation then turned to the interviewee's experience and perception of OCA. At the end of each interview, the interviewee was given an opportunity to review all that had been said and to comment if he/she so wished. Each interview took approximately 45 minutes and was subsequently transcribed. The data was then analysed to uncover common themes. The outcomes of the 17 interviews are 17 stories, with many commonalities but also with some unique aspects which provide rich and interesting narratives.

Findings

1. *Communicating in Different Contexts*

The approach adopted for the presentation of the findings in this section is to explore the views of the interviewees in each of the four sub-contexts by level of apprehension, beginning with those with low overall OCA and progressing to those with high OCA scores. Where relevant, the perceptions of the interviewees concerning the similarities or differences between communicating with a friend compared to a stranger are examined.

Communicating one-to-one. All the students interviewed, except one, feel comfortable when conversing in one-to-one situations with friends. They are relaxed and do not feel threatened or apprehensive. This was expected in the light of prior research, which indicated that overall OCA scores may be poor predictors of anxiety in situations where participants were likely to know one another (Parks, 1980). Nevertheless, one interviewee, Cliona, who has high OCA, reveals that she is very anxious even when communicating with friends:

> I am afraid of people. I am afraid of communicating.

This was unexpected and it will be evident later in the analysis that Cliona is very nervous, apprehensive, and fearful over communicating in all four contexts. Her responses are extreme as she describes how her apprehension affects her:

> Absolute butterflies. I can feel blushing, heat rising through my body and I am sweating. I find it very hard to express myself. Because I have millions of thoughts, there's so much going on that I can't get everything out at once.

In terms of communicating with a stranger, the majority of those with low or average apprehension are calm and assured. Ruth embodies this relaxed attitude, when she says:

> I'll go up and I'll talk to anyone.

Emma displays the openness of some of those with average apprehension when she describes how she behaves with a new acquaintance:

> If there was someone I had to get to know I would just sit down and tell them about my life and then ask them questions. I would have no problem.

All three students with high OCA are fearful of talking to a stranger. This fear may cause them to remain silent, as Daniel explains:

> It depends on who you are talking to. If people are not friendly, I tend to be an awful lot quieter. If someone did not make it informal and comfortable I'd probably not be able to talk whatsoever. It probably would be a disaster.

Their difficulty in talking to strangers is also well expressed by Mary, who finds it hard to open up to others:

> I am not one for starting to talk to people straight away. I am very cautious of people.

Cliona feels anxious talking with strangers and, consequently, babbles, which has been described in the prior literature as 'over-communication' (Richmond and McCroskey, 1998, p. 53).

Communicating in groups.   As in the one-to-one context, the majority of the interviewees experience little difficulty in taking part in group discussions with friends or when they have a friend in the group. Most feel comfortable with people they know and, as a result, express themselves freely, a view best expressed by Niall:

> It would be different if there were guys in the group that you did not know well. You would be wary of what you were saying. If I knew everyone I'd just say it anyway.

Even some of the students with high OCA have little difficulty communicating among a group of friends, as Daniel explains:

> If I'm in a group that I am familiar with, I'll tell them exactly what I think.

However, a small number of interviewees are not always comfortable in a group of friends. Paul (low OCA) holds the opposite view to Niall, as he explains:

> I'd be a lot more careful in a group where I knew everybody, because I wouldn't want to offend anyone or rub them up the wrong way.

Emma (average OCA) prefers to work in a group with strangers rather than friends, as she explains:

> If they don't know me, they don't know my background, they don't know anything about me.

When communicating in a group with strangers, most students with low OCA are relaxed and are unaffected by the attitude of others in the group. Negative reactions from others in a group do not overly affect those with low OCA, as Tom outlines:

> I think you are conscious of what the others are thinking when you are going to say something at first. But then as you slowly get your word in or start talking and go through the group I think that people start to relax more with each other.

In examining the perspectives of the students with average OCA, many reflect much of the same confidence as those with low OCA in communicating with strangers. Anna enjoys it, as she reflects:

> I like going into group discussions. You get to hear what other people think.

In contrast, students with high OCA are uncomfortable participating in groups with strangers. They do not enjoy it, have a negative attitude towards it and sometimes cannot complete the communication task. They describe their fears in varying ways. Mary confesses:

> You don't really know how to react around people that you don't know or what you can say without insulting them.

Both Cliona and Daniel are so intimidated when working with strangers that they find it very difficult to take part in group discussions and consequently may remain silent. Cliona says:

> [...] you wouldn't have me opening my mouth

and Daniel reports:

> [...] if I didn't know them at all, I probably wouldn't speak to them unless I was spoken to.

Often those with high OCA feel isolated, uncomfortable, and are fearful of how others will respond to them. Mary explains:

> If it's a lot of people in the group and you don't know anybody you feel intimidated and you don't really want to say anything.

Daniel expresses a more extreme view when he describes how he would react if a member in a group laughed at him:

> Cry! Well I'd probably not cry, I'd probably just shrink up into the back of the chair and that would be it. That would be me finished in that group and I wouldn't be in any group the next time. There wouldn't be any group that would want me.

Communicating at meetings. Twelve of the seventeen interviewees had experience of attending meetings in a work setting or in connection with group projects in school. However, the others had not attended any formal meetings and the feelings they express arise from the thought of attending meetings rather than actual attendance.

The majority of those with low OCA feel comfortable at the prospect of taking part in meetings. The students with average levels of OCA are, or think they would be, comfortable attending meetings. A number, including Kate, Lisa, and Anna, feel they would suffer a degree of initial anxiety before a meeting, as Kate states:

> If it was something a bit formal, I'd probably be a bit nervous going into it, but once you get started you just keep going and it's grand.

Both Colin and Orla express higher levels of concern, particularly about speaking in front of people they don't know, as Orla explains:

> If I had to talk in front of everyone, like formally talk in front of everyone, I would get very nervous.

As might be anticipated, the students with high OCA feel uncomfortable taking part in meetings. Mary had no previous experience of attending meetings but is fearful of the prospect. Both Cliona and Daniel have attended meetings in a job setting and they both get extremely nervous in this context. Cliona feels a sense of panic, which she describes:

> I am dreading my turn to speak, dreading it. When it comes to my area I say 'nothing to report' even if I have something to report.

Daniel also reflects this extreme tension and, even though he is proficient at his work, he still feels very anxious, as he explains:

> I'd always feel very nervous. I'd be sitting back trying to look somewhat confident but inside I'd be shaking really. I was doing a brilliant job and everyone was constantly saying that I was doing a brilliant job. So confidence was not an issue whatsoever in my job but in meetings that just all disappeared. I'd know exactly what everybody was talking about. But when somebody would ask me a question, I would know the answer in my head, I'd have a brilliant answer, but I would not be able to say it. I'd just make a mess of it. I'd just come out with jumbled words. I wouldn't be able to express myself especially if I had to stand up in front of everyone; it just doesn't work.

Public speaking. All of the interviewees share the experience of increased anxiety regarding public speaking compared to other communication contexts. For those with low overall OCA, the anxiety is manifested by nervousness beforehand and with some physical symptoms, such as butterflies in the stomach. However, they expect to be able to complete the task and so any nervousness subsides when they commence the speech or presentation and they quickly begin to relax, as Paul describes:

> I get a little bit nervous. I move my hands and my body a lot. Once I'm up there and once I've said the first line, it's grand.

These sentiments are echoed by Eileen when she explains:

> A few minutes beforehand my palms would get sweaty and all, but nothing like where I couldn't go up. I've no problem doing it. It's obviously just the butterflies a few minutes before.

Their views are supported by prior research which indicates that the increased apprehension in this context may be evidenced by a greater physiological arousal (perspiration, body and limb movement) in most people (Beatty and Dobos, 1997). However, where they feel they can meet the audience's expectations, the apprehension decreases (Heuett, Hsu and Ayres, 2003).

Four of the six students with low OCA (Paul, Eileen, Ruth, and Tom) consider themselves good at public speaking. The other two, John and Niall, consider that they are weak at it but they don't dwell on poor experiences. For example, Niall is not upset if he has done a bad presentation, as he explains:

> I'd just regret it and say I should have done it better. I should have got my facts together if I didn't do it well. If it went well you'd just feel very good about yourself afterwards. If it went badly there is nothing you can do. You have to live with it.

Some (David, Anna, and Lisa) of the students with average levels of OCA express similar feelings to the low OCA group; they get nervous but then relax after they start the presentation, as David admits:

> You'd be nervous starting off, but as you get into it you flow.

However, four students (Ken, Colin, Orla, Emma) with average OCA report much higher levels of anxiety with regard to the public speaking context. Orla is 'terrified' every time she thinks about standing up in front of a group. She finds that she is extremely nervous in advance of giving a speech and finds it difficult to concentrate during the speech. And finally, Emma finds presenting in front of people she knows debilitating, and she outlines the torment she experiences when doing a presentation:

I would be very nervous beforehand and my hands would be sweaty. But when I'm up I don't feel anything. It's just like I am not doing it, I don't feel I am actually doing it. My knees are shaking and I would have butterflies. I wouldn't be in my body. It's just my body would be doing it itself but it's like I would not be in my body.

Emma's anxiety reflects the responses of two of the students with high OCA, who both disclose how severely speaking in public affects them. Cliona feels that she talks

[…] absolute gibberish. I'd forget what I am saying and I might not be able to tell you one thing I said as soon as I sit down. It will be completely blanked out.

Daniel painfully describes a recent experience of giving a presentation:

I'd have just liked the ground to open and swallow me up. Pressure all over […] every point of my body is just shaking and it feels horrible, especially in my stomach to the point of almost feeling like I am going to get sick. I get really cold and even afterwards my hands would be shaking and I am just going crazy. Even though I prepared well with slides and additional notes I would not be able to elaborate on them at all. Once you get up there it all disappears, you just can't talk and it's just all jumbled up and it's a disaster.

It is clear that all the interviewees report greater apprehension concerning public speaking than in relation to the other three oral communication contexts. Nearly all of the students feel nervous before making a speech or presentation. However, those with low OCA and some with average OCA cope with the pressure and feel they perform effectively. In contrast, the remaining students find making a presentation very difficult and are not able to relax or perform effectively. They do not enjoy it; they find the experience very stressful and would avoid it if possible. Their physiological and emotional upset is much greater than experienced by the other students.

2. *Themes*

Having presented the experiences of students across the four communication settings, the analysis in this sub-section seeks to identify themes which either suggest the potential sources of students' apprehension and/or activities that aid or impede the reduction of OCA levels. The identified themes are: *fear of peer evaluation, prior communication experiences, and preparation.*

Fear of peer evaluation. An overarching theme emerging from the data is the extent to which fear of peer evaluation drives OCA. Prior studies indicate that this fear can lead to increased anxiety and apprehension, especially for those with high OCA. Many individuals fear that they will be perceived as unsatisfactory and will be rejected by their peers (Gardner *et al.*, 2005; Richmond and McCroskey, 1998). In this study, peer evaluation is a factor for the majority of the interviewees, particularly as they move into the more public aspects of communicating in groups, at meetings, and when engaged in public speaking activities. Not surprisingly, students who can acknowledge and deal with peer evaluation arising from communication situations typically report low or average OCA. In contrast, when students have intense fear of peer evaluation, higher OCA scores are reported. Ultimately, the fear that they will be negatively perceived or judged by others dominates the thinking of the highly-apprehensive students to such an extent that their ability to complete communication tasks satisfactorily is inhibited.

It seems that the reason why a small number of students have little apprehension concerning others' perceptions is because they consider those perceptions somewhat beyond their control or influence. For example, peers may just not like them due to personality issues, as Ruth comments:

I know I'm not everyone's cup of tea but you learn to deal with these things.

Alternatively, as illustrated by Lisa, the student can perceive the communication task as being about the conveyance of an objective message and so if he/she receives a negative reaction, they attribute it to the message rather than taking it personally:

If somebody doesn't like what I have to say, that's their problem.

However, many students feel they have some influence over other people's perceptions by virtue of what they say during the communication activity and/or how they say it. For example, Tom (low OCA) copes with fear of peer evaluation by:

[...] not thinking as much about what others are thinking of you, but instead thinking about the point you are making.

Tom seems to be positive in his attitude; he perceives that if he concentrates on the message and gets that right, there is little scope for others to have negative perceptions of him. However, the comments of many of those who report average OCA seem more negative in orientation:

You are always afraid you'll be wrong. I'd probably be worried that people thought that I got it wrong and that I made a fool out of myself. (Kate)

It's the reaction that you get afraid of. People are waiting for you to do things wrong. They notice when you do things wrong. (Orla)

Interestingly, both of the above quotations also indicate that the fear is not only that peers might hold negative perceptions of the student but that those negative perceptions might be made public and visible in some way (making a 'fool' of oneself and a fear of the 'reaction'). Thus, the fear of peer evaluation is closely followed by a fear of humiliation.

Not surprisingly, fear of peer evaluation is particularly prevalent among the students with high OCA. They feel they are unable to leave a good impression on others and so they can only envisage negative responses. What is particularly noticeable among the narratives of these students is their sense of inevitability and powerlessness regarding communication activities and the perceptions that their peers might hold, as Mary outlines:

It is your work. People are going to start to criticise you and you have to sit there and take it. You really can't get up and leave.

She is also highly fearful that their negative perceptions will be shared with others, as she discloses:

[...] if they think badly of you they are going to tell other people even if you haven't met the other people.

Cliona has similar fears about public exposure:

Everyone is afraid when speaking in public that people are going to laugh at them and that people will judge them.

Daniel, who finds it extremely difficult to converse with people he does not know, outlines that fear of peer evaluation is one of the main sources of his OCA. He hates being the focus of attention and is terrified that he will look 'completely stupid' and that people will laugh at him. When asked to provide examples of when this occurred, Daniel indicates that he is so scared of that scenario that he doesn't allow it to happen. Instead, he just 'shrinks up' and doesn't communicate. The invasiveness and intensity of the fear of peer evaluation for some students indicates that the issue may be intertwined with identity construction issues. However, this broader issue of identity was not pursued in the interviews, though it clearly provides opportunities for future research.

The qualitative analysis suggests that the higher a person's total OCA score the more negative s/he views peer evaluation. When positive feedback is expected, or at a minimum when negative feedback is not anticipated, the level of apprehension is relatively low. However, where a negative expectation of peer evaluation arises, the intensity of the apprehension is much greater. What the analysis has further demonstrated is that individuals with higher levels of OCA not only fear that peers will have negative perceptions following a communication situation, but are afraid that that their peers will display and share their negative perceptions in some public forum which will lead to a feeling of humiliation.

Prior experiences of communicating with new friends.   The analysis of interviewees' narratives reveals that communicating with strangers compared to interacting with friends, in any of the four contexts, leads to heightened anxiety. The 'stranger' effect is short-lived for some and so apprehension levels reduce quickly, with such students reporting low levels of OCA. Ultimately, those with low OCA have a very positive attitude and appear to see strangers as potential new friends. In contrast, for other students, strangers are any individuals with whom they do not have strong personal relationships. For example, those with high OCA view many classmates as strangers and have real fears of communicating in groups with those classmates.

Interviewees' past experiences of being in unfamiliar groups and making new friends seems to influence their comfort in communicating with 'strangers'. A number of them referred to prior experiences relating to school life which had a significant effect, in different ways, on their sense of self and their levels of CA. For example, the transfer from primary to secondary school had a negative effect on Tom (low OCA) as he outlines:

> I went to a very small primary school and I think the big environment in secondary school scared me a little bit. Up to third year I would just do my work and would not really talk to people as much.

However, Tom's participation in transition year (explained below) transformed him. In contrast, Daniel (high OCA) remembers feeling good about communicating until he was separated from his primary school friends and progressed to secondary school among a new peer group. He admits:

> That was a bit of a disaster. I was very upset with being put in with a lot of people I didn't really know.

When reflecting on prior occasions of meeting strangers/making new friends, many interviewees refer to their transition year (year between junior and senior cycle in the Irish second level system; typically students are age 15 or 16). Indeed, 10 of the interviewees completed transition year. Typically, in transition year, students are involved in different activities and so get to know more students than their traditional class group. Most found this a very worthwhile experience, giving them extra confidence in meeting and conversing with others and in making speeches and doing presentations. Many of those now reporting low or average OCA found it a very positive experience. The positive results of transition year, which allowed the students more time to communicate with their peers and to develop new friendships, reinforces the findings of prior literature regarding the importance of friendships in developing an understanding of communication (Evangelou *et al.*, 2009). Only one student with high OCA completed transition year (Mary) and she claims that it was no help to her in reducing her communication fears. Daniel and Cliona (both high OCA) cannot think of any prior occasion where they had a positive experience of settling into a new group, which helps to explain their high levels of apprehension in dealing with strangers in any communication context.

Preparation.   Another theme emerging from the OCA analysis is the effect of preparation on a student's level of apprehension when attending meetings or when facing a public speaking situation. Preparation captures students' sentiment about the need to feel comfortable with regard to the subject matter. This comfort can encourage confidence regarding understanding of a topic in an educational setting or a having a full grasp of facts or events in a workplace situation. There seems to be recognition among the interviewees that gaining comfort with subject matter requires time and effort but that the benefit of the preparation is reduced apprehension regarding the meeting or presentation. Niall's view is echoed by a number of students:

> I have to know about what I am doing, I wouldn't be able to just get up there and talk on a topic, like. If you were confident you knew everything [...] you'd be grand.

Even Mary, who has high OCA, feels that preparation can enable her to perform better, as she comments:

> Put me on the spot and put me in front of a crowd of people and give me a random topic and tell me to talk about it, I wouldn't be able to do it. But if I have prepared what I am going to talk about I wouldn't have as much bother doing it then.

The students who acknowledge a role for preparation often see it as a way of reducing the possibility of 'looking stupid' (John).

A number of students associate preparation with practice or gaining experience of communicating in more public fora (meetings, public speaking/presentations). Some have had exposure to some communication skills training (at school or via clubs and societies, etc.), but often they consider that such sessions occurred in an artificial environment and did not replicate the reality of meetings or public speaking. This is an interesting insight, as communication skills training which emphasises preparation and practice is often, perhaps naively, proposed as a remedy to OCA. Indeed, as mentioned in the literature review, it is often the only remedy offered by higher education institutions. However, prior studies have found that skills training may not provide any aid to those suffering with high OCA (Allen and Bourhis, 1996) and, indeed, it may exacerbate their apprehension levels. Two of the students with high OCA report that preparation and practice are of no benefit to them, as their anxiety persists regardless of their preparations.

Limitations of the Study and Directions for Future Research

This study was limited to an exploration of the experiences of 17 students at one higher education institution in Ireland. Thus, the findings are grounded in that particular setting. It is possible that a larger sample of students across different institutions may have provided additional and different insights into the phenomenon of OCA. In addition, the study focused on first-year students at a point in time; it did not attempt to examine changes in

OCA experience or to examine the impact of any particular communication activities or courses. It is very possible that, as the students mature, they will naturally experience changes in their levels of OCA, and that particular activities may also influence their levels of anxiety (these changes may be positive or negative). It must also be acknowledged that the study did not delve deeply into the origins of OCA for individual students. Furthermore, it did not examine the relationship of OCA with their actual communication skills. Thus, it was not possible to determine whether students' OCA levels would be classified as either 'rational' or 'non-rational', as described by McCroskey (1984).

In terms of perspective, this study has only examined OCA from the viewpoint of the student. There are other perspectives which may provide further insights into the phenomenon. For example, it is plausible that examining the way educators and peers view those struggling with high OCA may provide useful feedback to such students and it may influence the collaborative design of appropriate interventions.

There are many potential avenues for future research; some are aimed at addressing the limitations of the current study, whereas others seek to enhance further our understanding of OCA, which may influence educators' teaching practice in the future.

1. Research could be conducted with business and accounting students from other higher education institutions in Ireland and beyond to assess the robustness and generalisability of the current findings.
2. Engaging in comparative research with students from outside Ireland could help identify issues of shared concern and possible interventions.
3. There is an obvious need to examine the relationship between OCA and performance in communication tasks, and with overall academic achievement.
4. Research which explores the link between OCA and other background variables (e.g. culture, personality, socio-economic status) could reveal further insights into the antecedents of OCA.
5. Given the lack of qualitative research into OCA there is considerable scope to utilise this approach to examine issues such as the causes and consequences of OCA from the student's perspective.
6. Finally, the findings of this study indicate that research is needed to determine which pedagogical strategies are best suited to reducing high levels of OCA.

Conclusions

In summary, this paper qualitatively explored first-year business and accounting students' experiences of OCA. The findings clearly demonstrated that, while there is considerable variation in the apprehension experienced by different students, apprehension levels typically increase for all students in the more public communication settings. The analysis also illustrated that OCA is influenced by perceptions of peer evaluation, prior experiences of communicating with new people, and preparation activities.

In terms of assessing the contribution of this study, the value in documenting and communicating the range of students' experiences of OCA cannot be underestimated. So many prior studies on OCA have been solely quantitative in orientation and the lived experiences of CA have been absent. It is only by reading students' own words that the reality of the apprehension is effectively conveyed. In particular, the study contributes to sensitising educators to the very dramatic, emotional, and ultimately debilitating effect of high OCA. Given the range of student experiences and the depth of fear of those with high OCA, it is clear that a great deal of care and reflection is required if educators are to appropriately adapt their teaching practice and design effective interventions. Indeed, whether accounting and business educators can design such interventions without the direct support and assistance of specialist communication psychologists is questionable. Inappropriate interventions could exacerbate students' levels of anxiety.

The study illustrates that highly-apprehensive students are willing to discuss their communication fears, but may only do so when in a one-to-one confidential, supportive environment. This indicates that support for those with high OCA may need to happen at the individual level. Clearly, such a proposal will demand significant resources, which will be difficult to access in the current stringent financial environment being experienced in higher education. In the short-term, and at a minimum, business and accounting educators could measure the levels of OCA of their students so they are aware of the variation in OCA levels among their class group. Further, we suggest that educators might reflect on their pedagogy, the way in which they interact with students, and how they encourage students to engage with each other. Creating a non-threatening, supportive classroom environment may prevent classroom activities heightening OCA.

Notes

[1] Approval for the conduct of the study was granted by the appropriate body within the institution.

[2] The study was conducted in Ireland because it is where the researchers are based and where they can arrange data collection. While the study is exploratory in nature and is not seeking generalisable findings per se, the researchers contend that there is nothing particularly unique in terms of the setting of this study (i.e. type of degree programmes, institution, or wider higher education context). In other words, it is plausible that the findings reported in this study may have resonance with students in other settings. For further information on the educational system in Ireland, see White (2001) and Byrne and Flood (2003).

[3] In selecting the sample for this exploratory, qualitative study, the principal concern was to seek the participation of students who experienced various levels of OCA. Thus, the sample was not chosen to be representative of the population in the quantitative study. Full details of the population in the quantitative study are provided in Byrne, Flood and Shanahan (2009).

References

Allen, M. and Bourhis, J. (1996) The relationship of communication apprehension to communication behaviour: a meta-analysis, *Communication Quarterly*, 44(2), pp. 214–226.

Aly, I. and Islam, M. (2003) Audit of accounting program on oral communications apprehension: a comparative study among accounting students, *Managerial Auditing Journal*, 18(9), pp. 751–760.

Ameen, E., Bruns, S. and Jackson, C. (2010) Communication skills and accounting: do perceptions match reality?, *The CPA Journal*, 80(7), pp. 63–65.

Arquero, J., Hassall, T., Joyce, J. and Donoso, J. (2007) Accounting students and communication apprehension: a study of Spanish and UK students, *European Accounting Review*, 16(2), pp. 299–322.

Beatty, M. J. and Dobos, J. A. (1997) Physiological assessment, in: J. A. Daly, J. C. McCroskey, J. Ayres, T. Hopf and D. M. Ayres (Eds) *Avoiding Communication*, pp. 217–229 (Beverly Hills, CA: Sage Publications).

Borzi, M. and Mills, T. (2001) Communication apprehension in upper level accounting students: an assessment of skill development, *Journal of Education for Business*, 76(4), pp. 193–198.

Bowers, J. W. (1986) Classroom communication apprehension: a survey, *Communication Education*, 35(1), pp. 372–378.

Byrne, M. and Flood, B. (2003) Defining the present and shaping the future: the changing nature of accounting education in Ireland, *Journal of Accounting Education*, 21(3), pp. 197–213.

Byrne, M., Flood, B. and Shanahan, D. (2009) Communication apprehension among business and accounting students in Ireland, *Irish Accounting Review*, 16(2), pp. 1–19.

Cavanagh, R., Kay, K., Klein, D. and Meisinger, S. (2006) Are they really ready to work?, Employers' perspectives on the basic knowledge and applied skills of new entrants to the 21st century U.S. workforce. Available at p21.org/documents/FINAL_REPORT_PDF09-29-06.pdf (accessed 28 September 2010).

Council for Industry and Higher Education (2008) *Graduate Employability: What do Employers Think and Want?* (London: W. Archer and J. Davidson).

Du-Babcock, B. (2006) Teaching business communication: past, present, and future, *Journal of Business Communication*, 43(3), pp. 253–264.

Evangelou, M., Sylva, K., Kyriacou, M., Wild, M. and Glenny, G. (2009) *Early Years Learning and Development—Literature Review. Research Report DCSF-RR176. The Importance of Friendship for School-Age Children* (Oxford: Department for Children, Schools and Families).

Fordham, D. R. and Gabbin, A. L. (1996) Skills versus apprehension: empirical evidence on oral communication, *Business Communication Quarterly*, 59(3), pp. 88–97.

Gardner, C. T., Milne, M. J., Stringer, C. P. and Whiting, R. H. (2005) Oral and written communication apprehension in accounting students: curriculum impacts and impacts on academic performance, *Accounting Education: an international journal*, 14(3), pp. 313–336.

Gilkinson, H. (1942) Social fears as reported by students in college speech classes, *Speech Monographs*, 9(1), pp. 141–160.

Graham, A., Hampton, M. and Willett, C. (2009) What not to write: an intervention in written communication skills for accounting students, *International Journal of Management Education*, 8(2), pp. 67–74.

Gradireland (2010) Graduate Salary & Graduate Recruitment Trends Survey 2010. Available at www.gradireland.com (accessed 11 October 2010).

Hassall, T., Joyce, J., Arquero, J. and Donoso, J. (1999) Vocational skills and capabilities for management accountants, Management Accounting, 77(11), pp. 52–54.

Hassall, T., Joyce, J., Ottewill, R., Arquero, J. and Donoso, J. (2000) Communication apprehension in UK and Spanish business and accounting students, *Education and Training*, 42(2), pp. 93–100.

Heuett, B., Hsu, C. and Ayres, J. (2003) Testing a screening procedure in the treatments for communication apprehension, *Communication Research Reports*, 20(3), pp. 219–229.

Horwitz, B. (2002) *Communication Apprehension: Origins and Management* (Albany, NY: Singular-Thomson Learning).

Kougl, K. (1980) Dealing with quiet students in the basic college speech course, *Communication Education*, 29(3), pp. 234–238.

Kvale, S. (2007) *Doing Interviews* (London: Sage Publications).

Kvale, S. and Brinkmann, S. (2009) *Interviews. Learning the Craft of Qualitative Research Interviewing* (Thousand Oaks, CA: Sage Publications).

McCroskey, J. C. (1970) Measures of communication-bound anxiety, *Speech Monographs*, 37(4), pp. 269–277.

McCroskey, J. C. (1977) Oral communication apprehension: a summary of recent theory and research, *Human Communication Research*, 4(1), pp. 78–96.

McCroskey, J. C. (1984) The communication apprehension perspective, in: J. A. Daly and J. C. McCroskey (Eds) *Avoiding Communication*, pp. 13–38 (Beverly Hills, CA: Sage Publications).

McCroskey, J. C. (1997a) Willingness to communicate, communication apprehension, and self-perceived communication competence: conceptualisations and perspectives, in: J. A. Daly, J. C. McCroskey, J. Ayres, T. Hopf and D. M. Ayres (Eds) *Avoiding Communication: Shyness, Reticence and Communication Apprehension*, pp. 75–108 (Beverly Hills, CA: Sage Publications).

McCroskey, J. C. (1997b) Self-report measurement, in: J. A. Daly, J. C. McCroskey, J. Ayres, T. Hopf and D. M. Ayres (Eds) *Avoiding Communication: Shyness, Reticence and Communication Apprehension*, pp. 191–216 (Beverly Hills, CA: Sage Publications).

McCroskey, J. C. (2006) *An Introduction to Rhetorical Communication: A Western Rhetorical Perspective,* 9th ed (Boston, MA: Allyn and Bacon Pearson Education Inc).

McDaniel, S. and White, J. (1993) The quality of the academic preparation of undergraduate marketing majors: an assessment by company recruiters, *Marketing Education Review*, 3(3), pp. 9–16.

Mitchell, G., Skinner, L. and White, B. (2010) Essential soft skills for success in the twenty-first century workforce as perceived by business educators, *The Delta Pi Epsilon Journal*, 12(1), pp. 43–53.

O'Mara, J., Allen, J. L., Long, K. M. and Judd, B. (1996) Communication apprehension, nonverbal immediacy, and negative expectations for learning, *Communication Research Reports*, 13(1), pp. 109–128.

Parks, M. (1980) A test of the cross-situational consistency of communication apprehension, *Communication Monographs*, 47(3), pp. 220–232.

Plutsky, S. (1996) Faculty perceptions of students' business communication needs, *Business Communication Quarterly*, 59(4), pp. 69–76.

Quible, Z. and Griffin, F. (2007) Are writing deficiencies creating a lost generation of business writers?, *Journal of Education for Business*, 83(1), pp. 32–36.

Richmond, V. and McCroskey, J. (1998) *Communication Apprehension, Avoidance, and Effectiveness,* 5th edn (Needham Heights, MA: Allyn and Bacon).

Simons, K., Higgins, M. and Lowe, D. (1995) A profile of communication apprehension in accounting majors: implications for teaching and curriculum revision, *Journal of Accounting Education*, 13(2), pp. 159–176.

Smith, D. and Nelson, S. (1994) Written and oral communication apprehension: extent and influence on writing variables, *NABTE Review*, 21, pp. 29–34.

Stanga, K. G. and Ladd, R. T. (1990) Oral communication apprehension in beginning accounting majors: an exploratory study, *Issues in Accounting Education*, 5(2), pp. 180–194.

Warnock, K. and Curtis, E. (1997) Oral communication apprehension: a preliminary study of accounting students. Paper presented at the Annual Conference of the Irish Accounting and Finance Association, 8–9 May (Dublin City University).

White, T. (2001) *Investing in People—Higher Education in Ireland from 1960 to 2000* (Dublin: Institution of Public Administration).

Wrench, J., Brogan, S., McCroskey, J. and Doreen, J. (2008) Social communication apprehension: the intersection of communication apprehension and social phobia, *Human Communication*, 11(4), pp. 409–430.

Appendix

INTERVIEW GUIDE

Introduction

Introduction of the interviewer; explanation of the purpose of the interview; reiteration of the voluntary nature of student's participation—he/she may refuse to discuss any item raised and may conclude the interview at any stage; reassurance of confidentiality, etc.

Outline of topics:

1. Background (to relax the interviewee and to build rapport with the interviewer):

- Where were you born and where did you grow up?
- Tell me a little about your family, siblings, etc.?
- Where did you go to school? Did you enjoy your school experience? Had you many friends at school? Do you still keep in touch with school friends, etc.?
- How did you feel about the transition from primary school to secondary school?
- What has the transition from school to higher education been like? Course of study, making friends, social and extracurricular activities, living away from home, etc.
- What sort of hobbies and interests do you have?

The interview then explores the interviewee's attitudes to communicating in each of the four oral contexts.

2. One-to-one communication

- Tell me how comfortable you feel talking to a friend on a one-to-one basis.
- How does this compare with talking to a stranger?
- Have you ever found it difficult to talk to a stranger? Can you give an example? How did you overcome any such difficulties?
- If communication is difficult, what kinds of feelings are evoked? Can you describe a troublesome situation?
- Have you always felt comfortable/uncomfortable in such a situation?
- What might cause any apprehension?

3. Communicating in groups

- Tell me how you feel talking with a group of friends.
- How does this compare with talking within a group, some or all of whom you haven't met previously?
- Have you ever found it difficult to talk in groups? Can you describe a particular example? How did you overcome any such difficulties?
- If you find communication difficult in a group, what kinds of feelings are evoked?
- Have you always felt comfortable/uncomfortable in such a situation?
- What might cause any apprehension?

4. Communicating at meetings

- Have you any experience of attending meetings—formal or informal? Can you give some examples?
- Have you participated or contributed at a meeting?
- Was your participation voluntary, self-initiated or required?
- How do you feel if you have to participate?
- Can you give an example of a meeting at which you felt you participated effectively?
- Can you describe a meeting at which you felt your participation/contribution was poor?
- What influences your comfort/confidence to participate when at a meeting?
- What contributes to your apprehension regarding meetings?

5. Public speaking

- Can you describe some examples of when you have had to speak in public?
- Was your involvement voluntary or required?
- How did you feel in advance?
- Did you prepare or think about the activity in advance?
- During your speech/presentation, were you conscious of the audience, what role did the audience play? What were you thinking and feeling?
- Describe how effective you think you communicated? How did you feel afterwards?
- What contributes/causes your apprehension regarding public speaking?

6. Communication skills

- Have you ever attended a course or class focused on developing communication skills?
- Can you describe the course/class?
- Did you enjoy your involvement in the course/class?
- Did you benefit from your involvement?
- Did the course/class affect your thinking or feelings regarding various communication activities?

7. Conclusion
The interview concludes with an offer to the interviewee to contribute any further relevant details which may contribute to the study. Often interesting issues and discussions emerge at this point.

Finally, the interviewer thanks the interviewee and concludes the interview.

Developing Accounting Students' Listening Skills: Barriers, Opportunities and an Integrated Stakeholder Approach

GERARD STONE*,**, MARGARET LIGHTBODY*,** and ROB WHAIT*,**

*The University of South Australia, Australia; **Centre for Accounting, Governance and Sustainability, University of South Australia, Australia

ABSTRACT   Accountants and employers of accounting graduates consider listening to be among the most important communication skills that graduates possess. However, accounting education practices that develop students' listening skills are uncommon. Further, in the case of listening development, the current approach of prescribing that educators do more to rectify students' skill deficiencies overlooks barriers that prevent greater incorporation of listening instruction in the accounting curriculum. An alternative integrated stakeholder approach to develop students' listening skills is proposed. Informed by a broad range of education literature, the approach identifies cross-disciplinary listening development best practice and barriers to the widespread implementation of such practices in the typical accounting programme, before determining and assigning interrelated listening development roles to key stakeholders who will benefit from improved student listening. While student listening development is feasible under the proposed approach, shared contributions by accounting students, the profession and educators are needed to achieve enhanced skills outcomes.

Introduction

> Listening, well we don't have too much of it ... The only listening they do is when I talk to them and they write down whatever they can. (Tutor interviewed by Chand, 2007, p. 8)

Listening is an indispensable attribute in accounting practice and a highly sought-after skill among the employers of accounting graduates (see, for example, Hassall *et al.*, 2003; Tan, Fowler and Hawkes, 2004; Gray, 2010; Gray and Murray, 2011; Stone and Lightbody,

2012). An estimated two-thirds of accountants' communication with clients and colleagues consists of speaking and listening (Gouws and Terblanche, 1998). Due to the increasing importance of team and group work in many organisations, listening in business is a basic competency (Cooper, 1997). The significance of listening skills in practice is recognised by the professional accounting bodies who list the ability to 'listen effectively' as a core generic skill that is expected of accountants (The ICAA and CPA Australia, 2011, p. 11).

Nonetheless, of the communication skills of writing, speaking, reading, and listening,[1] listening is often neglected in both the formal development of curricula in accounting education and scholarly research, which informs pedagogical practice (Hartley, 2007; Lynch, 2011). Its characterisation as a so-called 'soft' skill by some educators and scholars tends to belie its standing among business professionals as a 'highly desirable workplace skill' (Flynn, Valikoski and Grau, 2008, p. 141). The parsimonious treatment of listening by educators and the designers of accounting curricula also stands in marked contrast to the recurring recommendation that accountants should be expert communicators who possess a range of communication attributes, including the ability to listen to and understand the needs of clients and colleagues (Hirsch, Anderson and Gabriel, 1994; Albrecht and Sack, 2000; Hancock *et al.*, 2009). As a result, it is not surprising that studies show that graduates are considered, by both themselves and their employers, to lack adequate listening skills (Tan, Fowler and Hawkes, 2004; de Lange, Jackling and Gut, 2006; Gray and Murray, 2011). This deficiency is not new; there have long been calls for a greater emphasis on communication skills, including listening in accounting programmes (Andrews and Sigband, 1984; Mathews, Jackson and Brown, 1990; Albrecht and Sack, 2000; Henderson, 2001; Jackling and de Lange, 2009). The ongoing and substantial coverage of the issue, however, indicates that there has been no major progress in closing the 'gap' between what the profession expects and what universities are delivering. While it is a relatively simple task to call for more attention to be given to improving students' listening and other communication skills, it is somewhat more challenging to determine how this might be accomplished.

Pedagogical developments in accounting tend to emphasise the role of the academic as educator and prescribe what educators ought to do in order to better teach students communication skills, including listening (Willcoxson, Wynder and Laing, 2010; Doran *et al.*, 2011; Jones, 2011; Keneley and Jackling, 2011). Relying predominantly on accounting educators to improve this aspect of students' skills base may, however, be ill-advised in light of research that identifies a number of factors in the contemporary university environment preventing the greater incorporation of listening instruction in accounting subjects (Bui and Porter, 2010; Lynch, 2011; Parker, 2011).[2] This paper proposes an alternative approach, which acknowledges the impact of these inhibiting factors and focuses on feasible opportunities to develop accounting students' listening skills during their university studies. The proposed integrated stakeholder approach is based on a review of the relevant accounting education literature and pertinent research conducted in other disciplines. It is contended that other stakeholders, in addition to educators, have a significant interest and accompanying role in developing students' listening skills. The approach identifies realistic roles for each stakeholder – educators, students, the professional accounting bodies and employers of accounting graduates – and outlines interrelationships in the stakeholders' roles which may result in tangible contributions to students' listening. The proposed roles of educators and students are informed by cross-disciplinary pedagogical listening initiatives and the substantial literature on the accounting profession's communication skills requirements. Finally, by sharing responsibility for the development of students' listening skills between educators, the student community and the profession, the proposed approach responds to calls to reassess the prevailing reliance on educators to enhance accounting students' generic attributes (de Lange, Jackling and Gut, 2006; Gray and Murray, 2011).

The next section summarises the current approach to developing accounting students' listening. An overview of the proposed integrated stakeholder approach to students' listening development follows. Subsequent sections provide a detailed discussion of the proposed approach. The penultimate section discusses the approach's implications for the stakeholders. Concluding comments, including suggestions for further research, are presented in the final section.

The Current Approach to Accounting Students' Listening Development

Accounting curricula prioritises the development of students' written communication proficiency (Sin, Jones and Petocz, 2007; Evans and Rigby, 2008; Graham, Hampton and Willett, 2009; Craig and McKinney, 2010). Oral communication instruction tends to concentrate on students' oral presentation and speaking skills (Grace and Gilsdorf, 2004; Kerby and Romine, 2009; Miller and Stone, 2009). Listening is generally treated as a secondary and passive activity and is given comparatively less attention (Vandergrift, 2004; Beall et al., 2008). Nonetheless, recent studies indicate that listening is being indirectly incorporated, albeit infrequently, in accounting subject design. While these practices are rare, they provide useful insights into the current approach to attempt to develop students' listening skills. The practices are summarised in Table 1.

The practices are characterised by high levels of educator involvement in developing, organising and executing the listening development opportunities that are made available to small groups of accounting students. The students' role varies considerably, from

Table 1. Listening development practices in accounting education.

Canadian accounting students believed that their listening skills were improved by a mixed teaching approach, comprising student role plays, presentations and cooperative learning tasks (Fortin and Legault, 2010).

Instructor intervention to ensure that small groups comprised students of varying academic achievement may have generated increased discussion and enhanced students' listening skills in a cooperative learning exercise in a final year UK accounting subject (Ballantine and Larres, 2009).

Australian accounting students who participated in a study tour believed that observing the communication skills of executives at the organisations the students visited reinforced the importance of listening to assist solve 'real world' problems (Webb, de Lange and O'Connell, 2009).

Cooperative learning in small groups of four in an Australian second-year accounting subject contributed to the development of students' interaction, discussion and accompanying listening skills (Farrell and Farrell, 2008).

Third-year Australian accounting students who mentored second-year students in small computer laboratory sessions reported that closely listening to students' questions improved their listening skills (Jackling and McDowall, 2008).

Final-year UK accounting students who undertook a business simulation in small groups in an elective subject perceived that their ability to listen to and evaluate the opinions of other group members was enhanced (Marriott, 2004).

Cooperative learning emphasises social interaction between students who are placed in small groups to undertake tasks (Ballantine and Larres, 2009). Educator intervention and direction influences group structure, with the objective of achieving the 'five basic elements' of cooperative learning (Ballantine and Larres, 2009, p. 390): interdependence between group members, individual accountability, face-to-face interaction, developing interpersonal and small group skills and member responsibility for monitoring group performance.

merely being present in class and, hopefully, participating in a group, to significant engagement as mentors and participants of study tours. The latter practices are normally restricted to high-achieving students (Jackling and McDowall, 2008; Webb, de Lange and O'Connell, 2009). In each case, the practices do not only aim to develop listening skills. Typically, listening development is incidental to educators' attempts to improve a range of generic attributes, including students' ability to express their opinion and evaluate the views of others (Ballantine and Larres, 2009; Fortin and Legault, 2010). In Marriott's (2004, p. 66) study, listening development is an unexpected and 'unplanned benefit'. No examples of structured listening practices being incorporated in the large student classes which typify the majority of accounting programmes were found in a review of the relevant literature. Apart from the one example of students observing executives in the Webb, de Lange and O'Connell (2009) study, no consideration is given to the potential roles of other interested stakeholders, such as employers or the professional accounting bodies. Thus, the overall impression given by the literature on listening skills in accounting education is that little is done and the responsibility to rectify the skills deficiency lies primarily with educators.

More generally, studies of generic skills development question whether other stakeholders should adopt a greater role in the process. The major role assigned to accounting educators has captured the attention of employers, who contend that the responsibility for communication skills development ought to be shared by employing firms, educators and students (Gray and Murray, 2011). Leading scholars in the field of accounting education also recommend reassessing the emphasis on educators' role in developing students' generic skills. de Lange, Jackling and Gut (2006) argue that the professional accounting bodies' contribution to skills development may need to expand, due to the congested accounting curriculum and increasing demands on educators. Fogarty (2010, p. 410) prompts parties with an interest in students' 'critical' communication skills to be realistic and mindful of the considerable impact of life and professional experience acquired after students' university education is completed on the development of this aspect of their skills set. There is thus a need to consider the roles that stakeholders other than educators could undertake in developing accounting students' listening skills.

An Integrated Stakeholder Approach to Accounting Students' Listening Development

In contrast to prevailing pedagogical practice and research on improving students' communication and other generic attributes, the proposed integrated stakeholder approach does not consider that accounting educators are primarily responsible for the development of students' listening. The approach proposes that other stakeholders who have a substantial interest in accounting students' listening undertake interrelated roles that may develop this desirable skill. Figure 1 provides a visual summary of the proposed approach.

Figure 1 shows how best practice listening initiatives from other disciplines may inform attempts to develop accounting students' listening skills. The liberal arts and English as an Additional Language (EAL) disciplines have a traditional focus on communication skills development and provide useful examples. The need to consult cross-disciplinary initiatives is emphasised by the scarcity of reported attempts to develop accounting students' listening. A number of factors which are considerable barriers to educators' attempts to develop accounting students' listening exist in the contemporary university environment (Bui and Porter, 2010; Lynch, 2011; Parker, 2011). These barriers inhibit what educators can accomplish and prevent the widespread adoption of listening initiatives in the current accounting curriculum, including best practice initiatives from the liberal arts and EAL

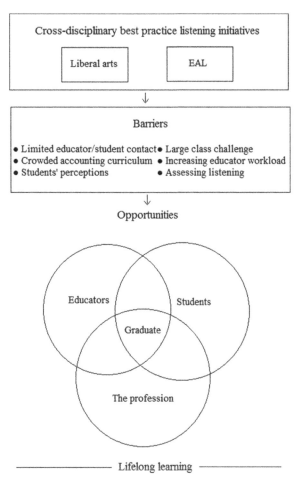

Figure 1. Integrated stakeholder approach

disciplines. Nevertheless, the proposed integrated stakeholder approach demonstrates that there are opportunities for all stakeholders to make realistic and interrelated contributions to students' listening skills. The focus on developing listening during students' time at university is represented by the accounting graduate at the centre of the overlapping circles in Figure 1. Finally, by recognising the impact of lifelong learning on listening development, the integrated stakeholder approach emphasises that listening is a complex activity, incrementally developed by a range of life and work experiences (Vandergrift, 2004; Fogarty, 2010). The following sections discuss the proposed approach in detail, commencing with a discussion of the best practice listening initiatives from other disciplines.

Cross-disciplinary Best Practice Listening Initiatives

A consideration of listening initiatives from the liberal arts and EAL disciplines is justified thus. Communication skills have long been a focus of liberal arts and language education. Many commentators argue for the need to liberalise the education of future accountants and identify the liberal arts as the core of a 'preferred approach' (Fogarty, 2010, p. 403). EAL educators' emphasis on listening is a consequence of the scholarly contention that improved listening skills significantly benefit the academic and non-academic endea-vours of students whose primary language in not English (Vandergrift, 2004; Graham, 2011; Lynch, 2011). The emphasis on listening in the liberal arts and language disciplines has generated initiatives which may be tailored to develop accounting students' listening. Two such examples of best practice, a liberal arts listening education model and bidirec-tional listening development in EAL education, are outlined below.

A Liberal Arts Approach to Developing Students' Listening

A simple, yet comprehensive, approach to listening development is incorporated in the curriculum at Alverno College through its Integrative Listening Model. Alverno College is 'a small, private, liberal arts women's college' in the United States (Thompson *et al.*, 2004, p. 227). The Alverno listening model consists of four sequential stages:

- listening preparation;
- applying the listening process;
- assessment of listening performance; and
- establishing new goals to further develop listening skills.

Listening preparation includes students determining the objectives they wish to accom-plish during listening activities. Examples of objectives include listening with the inten-tion to comprehend and evaluating the merit of a speaker's message. Educators who use the Alverno listening model expect that students will comprehensively prepare for classes and have a basic understanding of the subject matter to be discussed. This is essen-tial to ensure that students possess sufficient knowledge to 'attend to the shared messages and teaching examples of instructors and their peers' (Thompson *et al.*, 2004, p. 227). Applying the listening process in the second stage requires students to implement five components of listening: receiving, comprehending, interpreting and evaluating the verbal and non-verbal aspects of a speaker's message, before finally responding to the speaker. Students are advised to be conscious of the impact of 'listening filters', which Thompson *et al.* (2004, p. 232) describe as 'internal and external factors that influence all aspects of the listening situation'. Such filters include listener tiredness or preoccupa-tion with other matters that divert their focus away from the speaker's message. The Alverno model offers a number of 'coping strategies' to minimise the impact of listening filters (Thompson *et al.*, 2004, p. 233). For instance, students are encouraged to take brief notes to demonstrate that they are listening to and comprehending the speaker's message and to maintain eye contact with the speaker to improve their focus and concentration during class discussions. In the third stage, students' listening performance is assessed in three ways: instructor assessment, self-assessment and assessment by student peers. In the final stage, students utilise the feedback received in assessment to reflect on their performance and re-evaluate their goals as a listener. For example, students are required to identify strategies that they will employ to accentuate their strengths and rectify their weaknesses as a listener. Proponents of the Alverno model argue that the self-assessment and goal setting stages result in students being actively involved in developing their listen-ing skills (Thompson *et al.*, 2004).

The Alverno model's self-assessment and goal setting stages are supported by research that finds that students' oral communication skills are enhanced by self-assessment practices (Gabriel and Hirsch, 1992; Mitchell and Bakewell, 1995). By satisfactorily undertaking self-assessment, students' understanding of the basic tenets of effective communication, including listening, is likely to improve (Mitchell and Bakewell, 1995;

Morgan, 1997). Self-assessment also contributes to the development of students' self-regulated learning. Cassidy (2011, p. 996) extols self-regulated learning as a 'highly relevant and valuable concept' and a higher education 'priority'. Self-regulated learners value the acquisition of knowledge, are motivated to learn and recognise that learning is generally self-determinative and not dependent on the efforts of others (Cassidy, 2011). Self-assessment is a key process of self-regulated learning and provides students with an important 'feedback loop' to monitor the effectiveness of their learning strategies (Cassidy, 2011, p. 992). Feedback is also a basis for the goal setting and planning phase of students' self-regulated learning (Zimmerman, 2002; Cassidy, 2011). This is a significant phase, because students who set goals are more likely to achieve their learning objectives, acquire higher levels of motivation and the belief that they can successfully carry out learning tasks (Zimmerman, 2002; Graham, 2011).

In addition to encouraging students to engage with their listening development, the Alverno model emphasises the development of students' active listening skills (Thompson *et al.*, 2004). Active listening is a construct that receives considerable attention in the relevant literature (Pearce, Johnson and Barker, 1995; Morgan, 1997; Brown and Barker, 2001; Agrawal and Schmidt, 2003). It involves the listener giving the speaker their full attention and maintaining eye contact with the speaker to signify high levels of engagement and intent to grasp the meaning of what is being communicated (Brown and Barker, 2001). Active listening is an important skill to implement during the small group discussions and face-to-face communications that are commonplace in business (Agrawal and Schmidt, 2003).

While educators who use the Alverno model anticipate that students' listening skills will improve as they are continually exposed to the model's stages, there is recognition that developing students' listening is challenging. Thompson *et al.* (2004) acknowledge that student speakers are in the process of developing their oral presentation skills. They often lack confidence and are disorganised. As a result, it may be difficult for the listener to maintain focus and comprehend the speaker's message. Significantly, educators who utilise the Alverno model do not consider that this excuses students from attempting to exercise effective listening. In fact, they contend that it provides students with valuable exposure to the listening activities that occur in demanding settings which 'mirror real life listening' (Thompson *et al.*, 2004, p. 237).

EAL Listening Developments: Bidirectional Listening and Non-Academic Interactions

Students' listening is the subject of considerable discussion in EAL research, where there is substantial support for developing students' bidirectional or two-way listening (Vandergrift, 2004; Morell, 2007; Graham, 2011; Lynch, 2011). This mode of listening involves two or more participants taking turns, exchanging the roles of speaker and listener in a listening interaction (Morley, 2001). Bidirectional listening, through participating in conversations, is the most common form of listening (Graham, 2011; Lynch, 2011). It is also the form of listening that places the greatest cognitive demands on students. They need to interpret rapidly the speaker's verbal and non-verbal messages, clarify ambiguous messages, evaluate their understanding, respond as a speaker and repeat the process (Vandergrift, 2004; Lynch, 2011). Bidirectional listening may be developed in both small group discussions and student team project meetings, where students interact in conversations (Vandergrift, 2004; Lynch, 2011). Lynch (2011, p. 79) argues that these 'communicative events' represent a shift away from the traditional view of academic listening as one-way listening, epitomised by students taking notes in large lectures in which academics speak and students (hopefully) listen. By contrast, bidirectional listening interactions expose students to a broad and rich range of listening events.

Students' bidirectional listening may be extended and further developed by interactions outside the classroom. Lynch (2011, p. 87) observes that EAL students who engage in 'non-academic interactions' are more likely to enhance their English language listening skills than students who restrict their use of English to their studies. Valuable non-academic interactions include students having conversations and listening in English during part-time work, in informal social settings and club and sporting activities (Lynch, 2011). By exposing students to what Vandergrift (2004, p. 3) terms 'real-life listening', non-academic interactions extend students' bidirectional listening to settings beyond an academic context (Morell, 2007). Advocates of non-academic interactions and listening opportunities also contend that the practice is likely to be useful to students in their endeavours outside the classroom once their university education is completed (Vandergrift, 2004).

To summarise, the Alverno Integrative Listening Model and EAL's emphasis on bidirectional listening are examples of cross-disciplinary listening initiatives that may inform accounting educators' attempts to develop students' listening. The Alverno model's four stage structure provides listening development roles for both educators and students. The EAL non-academic interactions extend students' role to practising listening in real world settings. This is arguably significant, as the initiatives, when considered as a whole, require students to participate in the development of their listening in both academic and non-academic contexts.

Barriers to Developing Accounting Students' Listening Skills

The Alverno and EAL initiatives demonstrate how listening skills can be successfully developed in a university setting. However, research on accounting students' communication attributes has determined that it is important to recognise factors which are potential barriers to developing this aspect of students' skill set in the accounting curriculum (Arquero et al., 2007; Ameen, Jackson and Malgwi, 2010). While the existence and significance of these factors is acknowledged in the proposed integrated stakeholder approach (see Figure 1), it is contended that they should not be used as justification to disregard accounting students' listening development. Instead, under the proposed approach, it is argued that the barriers indicate that other stakeholders, in addition to educators, need to make a greater contribution to students' listening skills development.

Limited Educator/Student Contact and the Large Class Challenge

Accounting subjects typically comprise as few as three hours of contact time a week, of which one or two hours is absorbed by large group lectures. Educators who specialise in improving students' listening identify time limitations, particularly a lack of time to interact with students in small group face-to-face classes, as a major barrier to developing students' listening skills (Vandergrift, 2004; Chand, 2007; Lynch, 2011). Contact time in accounting subjects is unlikely to increase while universities operate in an increasingly competitive education market, characterised by providers that offer students distance learning with no requirement to attend classes and heightened student expectations for options that reduce time spent on their studies, including time at campus (Borden and Evenbeck, 2007; Finney and Finney, 2010; Parker, 2011).

Accounting educators' reliance on large group lectures is also unlikely to lessen as universities attempt to replace diminishing government funding by accepting substantial increases in enrolments (Parker, 2011). Bui and Porter (2010) and Cuseo (2007) argue that by increasing educators' dependence on the lecture method of instruction, large classes constrain educators from developing students' competencies. Largely monologue lectures contribute to 'passive spectating' by students who are prone to disengage from the learning process (Cuseo, 2007, p. 6). Student engagement is conducive to effective listening in class (Lynch, 2011). Nor do monologue lectures facilitate the interaction and discussion between educators and students, which is a significant factor in developing students' listening skills in the liberal arts and EAL initiatives outlined above (Vandergrift, 2004; Lynch, 2011).

The Crowded Accounting Curriculum

In addition to addressing conventional technical accounting content, accounting programmes are expected to teach a broad range of generic skills and provide students with the basis for ethical behaviour, leadership and intercultural sensitivity in their professional lives (Albrecht and Sack, 2000; Jackling and de Lange, 2009; Wessels and Steenkamp, 2009). An accompanying emphasis on the development of what Jones (2010, p. 14) describes as the 'higher order ... interwined', generic attributes of critical thinking, analysis, problem solving and communication has resulted in a 'crowded' curriculum (de Lange, Jackling and Gut, 2006, p. 382). As contact time in accounting subjects has not increased in parallel with these rising demands, efforts to develop students' communication and other generic skills must compete with technical accounting content for limited time and space (Jones, 2010). Technical content is considered by many accounting educators to be the essence of accounting programmes. Listening and other generic skills are perceived to be soft skills, which dilute programmes' technical rigour and warrant limited attention (Barrie, 2004; Jones, 2010). Educators' primarily technical emphasis has been the subject of debate. In response to the 'skill-shift' in the accounting profession (Jones and Lancaster, 2001, p. 276) and the rapid recognition of the need for listening and other generic skills, commentators have called on university educators to offer broad based programmes that improve students' generic attributes (Henderson, 2001; Jackling and de Lange, 2009). The study of technical content would be postponed and a substantial amount of this content would be transferred to the professional accounting bodies' further education programmes that graduates undertake to achieve professional membership (Henderson, 2001; de Lange, Jackling and Gut, 2006). Time and space to develop undergraduate students' sought after generic, including communication, skills would then result (de Lange, Jackling and Gut, 2006).[3] While there is merit in such proposals, they represent a significant shift from current practice and are unlikely to offer a timely solution to meet the demand for accounting graduates with enhanced listening skills.

Increasing Educator Workloads

Increasing student numbers, shrinking teaching staff-to-student ratios and the devolution of compliance and reporting tasks to academics has resulted in a 'generally dramatic increase in workload levels' (Parker, 2011, p. 444; Fredman and Doughney, 2012). In accounting, as with other disciplines, educators are also expected to participate in and produce research. Indeed, 'it is the research quantum which is the highly influential constant for tenure, promotion' and other aspects of academics' advancement (de Lange, 2005, p. 133). Vandergrift (2004), a foremost scholar in the field of academic listening, contends that listening is a difficult skill for students to learn and recommends substantial educator involvement in the listening development process. Confronted by rising workloads and with their focus on research output, accounting academics may be reluctant to devote time to design and implement the innovative teaching practices necessary to develop students' listening skills.

Students' Perceptions of the Relevance of Oral Communication Skills in Practice

Reluctance to devote time to developing students' listening skills may not be confined to the academic ranks. Researchers have consistently uncovered a widely-held view among students that oral communication skills are unimportant in accounting practice (Gardner *et al.*, 2005; Arquero *et al.*, 2007; Meixner *et al.*, 2009; Ameen, Jackson and Malgwi, 2010; Gray and Murray, 2011). This finding is strikingly evident in Ameen, Jackson and Malgwi's (2010) study of accounting students at four institutions in the United States during 1998 and 2006. The students nominated the level of oral communication proficiency they believed was required in 24 occupations. Accounting was ranked 19th by students surveyed in 1998. By 2006, accounting's ranking had fallen to 22nd. The profession and its representative bodies state repeatedly that they require practitioners who are adept oral communicators and effective listeners (Wessels and Steenkamp, 2009; Gray and Murray, 2011). This gap between the perceptions of students and the needs of practice may severely hamper attempts to engage students in the development of listening and other oral communication skills.

Assessing Listening

Accounting programmes increasingly seek to assess the skills they claim to teach in order to provide evidence of student learning outcomes for accreditation bodies such as The Association to Advance Collegiate Schools of Business (AACSB). The move towards assessment that evidences learning outcomes is part of an international trend towards an 'outcomes-based focus' among accounting higher education providers (Freeman and Hancock, 2011, p. 267). Listening is the least explicit of the communication skills (Vandergrift, 2004). The manifestations of good or poor, sophisticated or underdeveloped listening skills are often difficult to discern, unlike the product of a student's written activity or oral presentation (Rowley-Jolivet, 2002). Thus, student listening is difficult to assess. As Juchau and Galvin (1984, p. 29) observe, 'writing a report is more obviously assessable work than listening empathically to a fellow student'. Challenges associated with assessing an intangible activity such as listening are documented as a reason why it is frequently overlooked by educators (Juchau and Galvin, 1984; Zaid and Abraham, 1994; Morgan, 1997).

In summary, the barriers identified in this section indicate that the current structures of mass education, the demands on educators and the attitudes of students mean that improved listening outcomes will not be achieved by simply recommending that educators do more or that they adopt best practices from other disciplines in a wholesale manner. The barriers necessitate an alternative approach. As shown in Figure 1, under the proposed integrated stakeholder approach, there are opportunities for all stakeholders to undertake interrelated and realistic roles that jointly contribute to developing students' listening. It is to an examination of these opportunities and each stakeholder's role that the discussion now turns.

Opportunities to Develop Accounting Students' Listening Skills: Educators' Role

University educators' proposed role is the first to be considered. The section commences by outlining the benefits of educators informing and reinforcing the importance of listening in accounting practice to students. Aspects of the best practice listening initiatives from the liberal arts and EAL literature that may be realistically implemented by accounting educators are then discussed. Consistent with applying disciplinary context to students' listening development, these initiatives present further opportunities for educators to inform and reinforce listening's importance in practice to students. In turn, this provides educators with a contextual basis to develop students' listening skills and facilitates students recognising listening's relevance to their skills portfolio.

Informing and Reinforcing the Importance of Listening

The practice of educators both informing students and reinforcing the importance of listening in accounting practice is an important aspect of developing students' listening skills. The professional accounting bodies encourage educators to reinforce frequently 'the message' to students that listening and other generic skills are highly valued by the profession and employers (The ICAA and CPA Australia, 2011, p. 12). The practice contributes to developing accounting students' listening in two ways. First, student motivation to develop their listening is likely to increase when they recognise its value in the professional workplace (Howieson, 2003; D'Aloisio, 2006; de Lange, Jackling and Gut, 2006). Second, the practice assists in altering the above-mentioned perception among accounting students that accountants are 'solitary number crunching' individuals who do not require oral communication skills, including listening (Wessels and Steenkamp, 2009, p. 123). The academic and professional literature provide numerous examples that accounting educators may use in class discussions to emphasise the importance of listening. For instance, Flynn, Valikoski and Grau (2008) show that listening is an indispensable attribute within the manager and team leader ranks and essential to effective managerial communication with staff. This finding is likely to be of interest to students who aspire to be managers and partners.

Significantly, the large class size barrier to developing accounting students' listening skills should not hinder educators' attempts to inform and reinforce the importance of listening. The practice may be employed in both large group lectures and small class discussions. Further, the practice does not increase educators' workload, as it does not require the design of innovative teaching methodologies to enhance listening. Educators can also enlist the assistance of employers of accounting graduates to inform and reinforce the significance of listening to students. Presentations and guest lectures by employers are examples of interrelated contributions under the proposed integrated stakeholder approach that emphasise to students the importance of listening in practice and its status as a desirable graduate attribute (Tempone et al., 2012).

Extracting Cross-Disciplinary Best Practice Listening Initiatives

The Alverno Integrative Listening Model. The four-stage Alverno model offers accounting educators a potential foundation framework for the development of students' listening skills. While the Alverno model is presented as an exemplar of listening skills development, it is not suggested that the model can be effortlessly transplanted into accounting programmes. Alverno College is a private institution with a small student community and high staff-to-student ratios that do not reflect the large student numbers and resourcing issues confronting many publicly-funded universities that offer accounting programmes (Parker, 2011; Alverno College, 2012). Moreover, the educational focus of the liberal arts on its students' personal development is a marked contrast to the emphasis in accounting education on the acquisition of skills required to commence professional practice

(Henderson, 2001). As an alternative, Fogarty (2010, p. 412) proposes 'extracting' elements from the liberal arts that contribute to meeting the needs of the accounting profession and in which accounting education is deficient. He identifies the development of students' communication skills as one such liberal arts ideal that may be extracted to improve the accounting curriculum.

In order to provide communication skills education, many accounting programmes include a stand-alone generic communications subject. Given the already crowded accounting curriculum, these subjects are a logistically practical and pedagogically defensible venue to introduce accounting students to the first two stages of the Alverno model – listening preparation and applying the listening process – and to provide students with an overview of how to undertake self-assessment and goal setting, the model's third and final stages. It is accounting educators' role to build on this introduction by facilitating listening, self-assessment and goal setting opportunities for students in accounting subjects and by providing disciplinary 'guidance and scaffolding' to students' listening development (Jones, 2010, p. 13). This proposed role for accounting educators is supported by research that establishes that communication and other generic skills are best developed within a discipline's unique context (see, for example, Misko, 1995; Lucas et al., 2004; Carr, Chua and Perera, 2006; Jones, 2010). Studies conclude that attempts to develop accounting students' communication skills are most successful when they are informed by the accounting discipline's knowledge base, its particular discourse and the requirements of the employers of accounting graduates (Carr, Chua and Perera, 2006; de Lange, Jackling and Gut, 2006; Jackling and de Lange, 2009). Accounting educators are best placed to apply this important disciplinary context to the Alverno model during accounting subjects.

To demonstrate accounting educators' role, the model's strategies to minimise the impact of listening filters are symptomatic of attentive listening, a frequently used listening skill in accounting practice (Stone and Lightbody, 2012). Attentive listening is described by Morgan (1997) as the ability to interpret verbal and non-verbal information from another individual. By encouraging the use of the strategies in accounting subject class discussions, educators can develop students' attentive listening skills. The model's strategies also present educators with additional opportunities to inform and reinforce the importance of listening in accounting practice and convince students of listening's relevance as a valuable skill. Note-taking by accountants during client meetings is common and indicative of practitioners attentively listening to comprehend the verbal information conveyed by their clients. Educators can draw parallels between this professional skill and opportunities to practise note-taking during accounting subjects. Likewise, educators can remind students of the importance of paying attention to a speaker's non-verbal messages in addition to their spoken verbal messages in class discussions. Studies of accountants' listening skills show that successful accountants adroitly interpret the non-verbal information that clients' facial expressions convey (Stone and Lightbody, 2012). Non-verbal information transmits listeners' level of interest in a discussion and their intent to grasp the meaning of what is being communicated (Agrawal and Schmidt, 2003). Accountants interviewed by Stone and Lightbody (2012) claim to be adept at monitoring their clients' facial expressions for signs of confusion or disinterest and make appropriate adjustments to their communication approach to facilitate clients' understanding and interest.

Another aspect of the Alverno model that is applicable in the accounting classroom is its acknowledgement that student speakers are in the process of developing their oral presentation skills. This places demands on student listeners' ability to maintain focus and understand the speaker's message (Thompson et al., 2004). Stone and Lightbody's (2012) study of accountants' listening skills found that practitioners communicate with a spectrum of clients, a number of whom are disinterested in accounting information and hesitant to ask questions and engage their accountant in discussion. This poses challenges for practitioners who still need to identify their clients' needs in order to service them appropriately. Accounting educators may use such findings and the Alverno model's recognition that listening may occur in challenging circumstances to reinforce to students that effective listening is expected in practice 'in spite of the speaker' (Thompson *et al.*, 2004, p. 237).

Listening assessment alternatives. Accounting educators typically focus on educator-initiated assessment as evidence of learning (McGowan and Lightbody, 2008). However, the challenge in objectively assessing listening is an acknowledged barrier to wider integration of listening in the accounting curriculum. The Alverno model's self-assessment and goal-setting stages provide educators with useful assessment alternatives. The small number of accounting educators who have made tentative attempts to develop students' listening skills encourage students to undertake self-assessment through learning logs (Ballantine and Larres, 2009) and reflective journals (Webb, de Lange and O'Connell, 2009). Once again, accounting educators are well placed to apply disciplinary context to the benefits students may obtain from self-assessment. As discussed, self-assessment facilitates, and is a process of, self-regulated learning (Cassidy, 2011; Zimmerman, 2002). Self-regulated learning has received attention in the education literature because of its capacity to engender students with skills to acquire the knowledge needed for ongoing employment and the discipline required for lifelong learning (Cassidy, 2011). Professional accounting bodies and employers of graduates expect that students will acquire the ability to be self-regulated learners in order to adapt to a rapidly changing business environment (The ICAA and CPA Australia, 2011). Educators can emphasise to students that employers regard self-regulated learning skills as a distinguishing factor when they choose between graduate applicants with similar grades (Hancock *et al.*, 2009).

The significance of non-academic interactions. EAL bidirectional listening places great emphasis on the need to practise listening skills in diverse contexts and, particularly, in places other than the classroom. It is argued that non-academic interactions, where students practise listening away from the 'safe laboratory' of the classroom, have the potential to be of considerable benefit in attempts to develop accounting students' listening skills (Morell, 2007, p. 234). Accounting educators may need to make explicit the link between non-academic interactions and students' skills portfolio for students to realise their value. To emphasise the significance of this link, educators could draw upon the views of graduates' employers. For example, employers interviewed by Jackling and de Lange (2009, p. 378) indicate their 'strong support' for graduates engaging in activities outside university that assist in developing their communication attributes. KPMG, a major global employer of accounting graduates, nominates good listening skills and the ability to 'relate well to people who have a diverse range of skills, styles and approaches' as desirable graduate attributes (KPMG, 2012). Student involvement in clubs, team sports, not-for-profit committees, debating, volunteering and work experience are examples of non-academic interactions that develop these attributes. Universities may support accounting educators by publicising paid and voluntary employment and club activities to students.

Accounting Students' Role

A premise of extant pedagogic models is that educators and students are 'co-producers' of learning outcomes (Finney and Finney, 2010, p. 278). The accounting education literature tends to concentrate on the role of educators rather than proposing contributions that students may make to their learning. The importance of students contributing to their learning is highlighted by the reality that accounting programmes are unable to deliver all aspects of the skills development required for success in professional practice (Henderson, 2001; Jackling and de Lange, 2009). Employers acknowledge this and often indicate in their recruitment material that they are seeking graduates who identify and take advantage of a spectrum of opportunities to learn and 'seek out and act on feedback in relation to results at work or university' (KPMG, 2012). As co-producers, students need to participate actively in the learning process, which aims to develop 'habits of mind that will help them learn ... and succeed in their chosen fields' (Hassel and Lourey, 2005, p. 3). Accounting students have a substantial role in the development of their listening and other habits of mind that facilitate learning and are sought after in practice. This section considers students' role in developing their listening skills under the proposed integrated stakeholder approach, both within and outside the classroom.

Reasserting Student Preparation to Develop Listening

Educators who use the Alverno model have expressed the clear expectation that students will prepare for classes and, therefore, be equipped to listen and contribute to class discussion (Thompson et al., 2004). This expectation may be at odds with the experience of many educators who have long expressed concern that an increasing number of students do not adequately prepare for classes (Hassel and Lourey, 2005; Borden and Evenbeck, 2007). A reassertion of students' responsibility to prepare for classes is arguably overdue. As Hassel and Lourey (2005, p. 3) observe, the utility of classroom discussion 'radically degenerates' when students are unprepared. There are two consequences of inadequate student preparation that impair the development of students' listening skills. First, it is likely to result in less contributory discussion by fewer students. This deprives students of the opportunity to listen to a range of speaking styles and opinions. Students' ability to attentively listen is enhanced in classroom exercises where increased discussion 'arising from new and diverse perspectives' occurs (Ballantine and Larres, 2009, p. 397). Second, unprepared students are unlikely to understand the subject matter being discussed. This impedes their ability to be 'intellectually present' and participate in fulfilling discussion, both as a speaker and listener (Thompson et al., 2004, p. 228). The importance of student preparation is accentuated by limited educator/student contact in accounting subjects, a barrier to listening development that necessitates educators and students maximising limited small group discussion opportunities to develop listening.

Exploiting Non-Academic Interactions

While educators have a role in informing and reinforcing the benefits of these broader life experiences to students, it is each student's responsibility to exploit the opportunities that interactions outside of the classroom present. Research indicates that students who engage positively with extracurricular opportunities gain greater learning outcomes than their more reluctant peers (Kuh, 1995). An example of this is studies of supervised work experience, a non-academic interaction that is common in accounting programmes. Advocates of work experience contend that it assists in developing students' communication skills by introducing students to an environment that provides a practical dimension to classroom based learning (Kuh, 1995; Beck and Halim, 2008; Jackling and de Lange, 2009; Paisey and Paisey, 2010). According to Gracia's (2010) analysis of UK accounting students' work experience, these benefits are considerable. This is dependent, however, on the nature of students' engagement with their work experience. Students who recognise the importance of communication skills in accounting practice, and who attempt to develop these skills, describe their work experience as a 'dynamic, context-specific experience with which they actively engaged' (Gracia, 2010, p. 61). By contrast, students who approach their work experience with the expectation that it will enhance their rudimentary technical, rather than communication, skills tend to be 'passive recipients of knowledge', who are considerably less engaged in the workplace learning process (Gracia, 2010, p. 61). Gracia (2010) concludes that this cohort of students struggles to assimilate with the work environment, displays a resistance to workplace practices that challenge their basic technical knowledge and do not capitalise on opportunities to develop communication skills.

Students' Perceptions of Oral Communication Skills in Practice: The Need for Research

Research cited previously in the discussion of barriers identifies a widely-held perception among accounting students that listening and other oral communication skills are unimportant in the professional workplace (Arquero *et al.*, 2007; Meixner *et al.*, 2009; Ameen, Jackson and Malgwi 2010; Gray and Murray, 2011). This barrier to developing accounting students' listening skills conflicts with the profession's view that accountants need to be proficient oral communicators and effective listeners (Gray and Murray, 2011). Students' perceptions may be formed by stereotypes that influence their opinion of the attributes required to be an accountant (Ameen, Jackson and Malgwi, 2010). Hunt, Falgiani and Intrieri's (2004) study of accounting majors' perceptions of accountants finds that an anti-social stereotype exists, which is created by unflattering film and television portrayals. The stereotype infers that accounting is a haven for the uncommunicative and reclusive (Albrecht and Sack, 2000; Hunt, Falgiani and Intrieri, 2004). Ameen, Jackson and Malgwi's (2010, p. 42) assertion that 'when little is known about an occupation, stereotypes are all that remain for formulating [students'] opinion' warrants comment. Students need to carry out informed research on their career choices. It is arguably alarming that students are either drawn to or rejecting careers in accounting based on fictional portrayals in television and film. Students should be encouraged to discuss the profession and what it entails with practitioners and by researching accounting firms' and the professional bodies' websites. Where students are attracted to accounting due to the mistaken belief that it requires minimal oral communication, including listening, there exists 'a mismatch ... and potential for future frustration' (Arquero *et al.*, 2007, p. 317). This frustration has materialised in some graduates' high levels of resistance to their employers' attempts to develop their deficient oral communication skills (Gray and Murray, 2011). Work experience students interviewed by Gracia (2010, p. 59) who perceive that 'accountancy is really about being good with numbers and understanding the rules so I don't focus so much on the people around me' reported feelings of frustration, isolation and alienation about their work experience in an accounting firm and found it 'difficult to fit in'.

The Profession's Role

This section discusses the role of the third stakeholder in the proposed integrated stakeholder approach to developing accounting students' listening, the accounting profession, comprising the professional accounting bodies and employers of accounting graduates. The professional bodies have a role to play in altering students' perceptions that oral communication, including listening, skills are unimportant in practice and that students can attain sufficient skills to be successful in practice merely by having enrolled in a university programme. It is also contended that the professional bodies hold unrealistic expectations about educators' capacity to produce graduates who are effective listeners. An alternative approach is presented, which considers the impact of lifelong learning on the development of students' listening skills. The section concludes by considering employers' role in providing work experience that facilitates students' listening development.

Altering Students' Perceptions

Previous research recommends that more work is needed by the profession to rectify students' perception that accounting is a career that requires minimal oral communication (Hunt, Falgiani and Intrieri, 2004; Ameen, Jackson and Malgwi, 2010). Albrecht and Sack (2000, p. 29) caution that a lack of reliable information and considerable misinformation about what accountants do 'is serious because students' perceptions of accounting are not compatible with the creative, rewarding, people-oriented careers that many students envision for themselves'. Providing accurate information also minimises the potential for student disillusionment and frustration after graduation (Albrecht and Sack, 2000). Ameen, Jackson and Malgwi (2010) argue that it is the professional bodies' role to develop marketing strategies that emphasise the importance of listening and other oral communication skills in practice. In this regard, the Institute of Chartered Accountants in Australia's 'Number One in Numbers' marketing campaign (The ICAA, 2012) is a puzzling strategy, which may not contribute to shifting the image of accountants needing to deal only with numerical data.

The profession's role in altering students' perceptions about listening and other oral communication skills extends to engaging with students and their sources of career advice. As many students formulate their career plans and associated programme of study during high school, researchers advise the profession to engage with high school students, their parents and teachers, who influence students' decision-making (Hardin, O'Bryan and Quirin, 2000; Hunt, Falgiani and Intrieri, 2004). Studies show that high school teachers have a generally low opinion of accounting, viewing it as a career requiring little interaction with others and limited communication skills that offers students uninteresting and unsatisfying work (Hardin, O'Bryan and Quirin, 2000; Wells and Fieger, 2006). Wells and Fieger (2006) suggest that some teachers may in fact be guiding students who possess excellent communication skills away from accounting careers. Researchers recommend that the professional bodies address these negative perceptions by devoting resources to promoting career paths in accounting and the skills sought by the profession to high school students and their parents and teachers (Wells and Fieger, 2006; Ameen, Jackson and Malgwi, 2010). Hunt, Falgiani and Intrieri (2004) advocate a stronger presence by the profession at career events, where students and teachers form important impressions by meeting industry representatives. Students who have personal contact with accountants hold more favourable impressions of accounting as a career than students who base their impressions on the stereotypes that accounting is 'tedious numbers-related work' (Albrecht and Sack, 2000, p. 28; Hunt, Falgiani and Intrieri, 2004). This reinforces Hardin, O'Bryan and Quirin's (2000, p. 217) contention that the profession needs to 'personally deliver the message' to high school students and their parents and teachers that accounting offers stimulating people-oriented careers that require, among other attributes, strong oral communication and listening skills.

It is argued that the professional bodies and employers should also disseminate this important message to university accounting students during guest lectures and presentations and as a feature of the campaigns that seek to recruit new members and graduate employees. This would augment and add valuable endorsement to accounting educators' attempts to inform and reinforce the importance of listening. To further demonstrate the interrelated roles of the stakeholders in the proposed integrated stakeholder approach, the above-mentioned examples from the literature, which educators use to reinforce the importance of listening, may be utilised by the professional bodies and employers in the information disseminated to students.

Professional Bodies' Unrealistic Listening Expectations

Professional accounting body accreditation is critical for accounting programmes. Programmes with the imprimatur of accreditation demonstrate that their curriculum addresses the technical and generic skill base that the professional bodies regard as necessary 'to ensure the suitability of graduates' (The ICAA and CPA Australia, 2011, p. iii). As a result, the professional bodies significantly influence accounting education. Wessels and Steenkamp's (2009) transnational study of the skill requirements of seven national bodies identifies a common interest in accounting students' communication skills.[4] For example, the Australian professional bodies are adamant that communication skills, including listening, are 'essential' and that they should be '*effectively developed* throughout the full range of [university programme] courses' (The ICAA and CPA Australia, 2011, p. 3, emphasis added).

Whether the professional bodies' expectations are realistic is the subject of considerable debate. Irrespective of educators' best efforts, research 'casts doubt on the assumption that these [communication] skills can be effectively developed within classrooms' (Little, 2003; Cranmer, 2006, p. 172). Educators are unable to replicate the professional workplace's ongoing training, mentoring and daily exposure to disciplinary discourse. This dimension of the accounting workplace creates the optimal setting to develop listening and other communication skills (Courtis and Zaid, 2002; Cranmer, 2006; Jackling and de Lange, 2009; Jones, 2010). According to Henderson (2001, p. 399), expectations that educators will significantly develop students' communication skills is based on the 'heroic' and mistaken assumption that students have acquired sufficient preparatory communication skills at school. In the absence of this formative skills development, many accounting students' communication skills require substantial remedial attention. It is arguably unreasonable to expect university educators to first remedy this skills deficit and then effectively develop communication skills, while ensuring that students have satisfactorily completed the technical accounting content that the professional bodies prescribe, all within the confines of a typically three-year undergraduate programme.

The core education value of lifelong learning presents the professional bodies with a basis to set realistic expectations regarding the development of students' listening and other communication skills. Lifelong learning has been embraced by the professional bodies and many accounting higher education providers (Jackling and de Lange, 2009). Invoking its role in listening skills development does not require the adoption of unfamiliar learning concepts. The notion of lifelong learning contributing to accounting students' listening development is supported by studies that determine that communication skills are developed by a range of factors, including age, experience and maturity (Lucas *et al.*, 2004; Gray and Murray, 2011). Undergraduate accounting students interviewed by Lucas *et al.* (2004, p. 66) believe that such skills are acquired and developed as 'a part of growing up'. Consequently, it is the experience of many students that their communication skills development is unfulfilled during their university studies (Lucas *et al.*, 2004).

Fogarty (2010) eloquently summarises the impact of lifelong learning on students' and practitioners' skills. Accountants aspire to be professionals. Professionalism combines generic skills and the specific culture and knowledge base of the accounting profession and 'can only be mastered over a lifetime and through the guidance of more experienced members of the guild' (Fogarty, 2010, p. 411). Barrie's (2004) study of an Australian university's graduate attributes illustrates the favourable outcome of setting expectations with regard to lifelong learning. The University of Sydney subjected its graduate attributes, including communication, to a research based review. An outcome of this process is that the University now offers the employment market graduates who 'will recognise and value communication as a tool for negotiating and creating new understanding, interacting with others, and furthering their own learning' (Barrie, 2004, p. 270). The graduate attribute incorporates lifelong learning. Conspicuously, there is no suggestion of graduates entering the workplace with effectively developed listening and communication skills. Finally, by declaring that communication skills are to be recognised and valued, the statement sends a strong motivating signal to students.

By setting realistic expectations, it is contended that the professional bodies can make a significant contribution to students' listening development. The trickledown effect of the professional bodies' expectations is considerable. To demonstrate, Barrie (2004) is critical of the wording of universities' graduate attributes, which need to satisfy the professional accrediting bodies' expectations. According to Barrie (2004, p. 261), the claim made in graduate attributes that graduates will possess a range of well developed generic skills is 'rhetoric' that is not generally supported by successful outcomes and research findings. Realistic expectations would better guide and motivate educators who are confronted by a crowded curriculum and other barriers that inhibit wider incorporation of listening development in subject design (Jackling and de Lange, 2009). They would also better reflect the expectations of the professional bodies' member practitioners who employ graduates. Employers have stated that they do not expect that graduates will possess well developed listening and other oral communication skills (Gray, 2010) and acknowledge that such skills need further development through workplace training and continuing education (Cranmer, 2006; de Lange, Jackling and Gut, 2006).

Work Experience: Employers' Role in Facilitating Listening Development

As discussed, students' role in developing their listening skills includes recognising the value of listening and using work experience and other non-academic interactions as an opportunity to develop this skill (Gracia, 2010). Employers have an interrelated role in providing work experience that facilitates the development of students' listening and other oral communication skills. UK accounting students interviewed by Gracia (2009) perceive that communication skills were undervalued within the workplaces where their work experience occurred. This finding may be contrasted with Paisey and Paisey's (2010) study of Scottish accounting students and Beck and Halim's (2008) study of Singaporean students, who generally describe their work experience as a rewarding and engaging experience that developed their oral communication skills. Nonetheless, cases of students experiencing isolation, not meeting or seeing their supervisor and being required to spend an inordinate amount of time filing and photocopying warrant employers' attention (Gracia, 2009; 2010). Reports of student anxiety and uncertainty about what work experience will entail also merit attention (Gracia, 2010). Thus, in addition to providing meaningful work experience, the employers' role may extend to presenting to students and describing what the experience will involve and the skills that work experience can develop.

Implications for Stakeholders

Based on the preceding discussion, the proposed integrated stakeholder approach has a number of implications for each stakeholder, both individually and as joint contributors to students' listening development. To aid discussion of the approach's implications, the stakeholders' various roles are summarised in Table 2. This summary also provides the reader who is considering utilising the proposed approach with a useful tool by way of a concise point of reference.

Table 2 demonstrates a key feature of the proposed approach: that many of the stakeholders' roles are interrelated. To illustrate, the roles summarised in Table 2 about extracting EAL best practice involve the stakeholders undertaking interrelated roles to maximise the opportunities that work experience and other non-academic interactions offer to develop students' listening. Where a stakeholder does not engage in the proposed approach and execute their role, the potential to develop students' listening diminishes.

Turning to implications for educators, despite the crowded accounting curriculum, educators cannot delegate students' listening development to colleagues from other disciplines. This would disconnect students' listening development from the disciplinary context of accounting's knowledge base and the needs of graduates' employers. Table 2 indicates that educators are assigned the largest number of roles in the proposed approach. However, it is contended that the roles are realistic and achievable. Furthermore, they are developed with regard to the barriers that impede wider incorporation of listening development in the accounting curriculum.

The implications for students under the proposed approach are considerable. In a higher education sector that is increasingly adopting the hallmarks of commercialisation, including higher student fees, students are more likely to envision that they are clients (Parker, 2011). Students who hold this view are also likely to expect that educators will provide the student-client with a comprehensive service. The authors do not subscribe to this view. As shown in Table 2, the proposed approach assigns a number of explicit roles to students, both within and outside the accounting classroom. It is argued that for tangible listening development to occur during students' relatively short time at university, students need to engage with and participate in academic and non-academic listening development opportunities.

The accounting profession's interrelated role of augmenting educators' attempts to inform and reinforce the significance of listening is important. It adds the professional endorsement that listening is a valuable skill in practice. Potentially favourable outcomes include greater student engagement in listening development and a breaking down of the widely-held student perception that listening and other oral communication skills are unimportant in accounting careers. The profession needs to deliver this message in its communications and interactions with students, including the interactions proposed in the integrated stakeholder approach.

By bringing together the stakeholders, the proposed approach provides opportunities to devise assessment that evidences listening learning outcomes. Challenges to assessing listening are a barrier to listening instruction in the curriculum. Educators could consult and work with the professional bodies and their member practitioners to design listening role plays that mirror listening scenarios in the professional workplace. For instance, role plays where students act as practitioners and clients could occur in classes. Educators and practitioners would jointly assess the role plays and provide students with both academic and practical feedback on their listening performances.

Finally, it is recommended that each stakeholder should adopt realistic expectations. The highly-developed listening skills exhibited by experienced accountants are produced

Table 2. Stakeholders' listening development roles.

Accounting educators	Accounting students	The profession
Apply disciplinary context to listening development with regard to accounting's specific skills, discourse and the requirements of accounting employers	Engage with educators' attempts to apply disciplinary context to listening development	Use lifelong learning as a basis for realistic expectations for students' listening development to motivate and guide educators and reflect employers' expectations
Inform students and reinforce the importance of listening in accounting practice during large classes and small class discussions		Augment and add professional endorsement to educators' attempts to reinforce the importance of listening in accounting practice in interactions with students
Alter students' perception that listening and other oral communication skills are unimportant in practice	Conduct research to ascertain the importance of listening and other oral communication skills in practice. Critically assess stereotypes of accounting careers	Develop marketing strategies that reinforce the importance of oral communication, including listening, in practice. Engage with students to emphasise the communication aspects of accounting careers
Utilise examples from literature to reinforce the importance of listening in practice		Utilise examples from literature to reinforce the importance of listening in practice in interactions with students
Enlist employers of accounting graduates to present to students to reinforce the importance of listening in practice and its desirable graduate skill status		Present to students and conduct guest lectures to reinforce the importance of listening in practice and its status as a sought-after graduate skill
Extract liberal arts best practice: four stages of the Alverno model, with at least the first two stages taught in stand-alone communication subjects Accounting educators utilise the model's third and final stages in accounting classes. Emphasise that self-assessment and goal-setting facilitate self-regulated learning skills	Engage with the four stages of the Alverno model in stand-alone communication subjects and accounting subjects. Practice using the model's listening filters Undertake critical self-assessment and listening goal-setting to develop listening and self-regulated learning skills	Reinforce in interactions with students that self-regulated learning is a desirable graduate skill
Extract EAL best practice: make explicit the link between students' non-academic interactions and listening development	Undertake non-academic interactions, including work experience. Exploit non-academic opportunities to develop listening skills	Provide meaningful work experience that may develop students' listening skills. Present to students about what work experience involves and the skills that it may develop

(Continued)

Table 2. Continued

Accounting educators	Accounting students	The profession
Reinforce the expectation that students prepare for class discussions to facilitate listening development	Prepare for class discussions to enable contributions by a range of speakers and increased listening opportunities	

by substantial professional practice, workplace training and ongoing communication with clients and colleagues (Gray and Murray, 2011; Stone and Lightbody, 2012). Their developed listening exemplifies the lifelong learning that providers of accounting programmes and the professional accounting bodies espouse and which is recognised in this proposed approach to developing accounting students' listening skills (see Figure 1).

Concluding Comments, Limitations and Suggestions for Further Research

Today's accountant is expected to be a dexterous communicator and effective listener. Listening is part of the portfolio of generic skills that are highly regarded by the employers of accounting graduates. Hence, students' listening development is receiving increasing attention. Accounting education practices that contribute to developing students' listening skills are, however, uncommon. Simply recommending that educators do more to instil listening skills into students overlooks barriers to the greater incorporation of listening instruction in the accounting curriculum. Alternative approaches to develop students' listening warrant exploration. Based on a review of the relevant accounting education literature and related research conducted in other disciplines, this paper has proposed an integrated stakeholder approach to developing accounting students' listening skills. The proposed approach articulates and recognises the barriers to greater coverage of listening in accounting subjects and identifies resultant opportunities for educators and other stakeholders to make a feasible contribution to students' listening development. This is a significant departure from the prevailing reliance on educators to meet the demand for graduates who possess a range of generic attributes, despite the existence of barriers that inhibit what educators can realistically accomplish. A critical feature of the integrated stakeholder approach lies in the assignment of interrelated listening development roles to the stakeholders who stand to benefit from improved student listening skills. Accounting students and the profession join educators in undertaking realistic and interrelated roles that contribute to students' listening development.

There are limitations to this paper. However, these limitations provide a basis for future research, which indicates that listening development in the accounting curriculum is fertile ground for further scholarly enquiry. The development of the listening skills of accounting students who undertake distance learning and external study was not considered. This student cohort does not attend classes and is unable to participate in the classroom activities and discussions that facilitate listening development. Further research could investigate educator and student use of virtual face-to-face communication technologies, such as Skype, as a method to develop the listening skills of external and distance learners. The liberal arts and EAL listening initiatives that are identified as best practice listening initiatives demonstrate the potential to extract and apply listening developments from other disciplines in accounting education. Future studies could identify additional cross-disciplinary initiatives that may be applied by accounting educators to develop their students' listening skills. The debate among accounting educators about the emphasis on developing students' 'hard' technical skills over their 'soft' generic skills, including listening, presents interesting further research opportunities. Researchers may productively investigate practices which facilitate simultaneous development of both skills bases. Finally, space limitations have not permitted the exploration of developing the listening of the substantial number of students who undertake accounting programmes in languages other than English. *Accounting Education: an international journal*'s global readership is encouraged to join the authors in proposing pedagogical practices which may develop the listening of students across the rich spectrum of languages which comprise the international accounting community.

Acknowledgements

The authors wish to acknowledge the guidance of the anonymous reviewers and participants at the 2012 AFAANZ conference in Melbourne, Australia, which greatly improved this paper.

Notes

[1]Listening skills encompass the ability to interpret both the verbal information and the non-verbal information which that a speaker conveys by way of their facial and physical expressions during face-to-face communication (Agrawal and Schmidt, 2003; Brown and Barker, 2001).

[2]The term 'subject' refers to the courses, units or modules which that comprise a degree programme.

[3]Further consideration of this 'realignment of accounting education between universities and professional bodies' (Jackling and de Lange, 2009, p. 381) lies beyond the scope of this paper's focus.

[4]The bodies are the Institute of Chartered Accountants in Australia (ICAA), CPA Australia, the Canadian Institute of Chartered Accountants (CICA), the Institute of Chartered Accountants in England and Wales (ICAEW), the American Institute of Certified Public Accountants (AICPA), the New Zealand Institute of Chartered Accountants (NZICA) and the South African Institute of Chartered Accountants (SAICA).

References

Agrawal, M. L. and Schmidt, M. (2003) Listening quality of the point of service personnel (PSPs) as impulse trigger in service purchase: a research framework, *Journal of Services Research*, 3(1), pp. 29–43.

Albrecht, W. S. and Sack, R. J. (2000) Accounting education: charting the course through a perilous future, *Accounting Education Series*, p. 16 (Sarasota, FL: American Accounting Association).

Alverno College. (2012) Available at http://www.alverno.edu/aboutalverno/quickfacts/ (accessed 16 August 2012).

Ameen, E., Jackson, C. and Malgwi, C. (2010) Student perceptions of oral communication requirements in the accounting profession, *Global Perspectives on Accounting Education*, 7, pp. 31–49.

Andrews, J. D. and Sigband, N. B. (1984) How effectively does the 'new' accountant communicate? Perceptions by practitioners and academics, *Journal of Business Communication*, 21(2), pp. 15–24.

Arquero, J. L., Hassall, T., Joyce, J. and Donoso, J. A. (2007) Accounting students and communication apprehension: a study of Spanish and UK Ssudents, *European Accounting Review*, 16(2), pp. 299–322.

Ballantine, J. and Larres, P. (2009) Accounting undergraduates' perceptions of cooperative learning as a model for enhancing their interpersonal and communication skills to interface successfully with professional accountancy education and training, *Accounting Education: An International Journal*, 18(4-5), pp. 387–402.

Barrie, S. C. (2004) A research-based approach to generic graduate attributes policy, *Higher Education Research and Development*, 23(3), pp. 261–275.

Beall, M. L., Gill-Rosier, J., Tate, J. and Matten, A. (2008) State of the context: listening in education, *The International Journal of Listening*, 22(2), pp. 123–132.

Beck, J. E. and Halim, H. (2008) Undergraduate internships in accounting: what and how do Singapore interns learn from experience? *Accounting Education: An International Journal*, 17(2), pp. 151–172.

Borden, V. M. H. and Evenbeck, S. E. (2007) Changing the minds of new college students, *Tertiary Education and Management*, 13(2), pp. 153–167.

Brown, N. A. and Barker, R. T. (2001) Analysis of the communication components found within the situational leadership model: toward integration of communication and the model, *Journal of Technical Writing and Communication*, 31(2), pp. 135–157.

Bui, B. and Porter, B. (2010) The expectation-performance gap in accounting education: an exploratory study, *Accounting Education: An International Journal*, 19(1-2), pp. 23–50.

Carr, S., Chua, F. and Perera, H. (2006) University accounting curricula: the perceptions of an alumni group, *Accounting Education: An International Journal*, 15(4), pp. 359–376.

Cassidy, S. (2011) Self-regulated learning in higher education: identifying key component processes, *Studies in Higher Education*, 36(8), pp. 989–1000.

Chand, R. K. (2007) Same size doesn't fit all: insights from research on listening skills at the University of the South Pacific (USP), *International Review of Research in Open and Distance Learning*, 8(3), pp. 1–22.

Cooper, L. O. (1997) Listening competency in the workplace: a model for training, *Business Communication Quarterly*, 60(4), pp. 75–84.

Courtis, J. K. and Zaid, O. A. (2002) Early employment problems of Australian accounting graduates: an exploratory study, *Accounting Forum*, 26(3), pp. 320–339.

Craig, R. and McKinney, C. N. (2010) A successful competency-based writing skills development programme: results of an Experiment, *Accounting Education: An International Journal*, 19(3), pp. 257–278.

Cranmer, S. (2006) Enhancing graduate employability: best intentions and mixed outcomes, *Studies in Higher Education*, 31(2), pp. 169–184.

Cuseo, J. (2007) The empirical case against large class size: adverse effects on the teaching, learning, and retention of first-year students, *The Journal of Faculty Development*, 21(1), pp. 5–21.

D'Aloisio, A. (2006) Motivating students through awareness of the natural correlation between college learning and corporate work settings, *College Teaching*, 54(2), pp. 225–230.

Doran, J., Healy, M., McCutcheon, M. and O'Callaghan, S. (2011) Adapting case-based teaching to large class settings: an action research approach, *Accounting Education: An International Journal*, 20(3), pp. 245–263.

Evans, E. and Rigby, B. (2008) Integrating academic literacy skills in an elective intermediate accounting subject, *Asian Social Science*, 4(3), pp. 59–65.

Farrell, B. and Farrell, H. (2008) Student satisfaction with co-operative learning in an accounting curriculum, *Journal of University Teaching and Learning Practice*, 5(2), pp. 39–54.

Finney, T. G. and Finney, R. Z. (2010) Are students their universities' customers? An exploratory study, *Education + Training*, 52(4), pp. 276–291.

Flynn, J., Valikoski, T. and Grau, J. (2008) Listening in the business context: reviewing the state of research, *The International Journal of Listening*, 22(2), pp. 141–151.

Fogarty, T. J. (2010) Revitalizing accounting education: a highly applied liberal arts approach, *Accounting Education: An International Journal*, 19(4), pp. 403–419.

Fortin, A. and Legault, M. (2010) Development of generic competencies: impact of a mixed teaching approach on students' perceptions, *Accounting Education: An International Journal*, 19(1-2), pp. 93–122.

Fredman, N. and Doughney, J. (2012) Academic dissatisfaction, managerial change and neo-liberalism, *Higher Education*, 64(1), pp. 41–58.

Freeman, M. and Hancock, P. (2011) A brave new world: Australian learning outcomes in accounting education, *Accounting Education: An International Journal*, 20(3), pp. 265–273.

Gabriel, S. L. and Hirsch, M. L. (1992) Critical thinking and communication skills: integration and implementation issues, *Journal of Accounting Education*, 10(2), pp. 243–270.

Gardner, C., Milne, M. J., Stringer, C. and Whiting, R. (2005) Oral and written communication apprehension in accounting students: curriculum impacts and impacts on academic performance, *Accounting Education: An International Journal*, 14(3), pp. 313–336.

Gouws, D. G. and Terblanche, A. B. (1998) The accountant as a facilitator of communication, *Meditari Accountancy Research*, 6, pp. 91–119.

Grace, D. M. and Gilsdorf, J. W. (2004) Classroom strategies for improving students' oral communication skills, *Journal of Accounting Education*, 22(2), pp. 165–172.

Gracia, L. (2009) Employability and higher education: contextualising female students' workplace experiences to enhance understanding of employability development, *Journal of Education and Work*, 22(4), pp. 301–318.

Gracia, L. (2010) Accounting students' expectations and transition experiences of supervised work experience, *Accounting Education: An International Journal*, 19(1-2), pp. 51–64.

Graham, S. (2011) Self-efficacy and academic listening, *Journal of English for Academic Purposes*, 10(2), pp. 113–117.

Graham, A., Hampton, M. and Willett, C. (2009) What not to write: an intervention in written communication skills for accounting students, *International Journal of Management Education*, 8(2), pp. 67–74.

Gray, F. E. (2010) Specific oral communication skills desired in new accountancy graduates, *Business Communication Quarterly*, 73(1), pp. 40–67.

Gray, F. E. and Murray, N. (2011) 'A distinguishing factor': oral communication skills in new accountancy graduates, *Accounting Education: An International Journal*, 20(3), pp. 275–294.

Hancock, P., Howieson, B., Kavanagh, M., Kent, J., Tempone, I. and Segal, N. (2009) *Accounting for the Future: More Than Numbers. A Collaborative Investigation into the Changing Skill Set for Professional Accounting Graduates over the Next Ten Years and Strategies for Embedding Such Skills into Professional Accounting Programs* (Sydney: Australian Learning and Teaching Council).

Hardin, J. R., O'Bryan, D. and Quirin, J. J. (2000) Accounting versus engineering, law, and medicine: perceptions of influential high school teachers, *Advances in Accounting*, 17, pp. 205–220.

Hartley, J. (2007) Reading, writing, speaking and listening: perspectives in applied linguistics, *Applied Linguistics*, 28(2), pp. 316–320.

Hassall, T., Joyce, J., Arquero Montano, J., Donoso Anes, J. (2003) The vocational skills gap for management accountants: the stakeholders' perspectives, *Innovations in Education and Teaching International*, 40(1), pp. 78–88.

Hassel, H. and Lourey, J. (2005) The dea(r)th of student responsibility, *College Teaching*, 53(1), pp. 2–13.

Henderson, S. (2001) The education of accountants – a comment, *Accounting Forum*, 25(4), pp. 398–401.

Hirsch, M. L., Anderson, R. and Gabriel, S. (1994) *Accounting & Communication* (Cincinnati: South-Western Publishing Co).

Howieson, B. (2003) Accounting practice in the new millennium: is accounting education ready to meet the challenge? *The British Accounting Review*, 35(2), pp. 69–103.

Hunt, S. C., Falgiani, A. A. and Intrieri, R. C. (2004) The nature and origins of students' perceptions of accountants, *Journal of Education for Business*, 79(3), pp. 142–148.

Jackling, B. and de Lange, P. (2009) Do accounting graduates' skills meet the expectations of employers? A matter of convergence or divergence, *Accounting Education: An International Journal*, 18(4-5), pp. 369–385.

Jackling, B. and McDowall, T. (2008) Peer mentoring in an accounting setting: a case study of mentor skill development, *Accounting Education: An International Journal*, 17(4), pp. 447–462.

Jones, A. (2010) Generic attributes in accounting: the significance of the disciplinary context, *Accounting Education: An International Journal*, 19(1-2), pp. 5–21.

Jones, C. G. (2011) Written and computer-mediated accounting communication skills: an employer perspective, *Business Communication Quarterly*, 74(3), pp. 247–271.

Jones, R. A. and Lancaster, K. A. S. (2001) Process mapping and scripting in the accounting information systems (AIS) curriculum, *Accounting Education*, 10(3), pp. 263–278.

Juchau, R. and Galvin, M. (1984) Communication skills of accountants in Australia, *Accounting and Finance*, 24(1), pp. 17–32.

Keneley, M. and Jackling, B. (2011) The acquisition of generic skills of culturally-diverse student cohorts, *Accounting Education: An International Journal*, 20(6), pp. 605–623.

Kerby, D. and Romine, J. (2009) Develop oral presentation skills through accounting curriculum design and course-embedded assessment, *Journal of Education for Business*, 85(3), pp. 172–179.

KPMG. (2012) What we look for. Available at www.kpmg.com/au/en/joinus/graduates-students/what-we-look-for/Pages/default.aspx (accessed 1 September 2012).

Kuh, G. (1995) The other curriculum: out-of-class experiences associated with student learning and personal development, *The Journal of Higher Education*, 66(2), pp. 123–155.

de Lange, P. A. (2005) The long road to publishing: a user-friendly exposé, *Accounting Education: An International Journal*, 14(2), pp. 133–168.

de Lange, P., Jackling, B. and Gut, A. (2006) Accounting graduates' perceptions of skills emphasis in undergraduate courses: an investigation from two Victorian universities, *Accounting and Finance*, 46(3), pp. 365–386.

Little, B. (2003) International perspectives on employability, Briefing Paper, York, The Higher Education Academy. Available at http://www.heacademy.ac.uk (accessed 7 August 2011).

Lucas, U., Cox, P., Croudace, C. and Milford, P. (2004) Who writes this stuff? Students' perceptions of their skills development, *Teaching in Higher Education*, 9(1), pp. 55–68.

Lynch, T. (2011) Academic listening in the 21st century: reviewing a decade of research, *Journal of English for Academic Purposes*, 10(2), pp. 79–88.

Marriott, N. (2004) Using computerized business simulations and spreadsheet models in accounting education: a case study, *Accounting Education*, 13(S1), pp. 55–70.

Mathews, R., Jackson, M. and Brown, P. (1990) *Accounting in Higher Education: Report of the Review of the Accounting Discipline in Higher Education: Volume 1* (Canberra, ACT: Australian Government).

McGowan, S. and Lightbody, M. (2008) Enhancing students' understanding of plagiarism within a discipline context, *Accounting Education: An International Journal*, 17(3), pp. 273–290.

Meixner, W. F., Bline, D., Lowe, D. R. and Nouri, H. (2009) An examination of business student perceptions: the effect of math and communication skill apprehension on choice of major, *Advances in Accounting Behavioral Research*, 12, pp. 185–200.

Miller, T. C. and Stone, D. N. (2009) Public speaking apprehension (PSA), motivation, and affect among accounting majors: a proof-of-concept intervention, *Issues in Accounting Education*, 24(3), pp. 265–298.

Misko, J. (1995) *Transfer: Using Learning in New Contexts* (Leabrook, SA: National Centre for Vocational Education Research).

Mitchell, V. W. and Bakewell, C. (1995) Learning without doing: enhancing oral presentation skills through peer review, *Journal of Management Learning*, 26(3), pp. 353–366.

Morell, T. (2007) What enhances EFL students' participation in lecture discourse? Student, lecturer and discourse perspectives, *Journal of English for Academic Purposes*, 6(3), pp. 222–237.

Morgan, G. J. (1997) Communication skills required by accounting graduates: practitioner and academic perceptions, *Accounting Education*, 6(2), pp. 93–107.

Morley, J. (2001) Aural comprehension instructions: principles and practices, in: M. Celce-Mercia (Ed.) *Teaching English as a Second or Foreign Language*, 3rd edn, pp. 69–85 (Boston: Heinle & Heinle Publishers).

Paisey, C. and Paisey, N. J. (2010) Developing skills via work placements in accounting: student and employer views, *Accounting Forum*, 34(2), pp. 89–108.

Parker, L. D. (2011) University corporatisation: driving redefinition, *Critical Perspectives on Accounting*, 22(4), pp. 434–450.

Pearce, C. G., Johnson, I. W. and Barker, R. T. (1995) Enhancing the student listening skills and environment, *Business Communication Quarterly*, 58(4), pp. 28–33.

Rowley-Jolivet, E. (2002) Visual discourse in scientific conference papers: a genre-based study, *English for Specific Purposes*, 21(1), pp. 19–40.

Sin, S., Jones, A. and Petocz, P. (2007) Evaluating a method of integrating generic skills with accounting content based on a functional theory of meaning, *Accounting and Finance*, 47(1), pp. 143–163.

Stone, G. and Lightbody, M. (2012) The nature and significance of listening skills in accounting practice, *Accounting Education: An International Journal*, 21(4), pp. 363–384.

Tan, L., Fowler, M. and Hawkes, L. (2004) Management accounting curricula: striking a balance between the views of educators and practitioners, *Accounting Education*, 13(1), pp. 51–67.

Tempone, I., Kavanagh, M., Segal, N., Hancock, P., Howieson, B. and Kent, J. (2012) Desirable generic attributes for accounting graduates into the twenty-first century: the views of employers, *Accounting Research Journal*, 25(1), pp. 41–55.

The Institute of Chartered Accountants in Australia (The ICAA). (2012) Available at http://www.charteredaccountants.com.au (accessed 26 August 2012).

The Institute of Chartered Accountants in Australia (The ICAA) and CPA Australia. (2011) Professional Accreditation Guidelines for Higher Education Programs. Available at http://www.cpaaustralia.com.au/cps/rde/xbcr/cpasite/Professional_accreditation_guidelines_for_higher_education_programs.pdf (accessed 25 August 2011).

Thompson, K., Leintz, P., Nevers, B. and Witkowski, S. (2004) The integrative listening model: an approach to teaching and learning listening, *The Journal of General Education*, 53(3-4), pp. 225–246.

Vandergrift, L. (2004) Listening to learn or learning to listen? *Annual Review of Applied Linguistics*, 24, pp. 3–25.

Webb, L., De Lange, P. and O'Connell, B. (2009) A programme to expose students to senior executives in the world of accounting: an innovative learning method, *Accounting Education: An International Journal*, 18(2), pp. 183–205.

Wells, P. and Fieger, P. (2006) High school teachers' perceptions of accounting: an international study, *Australian Journal of Accounting Education*, 2(1), pp. 29–51.

Wessels, P. L. and Steenkamp, L. P. (2009) An investigation into students' perceptions of accountants, *Meditari Accountancy Research*, 17(1), pp. 117–132.

Willcoxson, L., Wynder, M. and Laing, K. L. (2010) A whole-of-program approach to the development of generic and professional skills in a university accounting program, *Accounting Education: An International Journal*, 19(1–2), pp. 65–91.

Zaid, O. A. and Abraham, A. (1994) Communication skills in accounting education: perceptions of academics, employers, and graduate accountants, *Accounting Education*, 3(3), pp. 205–221.

Zimmerman, B. J. (2002) Becoming a self-regulated learner: an overview, *Theory into Practice*, 41(2), pp. 64–70.

Accounting Students in an Australian University Improve their Writing: But How Did it Happen?

GILLIAN DALE-JONES*, PHIL HANCOCK* and KEITH WILLEY**

*University of Western Australia, Crawley, Perth, Australia; **University of Technology, Sydney, Australia

ABSTRACT   The ability to communicate – orally and in writing – is a graduate attribute that employers in many countries rank as number one in importance, aside from relevant qualifications. This paper reports the implementation and evaluation of a collaborative peer assessment and self-assessment learning and teaching (L&T) initiative, which was designed to improve postgraduate students' judgment of writing standards and to improve their own writing – according to that standard. The initiative was embedded in an introductory financial accounting unit in an Australian university. In a mixed methods study, the matched pair design revealed improvements in the written communication skills of students as determined by an independent assessor. There was also statistically significant improvement in the ability of students to apply assessment standards to grammatical, structural and presentation components of written communication. Whereas it was not possible to attribute the improvements entirely to the collaborative peer assessment initiative, our observations and students' self-reporting comments suggest that the L&T initiative was effective.

Introduction

The ability to communicate orally and in writing is probably the most important of the 'graduate attributes', which most universities aspire to, and it is certainly ranked first in the skills required/desired by employers of accounting graduates in Australia (Arnott and Carroll, 2012). However, the research literature on programs and strategies for teaching communications skills to higher education students is not compelling. Evans and Cable (2011, p. 324), reporting on research about discipline-based language interventions to improve English language skills, bemoan the lack of 'data sources that can be regarded as … robust, such as teachers' perceptions, diagnostic testing and improved pass rates'.

One of our reasons for undertaking the intervention and evaluation reported in this paper was to respond to Evans and Cable's exhortation. But our main motivation was the widespread criticism about the employability of many graduates from Masters conversion programs in Australia; these programs were initiated in the 1990s (and are still operating) to cater for the shortage of accountants in Australia. A report for CPA Australia (CPA Australia and Birrell, 2006, p. 16) claimed that many of the graduates from such conversion programs were not working in the profession because '[although] such graduates are generally technically proficient, and usually possess a strong work ethic, the problem lies with their communication skills'.

Our intervention, to improve the writing skills of 40 postgraduate students in a conversion program in an Australian university, was underpinned by assumptions about peer learning within a constructivist framework. We were encouraged by literature heralding the potential benefits from peer assessment and self-assessment activities, such as: it induces students to reflect and think critically about their assessment standards; and it improves students' judgment in applying such standards to their own writing (Boud, Cohen and Sampson, 1999; Brindley and Scoffield, 1998; Mowl and Pain, 1995; Searby and Ewers, 1997). Boud, Cohen and Sampson (1999, p. 415) also make the appealing claim that peer learning can yield the 'pragmatic' benefit of 'teaching and learning strategies to enable staff to cope without increasing their overall load'. We wish to acknowledge that our intervention was modeled on the one used in the Achievement Matters (AM) project – the external peer review of accounting learning standards jointly led by Freeman and Hancock (2011). As in the AM project, we used the Self and Peer Assessment Resource Kit (SPARK^{PLUS}) for the recording of assessors' decisions about a piece of work (Willey and Gardner, 2011a, 2011b).

In addressing the following two research questions, we relied on a combination of analysis of students' writing skills, surveys and self-reflection reports, aided by the capacity of SPARK^{PLUS} to assess judgment against benchmark standards:

(1) Does the use of peer and self-review and collaborative discussion improve students' ability to make better judgments about written communication skills?
(2) Does the use of peer review and collaborative discussion improve students' written communication skills?

The remainder of this paper is arranged into five sections. We begin with a *review of literature*, focusing on communication skills, constructivism and peer learning. Next we describe the *teaching and learning initiative*, evaluation *methods*, and the reporting and discussion of the evaluation *results*. Finally, in the *conclusion* we reflect critically on what was found and whether that makes a useful contribution to this important topic.

Literature Review

As mentioned in the introduction, in the 1990s several professional accounting programs were opportunistically created in Australian universities; these programs provided academic entry points for graduates without an undergraduate accounting or business degree who wished to enrol in the professional educational programs of CPA Australia (CPAA) and the Institute of Chartered Accountants in Australia (ICAA). The accreditation guidelines of these professional bodies, which represent the interests of the major employers of accounting graduates in Australia, incorporate the ALTC accounting learning standards, of which the ability of graduates to be able to 'justify and communicate accounting advice' is one (CPA and ICAA, 2012, p. 11). Interpersonal and communication skills are also included as professional skills in International Education Standard 3 (IES3) issued by the International Accounting Education Standards Board. IES 3 states professional accountants are expected to be able to 'present, discuss, report and defend views effectively through formal, informal, written and spoken communication' (IES 3, 2010, p. 50). We take these standards seriously and believe it is incumbent upon higher education providers to give high priority to the teaching of communication skills. However, we believe that striving for all graduates to be highly effective communicators is somewhat akin to 'the holy grail' – a goal that is revered but rarely achieved.

We now turn to the literature on communication skills, seeking examples of where teaching of communication in higher education has been effectively achieved, including projects concerned with students for whom English is an additional language.

Watty (2007) perceives a link between accounting academics' perceptions of the declining quality in accounting education and the low levels of students' English competency. The latter, she argues, affects students' ability to successfully complete assessment tasks such as essays, case studies and presentations listed under 'communication skills' (Watty, 2007, p. 26); hence lecturers have tended to shift from assessing students' ability to write, to assessing only their technical knowledge. The implication is that some students 'get the degree ... with an English language competency well below that expected for effective participation in the professional workforce' (p. 27).

However, there are examples in the higher education literature of successful interventions to address the literacy needs of diverse groups of students (e.g. Andrade, 2006; Evans and Cable, 2011; Lawrence, 2005; Shaw, Moore and Gandhidasan, 2007), and to integrate generic skills (e.g. Al-Mahmood and Gruba, 2007; Baik and Greig, 2009; Briguglio 2007). When reviewing interventions designed to improve students' communication skills, it is necessary to distinguish 'bolt-on' or remedial approaches from programs that are 'built in'. The 'bolt-on' programs tend to emphasise the 'deficit' in English competency of students from non-English linguistic and cultural backgrounds – in effect overlooking the often considerable linguistic skills of such students and, by implication, 'blaming' these students for their lack of English 'preparedness' (Lawrence, 2005, p. 244; see also Carroll, 2005; Wingate, 2006).

The preferred 'built in' or embedded approach entails content lecturers integrating their development of students' professional communication skills with their teaching of discipline content, and perhaps consulting with language or writing support teachers when special support is needed for some students. In this approach, ideally, integrated and adjunct workshops and small-group consultations are used to provide students with 'forms of social connection and activity that support learning' (McInnes, 2003, p. 14). Some researchers stress the importance of 'applied context' opportunities (i.e. contextually rich and professionally relevant) for students in developing their writing skills (Kern and Schultz, 2005; Tindale et al., 2006).

Baik and Greig (2009), working with architecture students, claim that their discipline-specific English language support programs improved students' academic performance. Other examples of successful collaborations at both a subject and program level include: the use of diagnostic tests marked by language teachers (Webb, English and Bonanno, 1995); and a whole-of-program approach in which language teachers worked with content lecturers on many aspects of teaching and assessment strategies for the majority of the subjects taught in the program (Evans et al., 2009). Sloan and Porter (2009) developed the CEM (contextualisation, embedding and mapping) program in the UK to provide English language support to international business students concurrent with their subject modules. In this program, *contextualisation* relates to the context in which the academic skills are presented and communicated to students; *embedding* entails the positioning within the overall academic program; and *mapping* refers to understanding students' needs in relation to language learning and timeliness of the 'English for academic purpose' delivery.

The reference above to McInnes' (2003) built-in intervention, with 'forms of social connection' alludes to theories of learning that are based on constructivist principles (cf. Oliver, 2000). Constructivism is conceived variously (e.g. Duffy and Cunningham, 1996; Simons, 1993), but what is common to its use is a shared emphasis on 'the role of the teacher, the student, and the cultural embeddedness of learning' (Nanjappa and Grant, 2003, p. 40). Constructivism is about active learning in a social context, where the learners are encouraged to draw on their experiences and interests to develop further understandings. Thus the learner constructs his/her knowing while endeavouring to make sense of the world on the basis of personal filters: experiences, goals, curiosities and beliefs (Cole, 1992). At the centre of the social construct theory is the notion that we all live in the world and, while we have our own experiences and beliefs, it is the individual who imposes meaning on the world rather than meaning being imposed on the individual (see Lucas, 2000; Lucas and Meyer, 2005; Lucas and Mladenovic, 2006a, 2006b).

We took the position that peer assessment and self-assessment are aligned with constructivism, although they are distinct concepts. Boud and Falchikov (1989, p. 529) define self-assessment as 'the involvement of learners in making judgments about their own learning, particularly about their achievements and the outcomes of their learning'. Presumably, the reflective nature of self-assessment has the potential to guide students in improving their own work. Topping (1998, p. 250) defines peer assessment as 'an arrangement in which individuals consider the amount, level, value, worth, quality, or success of the product or outcomes of learning of peers of similar status'.[1] Presumably, additional benefits are derived when the assessment of peers is done in a collaborative, teamwork context.

The benefits of self-assessment and peer assessment have been well documented.[2] In addition to their recognised ability to improve the operation and fairness of teamwork (Willey and Freeman, 2006a, 2006b), the two activities have been found to:

- increase student assessors' conscious understanding of the processes involved in the activity (even for strong students) (Searby and Ewers, 1997)
- improve students' understanding of assessment (Mowl and Pain, 1995)
- provide students with an opportunity to participate in the assessment process, which increases their motivation (Brindley and Scoffield, 1998)
- have the potential to assist students to develop important professional skills, such as reflection and critical thinking (Mello, 1993; Somervell, 1993).
- be a means of producing formative-learning-oriented feedback to complete the learning cycle and encourage the ongoing development of skills (Willey and Freeman, 2006a, 2006b)
- provide opportunities for students to develop and practise their judgment (Willey and Gardner, 2009).

In more general terms, Willey and Gardner (2010) report on the capacity of different types of self-assessment and peer assessment activities to engage students and promote learning; whereas Boud and Falchikov (2006) emphasise the long-term effects of these forms of assessment, linking them with the development of life-long learning skills.

However, some researchers have claimed instances when peer assessment was unsatisfactory and even deleterious, particularly in relation to essay writing (Mowl and Pain, 1995; Topping, 1998). For example, student assessors may not be willing to take responsibility for assessing their peers, particularly in small, socially cohesive groups (Falchikov, 1995; Topping, 1998). This effect is accentuated where students lack confidence in their competence to assess their peers, and where the feedback is required to be 'critical' (Ballantyne, Hughes and Mylonas, 2002). Associated with this concern is the effect (which is extremely difficult to detect and monitor) of conflicting power relationships between student assessors (Topping, 1998). Willey and Gardner (2010, p. 441) report on the competitive nature of some students in the learning environment, who may be reluctant to 'provide beneficial feedback to tasks that allow for resubmission, for fear of helping a fellow student to exceed their own final grade'. We tried to avoid these disadvantages by having students assess the written work of peers from a previous cohort, not of their current peers.

O'Donovan, Price and Rust (2001) found that from the students' perspective, the criteria assessment grid is a constructive means of providing feedback and improving the quality of work, providing the grid is part of a broader framework that includes 'explanation of the standards, examples and opportunities for discussion'. Sadler (2009, p. 178), on the other hand, is critical of assessment grids and contends that

> To simply reach for a rubric or construct a scoring key each time a complex work has to be appraised is both impractical and artificial in life outside academe. Equipping students with holistic evaluative insights and skills, therefore, would contribute an important graduate skill.

However, we contend that, even with holistic assessment, the use of criteria to guide the assessor may be appropriate. Sadler admits that 'clearly, there is more work to be done on this important issue of grading complex student responses to assessment' (p. 178). We now describe the implementation of the intervention reported in this paper.

The Teaching and Learning Initiative

The teaching and learning initiative was applied to a report-writing assignment embedded in a Masters-level introductory financial accounting unit, with an enrolment of 40 students.[3] The unit was taught over a period of 13 weeks in a weekly face-to-face three-hour workshop.

The Curriculum

As stated above, the two aims of the intervention were to provide the students with learning experiences, involving peer assessment and self-assessment in a collaborative setting, to (1) improve their ability to better judge writing against a marking rubric, and (2) improve their written communication skills. It was our intention to seamlessly embed these activities into the curriculum without reducing the content of the unit. This meant that the research topic for the students' report had to be one that was normally covered by the curriculum and of current relevance. 'Revenue recognition' was the research topic, and a suitable question was devised on this topic for the students' report. In addition, following the aforementioned Boud, Cohen and Sampson (1999), in these straitened times, we tried hard to not increase the workload of the unit coordinator. First the students submitted their own draft assignments. Then the intervention began.

The Examples

Preparatory work was undertaken by the unit coordinator to identify four suitable examples of written work and to establish a benchmark grade for those examples. The two pairs of examples were chosen through a two-stage process. In stage one 10 examples of work were selected[4] from the 65 reports that had been submitted in the previous year and then subjected to a process of pair-wise assessment. The pair-wise assessment is a method developed by Heldsinger and Humphry (2010), which requires two markers to compare each report with every other report to determine their ranking.

These comparisons were then converted onto a measurement scale using a logarithmic function by two independent markers – one being an educational expert (but not an accountant) and the other being one of the authors of this paper. While the internal validity of each marker was high, a disappointingly low correlation of 0.1 was achieved between the two markers' grades; but when one report (well written but technically poor), was removed, the correlation between the grades for the remaining nine reports rose to 0.7. Further discussion by the two assessors about the discrepancies in ranking revealed that the nine reports covered two distinct subtopics – one about the conceptual framework and the other about 'fair value accounting'. In some instances one subtopic was performed well by the students and the other was not. In these situations, the ranking of the overall report became contentious due to differences in the emphasis the markers put on the authors' knowledge. Thus stage one provided a degree of reliability in the grading, and four examples were selected at random for the students to assess before and after the face-to-face classroom discussion.

In stage two the four examples were subjected to a more conventional assessment process by two of the authors of this paper using a rubric (see Appendix A – Assessment Rubric) that had been developed over several years for the purpose of assessing written reports in this unit. The two authors first made individual assessments and then compared them. Out of six possible criteria for each of the four examples, the assessors gave exactly the same rating for 20 of the 24 points of assessment. The assessment for the other points differed by only one degree on the scale (e.g. acceptable vs. below acceptable), and after discussion between the markers consensus was reached on these. This two-stage process formed the 'benchmark' assessment for the two pairs (four) of examples (named A to D).

The four examples were then used in the intervention. First, students individually assessed two of the four examples (A and B) using a rubric and recorded their decisions on the SPARK[PLUS] (Self and Peer Assessment Resource Kit, Willey 2008). Students then worked in teams in a teacher-facilitated face-to-face workshop to discuss their individual assessments (that had been captured on SPARK[PLUS]). The process involved students sharing the reasons for their assessment of A and B and for coming to a consensus (consistent with the social construct theory). This process was the same as the one used in the Achievement Matters project (http://achievementmatters. starfishbowl.com) and similar to that reported by Willey and Gardner (2009), where it was found to induce an informed discussion about the criteria and the examples.

Following the face-to-face workshop, students assessed individually the second set of two examples (C and D) and recorded their decisions on SPARK[PLUS]. These assessments were then compared to the 'benchmark' marks reached by the two authors, as described above, with SPARK[PLUS] automatically awarding a mark for each judgment based on its closeness to the two authors' agreed marks. We deemed the assessment activities

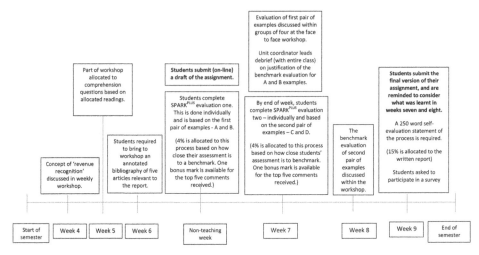

Figure 1. Timeline of process.

important, mindful of literature asserting that gaining an understanding of the assessment framework is likely to have a positive impact on learning (O'Donovan, Price and Rust, 2001).

Following the face-to-face classroom discussion of examples C and D, and the teacher's debriefing, the students then had the opportunity to revise their draft written report before its final submission. The conversations students had with other students about writing quality and the application of the marking rubric were meant to trigger revisions to the draft assignment.

This process is summarized in Figure 1.

Research Methods

As stated in the introduction, the research methods for the evaluation of the intervention comprised: analysis of writing skills, self-reflection by students, and a survey. The analysis of writing skills was conducted by an independent marker, who has expertise in assessing written communication. The marker used the same assessment rubric as the one used by the students in assessing examples A, B, C and D. She marked both the draft and final reports for the quality of the written communication; her focus was on the students' ability to communicate the information, as opposed to the knowledge component of the information presented by the students. The students' draft and final reports effectively formed another matched pair.

The second set of data was the self-reflective statements made by students, the analysis of which was a two-part manual process. First the statements were scanned to establish a list of the main points raised by authors. Second, each statement was read carefully and note was taken of which of the main points (as previously identified) the author had produced. We felt that this approach captured the essence of the students' statements more accurately than a computerised word analysis.

The final source of data was a survey given to students at the conclusion of the intervention. The survey (reported in Appendix B), which was entirely voluntary, was completed by 33 of the 40 students. It consisted of nine questions to which students responded using a five-point Likert scale ranging from strongly agree to strongly disagree. There were also four open-ended questions about the initiative.

Results

The aims of the research in this study were to evaluate the impact (if any) of the L&T initiative on the students' ability to form accurate judgments about written communication based on a set marking rubric, and of its impact on the students' written communication skills. We have used questions to structure the presentation of results.

Did the Self-Review, Peer Review and Collaborative Discussions Improve Students' Ability to Make Judgments about Written Communication Skills?

In this instance 'ability to make judgment' was measured by comparing the students' ratings of the examples against the benchmark ratings (that had been established in advance by the two authors).[5] For each example, almost 40 student ratings were collected against each of the six criteria. Examples A and B were performed concurrently before the intervention, and examples C and D were done concurrently after the intervention. The six criteria (taken from the rubric) are listed here for the reader's convenience:

K1	Knowledge 1	Relevant issues are raised and the discussion is convincing. Are the conclusions valid?
K2	Knowledge 2	Does the work contain reference to and reflect an understanding and application of appropriate, adequate literature?
W1	Writing style 1	Is the written work grammatically correct and well structured? (This includes sentence and paragraph structure and logical sequencing.)
W2	Writing style 2	Is the report well presented and in accordance with the requirements that were stipulated for the assignment?
W3	Writing style 3	Is the in-text referencing correctly applied?
W4	Writing style 4	Is the end referencing correctly applied?

The students recorded their assessments using SPARK[PLUS] which required the students to enter their ratings on a continuous spectrum, evenly sub-divided into the following categories[6]:

WB = well below acceptable

BA = below acceptable

AC = acceptable

AA = above acceptable

WA = well above acceptable

Since one aim of the intervention was to improve students' ability to make better judgments about communication skills, their assessments of each example were compared to the marks awarded by the two teachers. An indicator of an improvement in their

Table 1. Means of the differences between student and benchmark ratings before (A, B) and after (C, D) intervention.

	K1	K2	W1	W2	W3	W4
Examples A and B	18.53	16.10	15.48	26.46	25.42	14.73
Examples C and D	15.23	19.27	10.99	12.44	15.56	15.08
Improvement in judgment	Yes	No	Yes*	Yes*	Yes*	No

*Significant at 1%.

ability to better apply the marking rubric was for students to achieve marks for C and D that were closer to the marks of the teachers than for A and B.

Table 1 shows the means of the grouped results for the four examples (see Appendix C for more detailed statistics). An improvement in judgment (shown by a decrease in the differences between student and teacher marks) occurred for criteria K1, W1, W2 and W3; however, a two-tailed t-test indicated that these improvements were statistically significant for criteria W1, W2 and W3.

A control test was performed on examples A and B to ensure that there was a degree of internal stability in the rating difference before the intervention. (Likewise, examples C and D were compared to ensure stability in the ratings after the intervention.) For criteria W1 and W2, in which it is thought that an improvement had occurred, the t tests showed that there was no significant internal inconsistency in the ratings before and after the intervention. However, for criterion W3, the rating difference for A and B (i.e. before the intervention) were significantly different from each other (as they were also between C and D). This lowered the credibility of the finding reported in the previous paragraph for criterion W3. In summary: there was an improvement in students' ability to make better judgments about written communication skills for criteria W1 and W2.

Did the Use of Self-Review, Peer Review and Collaborative Discussion Improve Students' Written Communication Skills?

As stated above, the students' draft and final reports were assessed by the independent marker.[7] The results are reported in Table 2.[8]

As shown in Table 2, the total assessment for the final report exceeds the assessment for the draft report in 32 of the 35 cases. In one case there was no apparent change, and in the other two cases there was only a slight decrease in the assessment. However, on average, the results show a significant improvement between the draft and final reports for W1 and W4, with 95% confidence, and for all the other criteria, with 99% confidence.

Intriguingly, whereas these results show a definite improvement in the students' written communication, it is not clear how this improvement came about. It was not possible to run a control group of students who did not undergo the L&T initiative; therefore, we can only surmise that improvement occurred because of the initiative's assessment and other activities described above; but we cannot be certain which part of the initiative provided the most improvement or had the biggest impact on improvement – for example, the

Table 2. Summary of independent examiner's assessment of draft and final student reports.

	K1	K2	W1	W2	W3	W4	Total
Possible score	**5.00**	**5.00**	**2.00**	**1.00**	**1.00**	**1.00**	**15.00**
Before							
Mean	2.74	3.22	1.12	0.61	0.53	0.62	8.84
Median	2.80	3.20	0.80	0.60	0.40	0.60	8.80
Standard deviation	0.76	1.08	0.49	0.26	0.29	0.28	2.23
After							
Mean	3.23	3.87	1.20	0.75	0.73	0.71	10.49
Median	3.00	3.80	1.00	0.80	0.80	0.80	9.80
Standard deviation	0.80	0.80	0.51	0.19	0.26	0.29	2.07
Score (after – before)	**0.49**	**0.65**	**0.08**	**0.14**	**0.20**	**0.09**	**1.65**
Number of report pairs	35	35	35	35	35	35	35
Instances where no change	9	5	16	15	10	17	1
Instances of improvement	23	24	14	16	23	13	32

discussions, assessing others' work, or the feedback provided by the facilitator. Further-more, it is possible that some students undertook another communication unit, either con-currently or previously, which may have positively influenced their improvement. So we are left with the provisional finding that the L&T initiative enabled the students to improve their written reports because of some combination of their learning activities. We will return to the question of cause in the conclusion. Now we comment on the data produced by the students' self-reflection statements and survey responses.

What can be Inferred from the Students' Self-Reflection Statements?

The self-reflection requirement stated: 'the final version of the report must include a state-ment, of not more than 250 words, explaining how the intervention process changed your work from draft to the final version.' The aim here was to get the students to reflect on the process of peer assessment and self-assessment and judge whether they found it of value. The students' reflective statements were completely free form. The content of the 33 (out of a possible 40) self-reflective statements was analysed as described in the research methods section to establish the most common points raised by the students,[9] which were as follows;

- Students reported having improved the content of their report to some degree in 81% of the statements.
- Students specifically credited the intervention with providing insight into some com-ponent of their written work in 62% of the statements.
- Students made the claim that understanding the expected criteria and standards assisted their self-assessment in 46% of the statements.
- Students made statements about improvements to their: referencing techniques (73%), structure/style of writing (68%), and grammar (38%)
- Nine students (24%) claimed that the self-evaluation process[10] was something they would use in the future.

What follows is one of the more expressive student self-reflections:

> I found that the process of having to write a draft for our own benefit was actually very useful. I do not normally take the time to read through, reflect and edit after I write and I think that because I did this I have a final product that better reflects the ideas of the assignment. For my second report I took the time to read more and gain a better understanding of revenue recog-nition and think that I formed a more concrete argument. Also, coming from an art and design background, I had not written a report like this in a long time and I found the process of eval-uating other students' work very effective in seeing what was expected within the report, par-ticularly in regards to referencing. My referencing approach changed quite dramatically in the second report. As a former Arts student, I was quite used to writing predominantly my own opinions so I had to take a step back and try and include more of the literature I had come across in my research. Hopefully I managed to do this. Along with that, marking others' work forced to get a deeper awareness of the marking grid which ultimately means that I am now much more conscious of what is expected from my work.

What Did the Students' Survey Responses Show?

The responses to the voluntary survey questions are summarized in Table 3 below. It can be seen that students rated questions 1–6 (which concentrate on the example assessment process itself) somewhere between 'agreement' and 'strong agreement'; whereas for ques-tions 7–9 (which concentrate on *application* of what they may have learned through the

Table 3. Summary of average responses to survey.

	Q1	Q2	Q3	Q4	Q5	Q6	Q7	Q8	Q9a
Average score	4.03	4.31	4.08	4.08	4.03	4.28	3.68	3.92	3.79
Number of responses	38	39	39	39	38	39	39	39	39

example process to improve their work) their average rating lies somewhere between 'neutral' and 'agree'. Interestingly, students credited improvement in their understanding of the assessment criteria to all three parts of the example process – their individual reviews (Q4), their collaborative peer review (Q5) and the instructor's debrief (Q6); although it should be noted that a statistically insignificant preference was shown for the effect of the instructor's debrief.[11]

To sum up: it would appear that, based on responses to the survey, the whole intervention process was perceived by the students to have improved their confidence in assessing written material, their understanding of assessment criteria, and their ability to apply these skills to their written work. In their answers to question ten: 'What were the positive aspects (if any) of undertaking the peer review exercise?' 67% of students referred to the challenge and learning that had resulted from the process of having to assess other students' written work, using specific criteria.

Conclusion

We had several reasons for undertaking the L&T initiative described in this paper, not the least of which was the increasing number of students doing accounting conversion degree programs in Australia. Mindful of concerns expressed about the poor communication skills of students in such a program by colleagues and in the literature (e.g. CPA Australia and Birrell, 2006), we felt obliged to make an intervention in this area – settling for an introductory financial accounting unit in a conversion Master degree program. At this point the literature came into play, providing us with a constructivist underpinning for the initiative (Lucas, 2000; Lucas and Meyer, 2005), and for the collaborative learning and peer assessment activities that were the centrepiece of the initiative (Evans *et al.*, 2009; O'Connell *et al.*, 2013; Sloan and Porter 2009; Willey and Gardner, 2010).

We now reiterate the two research questions we address in the paper, followed by a brief account of their related findings. The first question: *Does the use of peer review and collaborative discussion improve students' ability to make better judgments about written communication skills?* Our L&T initiative required students to do a 'before' and 'after' assessment of writing examples (recording their assessments on SPARK[PLUS]) of previous student answers to a research question that had been independently marked by two of the authors (of this paper). The 'meat in the sandwich' was the collaborative discussion and teacher debriefings. The results show that the 'after' student assessments had improved, being closer to the teachers' agreed assessment in four of the six criteria and statistically significant for the grammar, spelling and structure (W1), presentation (W2) and in-text referencing (W3). In addition there was anecdotal evidence from the teacher that these activities helped students to extend their vocabulary for discussing the assessment artefacts, asking questions of the instructor, and more reliably interpreting the feedback they received on their own writing. This provisional finding corresponds with those of Searby and Ewers (1997), who contend that peer assessment induces student assessors to develop a more conscious understanding of the processes involved in the activity, and Mowl and Pain (1995) who argue that peer assessment improves the students' understanding of assessment.

The second question: *Does peer review and collaborative discussion improve students' written communication skills?* The students' draft and final written reports were marked blind by an experienced communications staff member, who found statistically significant improvement in writing for all six of the criteria and in 32 of the 35 matched pairs. But why did this improvement occur? There were only three weeks between the submission of the draft and final reports so it would seem that the intervention of peer assessment and collaborative discussion had some impact on the improvement – consistent with social construction theory. Furthermore, our analysis of the qualitative data adds support to the impact of the intervention. For example, in their reflective statements 62% of the students specifically credited the intervention with providing insight into some component of their written work.

There were several challenges and limitations in our study. Firstly, the preparation for the intervention was considerable – contrary to our intentions; although once the project was underway it created only a slightly higher workload than the previous year's teaching for that unit. Secondly, the benchmark rating was a challenging exercise because justifying and explaining what had hitherto been a tacit (not fully conscious) assessment process was somewhat daunting. This meant that the debriefing sessions were challenging (if they were to be meaningful). The coordinator was required to moderate all the discussions while providing and defending the correct mix of guidance and justification of the benchmark – consistent with the Achievement Matters project (O'Connell *et al*. 2013).

The overall results indicate that there were benefits for the students both in terms of their ability to make better judgments about written communication skills and their written communication skills. It was obvious in the assessment work that the majority of students progressed from initial hesitation and bewilderment to being more confident about assessing the quality of the examples. The following two remarks embedded in reflective statements from strong, mature-aged students are somewhat atypical but worth noting: the first said he wished he had undergone this process *before starting employment*; and the second commented that in all her years of study she had never previously learned the *power of learning through [group] participation.*

In closing, it has occurred to us that despite the perceptual benefits derived by the students in this exercise, it is we the authors who have also benefited and perhaps even more than the students. We are already contemplating future research endeavours, such as whether the benefits to students reflected in this initiative might go beyond the short term. And one of the authors is currently working with many of the same students in another peer-learning initiative. The early indications are that these students are positively engaged with their in-class learning activities and the quality of their writing.

Acknowledgements

The authors would like to thank John Hall, Kaye Haddrill and Eileen Thompson for their valuable input into this paper. We also wish to thank the two anonymous reviewers for very helpful comments.

Notes

[1] More recently, peer assessment is defined as 'an arrangement for learners to consider and specify the level, value or quality of a product or performance of other equal-status learners' (Topping, 2009, p. 20).

[2]Depending upon how the peer assessment is organised, the types of variables that could conceivably cause these benefits to students' learning include level of time spent on task, increased engagement of students, increased practice by students and the fact that there is a greater sense of accountability and responsibility. Additionally, there may be beneficial effects for faculty arising from the requirement for peer assessment to initiate reflection on the objectives of the marking criteria and, more generally, the unit as a whole (Topping et al., 2000, p. 149).

[3]A significant proportion of the students have a language other than English as their first language.

[4]Systematic random sampling (i.e. every *n*th student from a random starting point) was applied to a list of the previous year's students. The list was in report grade order, so that a wide range of quality was represented in the sample of ten.

[5]Although both of these authors have considerable experience in grading tertiary Accounting work, it is acknowledged that the inherent presumption (which may be challenged) is that experience in grading leads to more reliable judgment.

[6]The students were made aware, through a trial run with SPARK[PLUS], that the spectrum is a continuous measure.

[7]Every effort was made to remove any indication from the reports as to whether they were draft of final versions. In addition, they were all anonymised and randomised.

[8]There were 35 pairs of reports, out of the 40 students. In a few instances the reports were not submitted electronically, and some students failed to provide a draft report.

[9]The analysis was a two-part process. The statements were scanned to establish a list of the recurring themes. Then each statement was re-read, and note was taken of whether each of the themes (noticed in step one) occurred in that particular statement.

[10]It is not entirely clear if the students meant the self-evaluation process, itself, the exemplar evaluation process, or some combination of the two.

[11]At first glance this may appear to contradict the findings from a similar study by Willey and Gardner (2010, pp. 429–443). In their study the highest percentage (37%) of the students reported that 'discussing the specification marking within the group and then re-marking it collaboratively was the part of the process that improved their understanding and ability the most'. The different result may arise because their survey instrument required the students to identify 'which (one) part of the process improved their understanding the most', while the current study asks a similarly worded question three times, enabling the students to rate the various factors more evenly. In addition, the debrief sessions was performed by completely different people.

References

Al-Mahmood, R. and Gruba, P. (2007) Approaches to the implementation of generic graduate attributes in Australian ICT undergraduate education, *Computer Science Education*, 17(3), pp. 171–185.

Andrade, M. S. (2006) International students in English-speaking universities: adjustment factors, *Journal of Research in International Education*, 5(2), pp. 131–154.

Arnott, J. and Carroll, D. (2012) *Graduate Outlook 2012. Report of the Graduate Outlook Survey: Employers' Perspectives on Graduate Recruitment*. Available at http://search.proquest.com.ezproxy.library.uwa.edu.au/docview/866416442/fulltextPDF/13E251318CE1D7C9AAA/2?accountid=14681 (accessed 20 May 2013).

Baik, C. and Greig, J. (2009) Improving the academic outcomes of undergraduate ESL students: the case for discipline-based academic skills programs, *Higher Education Research and Development*, 28(4), pp. 401–416.

Ballantyne, R., Hughes, K. and Mylonas, A. (2002) Developing procedures for implementing peer assessment in large classes using an action research process, *Assessment & Evaluation in Higher Education*, 27(5), pp. 427–441.

Boud, D. and Falchikov, N. (1989) Quantitative studies of student self-assessment in higher education: a critical analysis of findings, *Higher Education*, 18(5), pp. 529–549.

Boud, D. and Falchikov, N. (2006) Aligning assessment with long-term learning, *Assessment & Evaluation in Higher Education*, 31(4), pp. 399–413.

Boud, D., Cohen, R. and Sampson, J. (1999) Peer learning and assessment, *Assessment & Evaluation in Higher Education*, 24(4), pp. 413–426.

Briguglio, C. (2007) Educating the business graduate of the 21st century: communication for a globalised world, *International Journal of Teaching and Learning in Higher Education*, 19(1), pp. 8–20.

Brindley, C. and Scoffield, S. (1998) Peer assessment in undergraduate programmes, *Teaching in Higher Education*, 3(1), pp. 79–79.

Carroll, J. (2005) Lightening the load: teaching in English, learning in English, in: J. Carroll and J. Ryan (Eds) *Teaching International Students: Improving Learning for All*, pp. 35–42 (London; New York: Routledge).

Cole, P. (1992) Constructivism revisited: a search for common ground, *Educational Technology*, 33(2), pp. 27–34.

CPA Australia and Birrell, B. (2006) *The Changing Face of the Accounting Profession in Australia*, CPA Australia, November (Melbourne: CPA Australia).

CPA Australia and The Institute of Chartered Accountants in Australia. (2012) *Professional Accreditation Guidelines for Australian Accounting Degrees* (Melbourne: CPA Australia and the Institute of Chartered Accountants in Australia).

Duffy, T. M. and Cunningham, D. J. (1996) Constructivism: implications for the design and delivery of instruction, in: D. H. Jonassen (Ed.) *Educational Communications and Technology*, pp. 170–199 (New York: Simon & Schuster Macmillan).

Evans, E., and Cable, D. (2011) Evidence of improvement in accounting students' communication skills, *International Journal of Educational Management*, 25(4), pp. 311–327.

Evans, E., Tindale, J., Cable, D. and Mead, S. H. (2009) Collaborative teaching in a linguistically and culturally diverse higher education setting: a case study of a postgraduate accounting program, *Higher Education Research & Development*, 28(6), pp. 597–613.

Falchikov, N. (1995) Peer feedback marking: developing peer assessment, *Innovations in Education & Training International*, 32(2), pp. 175–187.

Freeman, M. and Hancock, P. (2011) A brave new world: Australian learning outcomes in accounting education, *Accounting Education*, 20(3), pp. 265–273.

Heldsinger, S. and Humphry, S. (2010) Using the method of pairwise comparison to obtain reliable teacher assessments, *Australian Educational Researcher*, 37(2), pp. 1–19.

International Accounting Education Standards Board. (2010) *International Education Standard 3: Professional Skills and General Education*, pp. 46–52. Available at http://www.ifac.org/publications-resources/handbook-international-education-pronouncements-2010-edition (accessed 13 May 2013).

Kern, R. and Schultz, J. M. (2005) Beyond orality: investigating literacy and the literacy in second and foreign language instruction, *The Modern Languages Journal*, 89(3), pp. 381–392.

Lawrence, J. (2005) Addressing diversity in higher education: two models for facilitating student engagement and mastery. Paper presented at the HERDSA 2005 Conference, Sydney, 3–6 July 2005. Available at http://conference.herdsa.org.au/2005/.

Lucas, U. (2000) Worlds apart: students' experiences of learning introductory accounting, *Critical Perspectives on Accounting*, 11(4), pp. 479–504.

Lucas, U. and Meyer, J. H. F. (2005) Towards a mapping of the student world: the identification of variation in students' conceptions of, and motivations to learn, introductory accounting, *The British Accounting Review*, 37, pp. 177–204.

Lucas, U. and Mladenovic, R. (2006a) Reflections on accounting education research: how accounting education research on approaches to learning has contributed to educational practice, in: L. Murphy Smith (Ed.) *Reflections on Accounting Education Research*, pp. 46–56 (Sarisota: American Accounting Association (AAA)).

Lucas, U. and Mladenovic, R. (2006b) Developing new 'world views': threshold concepts in introductory accounting, in: J. H. F. Meyer and R. Land (Eds) *Overcoming Barriers to Student Understanding: Threshold Concepts and Troublesome Knowledge*, pp. 148–159 (Oxford: Routledge).

McInnes, C. (2003) New realities of the student experience: how should universities respond? Paper presented at the 25th Annual Conference of the European Association for Institutional Research, Limerick, 24–27 August.

Mello, J. A. (1993) Improving individual member accountability in small work group settings, *Journal of Management Education*, 17(2), pp. 253–259.

Mowl, G. and Pain, R. (1995) Using self and peer assessment to improve students' essay writing: a case study from geography, pp. 324–335.

Nanjappa, A. and Grant, M. M. (2003) Constructing on constructivism: the role of technology, *Electronic Journal for the Integration of Technology in Education*. Available at http://ejite.isu.edu/Volume2No1/nanjappa.htm (accessed 13 May 2013).

O'Connell, B., DeLange, P., Abraham, A., Freeman, M., Hancock, P., Howieson, B. and Watty, K. (2013) *Assessment Matters: Developing Collaborative Peer Assessment Of Accounting Learning Standards* (Paris: European Accounting Association Conference).

O'Donovan, B., Price, M. and Rust, C. (2001) The student experience of criterion-referenced assessment (through the introduction of a common criteria assessment grid), *Innovations in Education and Teaching International*, 38(1), pp. 74–85.

Oliver, R. (2000) When teaching meets learning: design principles and strategies for web-based learning environments that support knowledge construction. Proceedings of the ASCILITE 2000 conference, Coffs Harbour, 9–14 December, pp. 1–12. Available at http://www.ascilite.org.au/conferences/coffs00/.

Sadler, R. (2009) Indeterminacy in the use of preset criteria for assessment and grading, *Assessment & Evaluation in Higher Education*, 34(2), pp. 159–179.

Searby, M. and Ewers, T. (1997) An evaluation of the use of peer assessment in higher education: a case study in the School of Music, Kingston University, *Assessment and Evaluation in Higher Education*, 22(4), pp. 371–383.

Shaw, J., Moore, P. and Gandhidasan, S. (2007) Educational acculturation and academic integrity: outcomes of an intervention subject for international post-graduate public health students, *Journal of Academic Language and Learning*, 1(1), pp. 55–67.

Simons, P. R. J. (1993) Constructive learning: the role of the learner, in: T. M. Duffy, J. Lowyck and D. H. Jonassen (Eds) *Designing Environments for Constructive Learning*, pp. 291–313 (Berlin; New York: Springer-Verlag).

Sloan, D. and Porter, E. (2009) The management of English language support in postgraduate business education: the CEM model (contextualisation, embedding and mapping), *International Journal of Management Education*, 7(2), pp. 51–58.

Somervell, H. (1993) Issues in assessment, enterprise and higher education: the case for self-peer and collaborative assessment, *Assessment & Evaluation in Higher Education*, 18(3), pp. 221–233.

Tindale, J., Evans, E., Cable, D. and Mead, S. H. (2006) Operationalising collaboration, *International Journal of Knowledge, Culture & Change Management*, 6(4), pp. 81–88.

Topping, K. (1998) Peer assessment between students in colleges and universities, *Review of Educational Research*, 68(3), pp. 249–276.

Topping, K. (2009) Peer assessment, *Theory into Practice*, 48(1), pp. 20–27.

Topping, K. J., Smith, E. F., Swanson, I. and Elliot, A. (2000) Formative peer assessment of academic writing between postgraduate students, *Assessment and Evaluation in Higher Education*, 25(2), pp. 149–169.

Watty, K. (2007) Quality in accounting education and low English standards among overseas students: is there a link?, *People and Place*, 15(1), pp. 22–29.

Webb, C., English, L. and Bonanno, H. (1995) Collaboration in subject design: integration of the teaching and assessment of literacy skills into a first-year accounting course, *Accounting Education*, 4(4), pp. 335–350.

Willey, K. and Freeman, M. (2006a) Completing the learning cycle: the role of formative feedback when using self and peer assessment to improve teamwork and engagement. Proceedings of the 17th Annual Conference of the Australasian Association for Engineering Education, Auckland University of Technology, 10–13 December 2006, pp. 751–758.

Willey, K. and Freeman, M. (2006b) Improving teamwork and engagement: the case for self and peer assessment, *Australasian Journal of Engineering Education*. Available at http://www.aaee.com.au/journal/2006/willey0106.pdf.

Willey, K. and Gardner, A. (2009) Using benchmarking to improve students' learning and make assessment more student centred. Proceedings of the 20th Australasian Association for Engineering Education Conference, University of Adelaide, 6–9 December, pp. 726–734. Available at https://www.engineersaustralia.org.au/sites/default/files/shado/2009_the_university_of_adelaide.pdf.

Willey, K. and Gardner, A. (2010) Investigating the capacity of self and peer assessment activities to engage students and promote learning, *European Journal of Engineering Education*, 35(4), pp. 429–443.

Willey, K. and Gardner, A. (2011a) Building a community of practice to improve inter marker standardisation and consistency. Proceedings of the SEFI 2011 Annual Conference: Global Engineering Recognition, Sustainability, Mobility, Lisbon, Portugal, 27–30 September, pp. 666–671.

Willey, K. and Gardner, A. (2011b) Getting tutors on the same page. Proceedings of the 22nd Annual Conference for the Australasian Association for Engineering Education (AAEE 2011) – Developing Engineers for Social Justice: Community Involvement, Ethics and Sustainability, Fremantle, Western Australia, 5–7 December, pp. 454–459.

Wingate, U. (2006) Doing away with 'study skills', *Teaching in Higher Education*, 11(4), pp. 457–469.

Appendix A. Assessment Rubric

	Marks	Well below acceptable	Below acceptable	Acceptable	Above acceptable	Well above acceptable
Knowledge						
1. Relevant issues are raised and the discussion is convincing. Are the conclusions valid?	5	The majority of the report has no bearing on the discussion. The report fails to provide information or to clearly articulate the value of the conclusions.		The key points related to this discussion are considered by the report. The work contains detailed information but it is not organised around the value of the conclusions.		The report raises most key points related to the discussion and introduces a few more. All of the report is relevant to discussing the question. The work convinces the reader of the reasonableness of the conclusions.
2. Does the work contain reference to, and reflect an understanding and application of appropriate, adequate literature?	5	Very few, if any, sources are shown, either in text or end text.		An adequate quality and quantity of sources has been used.		The quality and quantity of sources used in the report reflect considerable research. The literature has been assimilated into the report.
Writing Style						
1. Is the written work grammatically correct and well structured? (This includes sentence and paragraph structure and logical sequencing.)	2	Spelling, English grammar, sentence structure and paragraph structure is poor. The thread of logic in the report is very difficult to follow		Grammar, sentence structure and logical sequence are satisfactory. Ideas are mostly clearly stated.		All points are clearly made and the information is assimilated and collated into an interesting read. It contains minor, if any, grammatical or structural errors. Sentence and paragraph structure is tight (parsimonious).

(Continued)

Appendix A. Continued

Well above acceptable	Marks	Well below acceptable	Below	acceptable	Acceptable	Above acceptable
2. Is the report well-presented and in accordance with the requirements that were stipulated in the assignment?	1	Incorrect font or spacing used. Layout is confusing. Significantly over or under the word limit.		Font and spacing used is correct. Layout is readable.		Excellent layout Font and spacing correct. Word limit is achieved.
3. Is the in-text referencing correctly applied?	1	In text referencing is not applied or is applied incorrectly.		The technique of in text referencing is applied nearly perfectly.		In text referencing is applied correctly. In text referencing is applied in the report in a variety of styles. It is absolutely clear what is being referenced.
4. Is the end-text referencing correctly applied?	1	End text referencing has not been applied or is applied incorrectly.		The technique of end text referencing is applied nearly perfectly.		End text referencing is applied correctly.
	15					

Appendix B. Survey Instrument

Questionnaire in relation to the Peer Review exercise

Completion of this survey indicates my consent to participate

Demographic information

Gender:

Previous discipline(s) of study:

Country of previous education:

Level of previous education:

Years spent in workforce:

Questions about the Peer Review exercise (Please circle your response)	Strongly disagree		Neutral		Strongly agree	Not applicable
1 After the peer review exercise, I feel more confident about assessing written communication than I felt before the process.	SD	D	N	A	SA	NA
2 After the peer review exercise, I understand the meaning of the assessment criteria better than I did before the exercise.	SD	D	N	A	SA	NA
3 After the peer review exercise, I understand the expected standards for written communication conveyed by the assessment criteria better than I did before the exercise.	SD	D	N	A	SA	NA
4 My understanding of the assessment criteria increased as a result of having to complete an individual assessment of the exemplars.	SD	D	N	A	SA	NA
5 My understanding of the assessment criteria increased as a result of discussing the exemplars with peers.	SD	D	N	A	SA	NA
6 My understanding of the assessment criteria increased as a result of the debrief facilitated by the unit coordinator.	SD	D	N	A	SA	NA
7 The peer review exercise enabled me to improve my written communication assignment.	SD	D	N	A	SA	NA
8 The peer review exercise improved my judgment in rating against the assessment criteria.	SD	D	N	A	SA	NA
9a The peer review exercise has changed the way I would write in future professional contexts (job applications, reports, assignments etc).	SD	D	N	A	SA	NA
9b Briefly explain how:						

10 What were the positive aspects (if any) of undertaking the peer review exercise?

11 What were the negative aspects (if any) of undertaking the peer review exercise?

12 Any other comments

Appendix C. Detailed Statistics related to Table 1 'Judgment Differences'

Table A. Detailed statistics of differences between student and benchmark ratings before and after intervention.

	AB K1	AB K2	AB W1	AB W2	AB W3	AB W4
Mean	18.532	16.104	15.481	26.455	25.416	14.727
Standard error	1.538	1.456	1.341	1.916	1.745	1.235
Median	16	14	13	26	21	12
Mode	9	7	7	36	17	4
Standard deviation	13.494	12.778	11.768	16.811	15.312	10.839
Sample variance	182.094	163.279	138.490	282.620	234.457	117.490
Kurtosis	−0.297	0.810	1.327	−0.109	−0.336	0.255
Skewness	0.792	1.110	1.275	0.463	0.560	0.853
Range	51	53	52	69	68	46
Minimum	0	0	0	0	2	0
Maximum	51	53	52	69	70	46
Sum	1427	1240	1192	2037	1957	1134
Count	77	77	77	77	77	77

	CD K1	CD K2	CD W1	CD W2	CD W3	CD W4
Mean	15.231	19.269	10.987	12.436	15.564	15.077
Standard error	1.155	1.450	1.051	1.274	1.348	1.445
Median	15	19.5	9	9	14	9.5
Mode	18	0	6	5	3	6
Standard deviation	10.199	12.802	9.280	11.251	11.908	12.764
Sample variance	104.024	163.888	86.117	126.587	141.808	162.929
Kurtosis	−0.065	−0.935	2.955	1.362	−0.522	0.708
Skewness	0.566	0.256	1.449	1.357	0.609	1.120
Range	46	47	49	47	44	55
Minimum	0	0	0	0	0	0
Maximum	46	47	49	47	44	55
Sum	1188	1503	857	970	1214	1176
Count	78	78	78	78	78	78

Index

Printed and bound by CPI Group (UK) Ltd, Croydon, CR0 4YY

08/05/2025

01864327-0011